Global Constitutionalism in International Legal Perspective

Queen Mary Studies in International Law

Edited by

Malgosia Fitzmaurice and Phoebe Okowa

VOLUME 4

Global Constitutionalism in International Legal Perspective

By

Christine E. J. Schwöbel

MARTINUS
NIJHOFF
PUBLISHERS

LEIDEN • BOSTON
2011

This book is printed on acid-free paper.

Library of Congress Cataloging-in-Publication Data

Schwöbel, Christine E. J.
Global constitutionalism in international legal perspective / by Christine E.J. Schwöbel.
p. cm. -- (Queen mary studies in international law, 1877-4822 ; v. 4)
Includes bibliographical references and index.
ISBN 978-90-04-19115-0 (hardback : alk. paper) 1. International law. 2. Constitutional law.
I. Title.
KZ3410.S378 2011
341'.1--dc22

2010051348

ISSN 1877-4822
ISBN 978 90 04 19115 0

For my parents

CONTENTS

ACKNOWLEDGEMENTS

This book began its life as a PhD thesis at King's College London. First and foremost, I would like to thank my dissertation supervisor Susan Marks, who has helped shape this work in many ways. Her thoughtful feedback and ideas were invaluable to making this book what it now is. I cannot overstate the attention to detail as well as the remarkable sense of overall structure that Susan generously brought to my work and that have made this book far more comprehensible than I could have achieved alone. I consider myself extremely fortunate to have been supervised by such a brilliant scholar and am endlessly proud that Susan still finds time to discuss my work.

The examiners in my *viva voce*, Patrick Capps and Malgosia Fitzmaurice deserve a special expression of gratitude. Their detailed and illuminating comments as well as probing questions proved to be extremely useful for bringing the thesis into book form. Malgosia has been particularly patient with me and her encouragement has made the process from thesis to book much swifter and less painful than I had feared.

Special thanks go to Martti Koskenniemi, whose comments inspired a significant turn in my research. Without his (thought-)provoking comments, which came at a crucial stage in my research, this book would not exist.

I am deeply grateful to the participants of various conferences and research groups that patiently listened to my ideas on various aspects of global constitutionalism and gave valuable feedback. I wish to mention here Henrique Carvalho, Eddie Bruce-Jones, Joseph Raz, Chris Townley, Leif Wenar, and Omer Direk.

My thanks also go to my friends and colleagues Jason Beckett and Sara Kendall, who provided me with valuable feedback and guidance – in Sara's case, even editorial help - for the final stages of this work.

The acknowledgments would not be complete without mentioning my dearest Axit who followed the progress – and setbacks – of this work from the very beginning. He has patiently and generously endured the late nights of typing, the endless number of radio plays that were to be heard from wherever I set up camp with my computer, and the highs and lows of my emotions in this time. I am truly lucky to share my life with such a wonderful person.

My final thanks go to my parents, who have listened to my ideas (to the extent that they have themselves become experts in global constitutionalism), given advice (luckily for me, from the perspective of both academics as well as parents), and provided the unconditional love and support in a way that only parents can.

INTRODUCTION

Global constitutionalism is the international legal term *du jour*. The last years have seen a great influx of debates on constitutionalism in international law, sparked by various globalisation processes. All manner of terms, ranging from 'international community', 'global rule of law' to 'global governance' have been engaged to explain increased interdependence, cooperation, and collaboration in the *inter*national, *intra*national and *trans*national sphere. The increased multifariousness of activities in the sphere that transcends the national has made the idea of a legal umbrella to frame the various activities and impulses an attractive enterprise. The unifying terminology is all the more interesting amidst the growing importance of the fragmentation of international law. One such legal umbrella that has been suggested is that of a global constitution.

This book critically examines public international law contributions to the debate on global constitutionalism. There is of course no single recognised global constitution; rather there are a number of visions of what a global constitution is and should be and what constitutionalisation in the international sphere is spurred by. The following takes a step back from the debate to call into question these prevailing visions, attempting to bring into focus the ideas which they entail. A critical examination highlights that contemporary visions of global constitutionalism are predominantly shaped by central tenets of the political form of government referred to as liberal democracy which is predicated on the ideology of political liberalism. Liberalism in this sense is characterised by the two elements of formal autonomy and abstract equality; democracy is characterised by popular representation in the public sphere. Public international law contributions to the debate on global constitutionalism are largely animated by a belief that these liberal democratic ideas define not only constitutionalism in nation States, but also constitutionalism for a global order. Indeed, they are often regarded as the only available ideas. This leads to significant limitations including the creation of an environment that favours hegemonic ambitions at the possible expense of diversity. In an effort to reengage with constitutionalism on a global scale, a suggestion is made as to how such limitations can be reduced, by employing an approach that I refer to as 'organic global constitutionalism'.

What then is global constitutionalism? So as to avoid exclusions from the outset, the term 'constitution' is not predetermined here. I will predominantly refer to 'constitutionalism' as the theory and practice pertaining to something that is 'constitutional'. In order not to leave readers completely in the dark (although this is unlikely, even impossible, since the term itself evokes a number of associations), as a first step to examining the idea of global constitutionalism, one can break the term down to its components of 'global' and of 'constitutionalism'. The word 'global' refers to the assumption of the universality of the concept. In the very broadest sense, the word 'constitutionalism' pertains to a certain social, political, cultural, economic, and legal system of ideas. The suffix 'ism' denotes a belief in or a practice of the system of ideas. At this stage, this extremely broad definition of global constitutionalism as a universal system of certain social, political, cultural, economic and legal ideas will have to suffice. This study aims at being as inclusive as possible and therefore shies away from exclusion through definitions. The constitutionalism that is the object of this book has been referred to as 'international constitutionalism', 'transnational constitutionalism' or 'global constitutionalism'. Although these terms are often used synonymously, the following discusses constitutionalism that is believed to concern matters *between* States (*inter*-national constitutionalism) as well as constitutionalism that is believed to concern matters *beyond* States (*trans*national constitutionalism). *Worldwide* visions of constitutionalism are examined; this means that although the discussions on regional visions of constitutionalism (such as the constitutional treaty for the European Union) are mentioned, indeed are key to some of the ideas of global constitutionalism, this book focuses on visions concerning the whole world. The term 'global constitutionalism' thus seems most fitting.

There are two main reasons for the timeliness of this book. Firstly, although there have been many contributions by international lawyers to what they view as 'the global constitution' or what they view as features of 'global constitutionalism', there has been no comprehensive analysis of these contributions, particularly in terms of situating them within a particular political tradition. The second reason for the timeliness is a shift that has supposedly taken place through the events surrounding 9/11. While in the 1990s there was much debate about diversity, recognition, and inclusion, the 9/11 attacks have arguably provoked something of a reorientation towards a search for a global common set of values and the exclusion of those that do not share these values. The Western States, led by the United States, have engaged in a policy of identifying allies and enemies respectively in the fight against terrorism. This has been the source of the emergence of a clear and accepted divide between those who operate within the liberal democratic consensus and those who are wary of its possible hegemonic implications. Against this background, there has crystallised a feeling that there is no need to question the premises on which liberal democracy is predicated. This book hopes to heighten awareness that it is still (or perhaps even more so) necessary to question dominant political forms. I hope to sensitise the reader to the fact that such political forms should not be applied to a global sphere – and, to that extent, universalised – without questioning the validity and generality of their premises.

As is customary with such research, the first Chapter sets the scene: It identifies and categorises the contemporary debates on public international law visions of global constitutionalism, and highlights the different issues that are addressed therein. This chapter reviews a wide variety of contributions, introducing the distinction between what I have called the four dimensions of constitutionalism: *Social Constitutionalism*, *Institutional Constitutionalism*, *Normative Constitutionalism*, and *Analogical Constitutionalism*.[1] These categories are an attempt to group the various approaches or schools of thought by reference to the key themes of global constitutionalism. The categories are, of course, only one way of describing the debate on global constitutionalism in international legal perspective.[2]

Social Constitutionalism is a vision of constitutionalism that views the international sphere as an order of coexistence. Concerns about participation, influence, and accountability are at the centre of these visions of global constitutionalism. A distinction is made between Social Constitutionalism that focuses on the international community as a global constitutional order and the form that focuses on global civil society. Hermann Mosler, Bardo Fassbender and Christian Tomuschat are identified as promoting the former; Gunther Teubner, Andreas-Fischer Lescano, and Philip Allott the latter. Visions of *Institutional Constitutionalism* are predominantly centred on the ways in which power is allocated among institutions in the international sphere. A distinction is made here between global governance ideas of constitutionalism (advanced for example by Anne Peters and Jürgen Habermas), ideas that put forward United Nations law as global constitutional law (advocated by Ronald St. John Macdonald and Bardo Fassbender), and ideas that suggest World Trade Organisational law and International Labour Organisational law as global constitutional law (described by Ernst-Ulrich Petersmann and Stefan Kadelbach/Thomas Kleinlein respectively). *Normative Constitutionalism* encompasses those visions that focus on the existence of a common normative (value) system. This section is divided into three types of Normative Constitutionalism. First, visions of a world law, as portrayed by Angelika Emmerich-Fritsche and Jost Delbrück; second, visions pertaining to a hierarchy of norms put forward by Brun-Otto Bryde and Luigi Ferragoli; and third, visions of fundamental norms will be presented as ideas stemming from Michael Byers, Erika de Wet and Jost Delbrück. Finally, *Analogical Constitutionalism* includes visions of global constitutionalism that are modelled on existing constitutional orders. Analogical Constitutionalism can focus on meta-rules (as suggested by the early writings of Alfred Verdross and

---

[1] Christine E. J. Schwöbel, 'Situating the Debate on Global Constitutionalism' (2010) 8 (3) International Journal of Constitutional Law *forthcoming*; Christine E. J. Schwöbel, 'Organic Global Constitutionalism'(2010) 23 Leiden Journal of International Law (LJIL) 530–533.

[2] For another way of ordering the debate, see Jeffrey L. Dunoff and Joel P. Trachtman, 'A Functional Approach to International Constitutionalization' in *idem* (eds), *Ruling the World: Constitutionalism, International Law, and Global Governance* (CUP, Cambridge 2009) 3–35.

Christian Tomuschat), on domestic constitutional orders (as suggested by Robert Uerpmann), or on European constitutionalism (as put forward by Mattias Kumm). It emerges from this that there are five key themes of constitutionalisation that shape the contemporary debate on global constitutionalism: the limitation of power, the institutionalisation of power, social idealism (meaning an idea for the future that is based on societal values), the standard-setting capacity of constitutions in the sense of a systematisation of law, and the recognition of individual rights. The five key themes can be found in various combinations in the four dimensions of global constitutionalism. One can compress the four dimensions of global constitutionalism further down to visions centring either on ideas of democratic processes or on ideas of liberal processes.

Chapter 2 examines the intellectual origins of the five key themes. The examination begins with thinkers of Ancient Greece and their influence on notions of the universality of certain principles. Whereas in those days there were no written constitutions as we know them today, many modern views on constitutionalism have their roots in the writings of philosophers of classical antiquity. The oldest key theme, closely connected to conceptions of natural law and ideas of universality, is the *limitation of power*. This key theme is related to the second key theme, attributed to Aristotle, the *institutionalisation of power*. The limitation and the institutionalisation of power foreground participation, accountability, governance, and representation. The third key theme, *social idealism*, is also rooted in Ancient Greece. It emerged with the teachings of the Stoics of the 3rd to 1st centuries BCE, who introduced notions of virtue and morality as dimensions of a universal law. The fourth key theme of *standard-setting* can be regarded as instituted by the Romans. In the 6th century CE, the Roman Emperor Justinian ordered the closing of the philosophical schools and thereby facilitated the practical application of law that was from there on distinct from philosophy. Legal principles were increasingly regarded as part of a legal system that society had to orient its conduct by. It was not until the 16th century CE that the fifth key theme of global constitutionalism emerged: the significance of the *protection of individual rights*. The spread of Christianity placed the individual at the centre of ideas on law and morals. These thoughts evolved further in the Enlightenment, which facilitated the development of the idea of certain fundamental rights that were inherent in every human. While the European thinkers were dwelling on questions of fundamental rights, their respective nation States were establishing colonies and empires throughout the world. For the first time, global constitutional history looks beyond Europe. It is illustrated how international law is instituted as an area of law and how its concept and concepts of constitutionalism were utilised to legitimise European imperial ambitions. The present day is only portrayed briefly since this is the focus of Chapter 1. It is noted that the domain of the universal is predominant in many other fields of research that award attention to globalisation. Much academic work today is dominated by reflections on changes regarding the significance of the nation State and the international sphere.

Having mapped the landscape in this way, the next chapter seeks to highlight what is missing from it – the omissions and biases of the prevailing notions of global constitutionalism. The aim is both to expose the limitations of global constitutionalist discourses, and to indicate what is at stake if visions of global constitutionalism are subject to those limitations. It is observed that many of the limitations are linked to the fact that the central ideas of global constitutionalism are at the same time central tenets of liberal democracy. This work does not intend to challenge liberal democracy itself (which in any event encompasses a wide diversity of political practices and arrangements), but it does point to the weakness of visions that depend exclusively on established traditions in liberal democratic thought, believing that they can be applied to global constitutionalism without further scrutiny. The Chapter begins with an examination of some common assumptions about global constitutionalism and then goes on to examine the different focal points of the contributors, in the form of the key themes of global constitutionalism. At the beginning of the chapter it is revealed that, despite the differences, there exist a range of common assumptions. These include: the belief that constitutions can exist beyond the nation State; the assumption of a certain unity or even homogeneity of the international sphere; and the assumption that the idea of global constitutionalism is itself universal. Under critical scrutiny, it becomes evident that the first assumption rationalises and idealises the existence of an international legal community in a manner that tends to overlook both the complexity of the international sphere and the political dynamics that are unique to it. The second assumption has the effect of downplaying ongoing concerns about the fragmentation of international law, hegemonic power struggles, self-awarded legitimacy, and cultural diversity. The third assumption encourages us to ignore the fact that much of the literature comes from European, particularly German, writers. It is questioned whether a concept that is so closely tied to a particular legal culture, or particular legal cultures, can really be described as universal. The five key themes of global constitutionalism as determined in Chapter 1 are subsequently scrutinised for their limitations. It is argued that the constraint of power always also includes the granting of power, and that the constraint of power by means of purely legal equality could lead to a marginalisation of minorities. The second key theme of global constitutionalism, the institutionalisation of power, is criticised as having the potential to create a chasm between the public and the private spheres, which could lead to a downgrading of abuses in the workplace and home, often of particular concern to women. Social idealism, as the third key theme, is criticised in terms of its focus on normative ideals of society, exclusively based on human rights. It is observed that human rights have been accused of conceptual or ideological imperialism, overlooking the benefits of diversity, if they are interpreted in a way that is particular to a certain philosophical, historical, and ethical viewpoint. The fourth key theme – standard-setting – is criticised for its bias towards ideas associated with a certain political tradition, privileged as those most 'progressive'. Finally, it is observed that individual rights carry with them an indeterminacy that invites political decision-makers to interpret the content of a norm, and therewith encourages hegemonic approaches that may disadvantage minority traditions. To conclude the chapter, it is noted that limitations of the predominant liberal democratic traditions would be manifested and reinforced on a global scale if applied to global constitutionalism.

With these critical points in mind, Chapter 4 suggests a reconfiguration of global constitutionalism, in terms of what I call 'organic global constitutionalism'. The chapter opens by asking whether, given the limitations of prevailing approaches, the project of global constitutionalism should be simply abandoned. The discourse on global constitutionalism is however established within international legal work to such an extent that it cannot viably be abandoned. What then accounts for this? How are we to understand the appeal of global constitutionalist thinking? It is asserted that the tenacity of the idea of global constitutionalism finds its reason in the rationalisation of new *allocations of power* in the international sphere, their belief that law has the *potency to impact on social reality* and the appeal of finding a means of *legitimising international law* itself. Towards the end of the chapter an alternative way of framing global constitutionalism - 'organic global constitutionalism' – is outlined. Underpinning it are four key elements: first, the idea of constitutionalism as *process*. By this is meant that, instead of viewing global constitutionalism as a fixed framework, and one organised with reference to a single and ultimate source of authority, constitutionalism is regarded as flexible and adaptable. Second, the idea of constitutionalism as *political*. This points to the possibilities for challenging technocratic decision-making, and for rendering that which has become rigid revisable through discourse. The emphasis is on a normative order that is determined discursively rather than being presupposed by pre-political convictions. Third, the idea of constitutionalism as a '*negative universal*'. Referencing the work of Ernesto Laclau on democracy, it is suggested that global constitutionalism should remain an 'empty space' in the sense that it has no 'positive' content, but instead is shaped in and through particular practices and institutions. And fourth, the idea of organic global constitutionalism as a *promise for the future*. A notion of 'constitutionalism to come', analogous to Jacques Derrida's idea of 'democracy to come', is advocated, as a way of suggesting the importance of orienting change without fixing its precise course.

Although this is predominantly a theoretical study, the final chapter attempts to address the many practical issues that would attend the implementation of organic global constitutionalism. This comes with a disclaimer that the study does not offer a comprehensive 'solution' to the problems of global constitutionalism; rather, it attempts to elucidate those problems, and to suggest possible ways of re-thinking global constitutionalism so as to get beyond them. Chapter 5 attempts to do this by revisiting the four dimensions of global constitutionalism and considers first how these are likely to play out in practice and then how this may be corrected by means of a more organic approach.

In the first two chapters, the authors relied upon are those that seemed most representative of a certain time or of a certain idea. This was in a way easiest for the contemporary debate illustrated in the first Chapter. I merely collected as much literature on global constitutionalism by international lawyers and those scholars thinking about international law as possible. I was however restricted by language, focussing largely on German and English publications. For considering the history of key constitutional themes I began with Aristotle of Classical Antiquity. When the examination moves to the Enlightenment, the work of Kant is referenced as the work of a thinker who had enormous impact on contemporaries and successors. The literature that was most influential for the critique of global constitutionalism (Chapter 3) stems from scholars that are critical of the predominance of liberal democratic themes in matters concerning power structures. The work of political philosophers such as James Tully, feminist social theorists such as Carol Gilligan, postmodernists such as Derrida, and international lawyers such as Martti Koskenniemi, was employed. The arguments draw on, *inter alia*, notions of participatory democracy, Marxist theories, approaches that grapple with the accommodation of cultural diversity, and anti-imperialist thought. Interestingly, while much of the literature on global constitutionalism is very recent, the relevant critical literature comes predominantly from the 1990s. In the 1990s, there was a wave of critical work that proved extremely valuable for this book. Concerns about the marginalisation of minorities, about governance by experts and bureaucrats, and about the dominance of male over female interests, were voiced in critical literature. Recalling these concerns, the fourth chapter suggests a new approach to global constitutionalism. This chapter draws largely on the thoughts of philosophers and political scientists such as Jürgen Habermas, James Tully, Ernesto Laclau and Jacques Derrida, and extrapolates them to the discourse on global constitutionalism.

Public international lawyers have long been attracted to the idea of global constitutionalism. Alfred Verdross was among the first to treat constitutionalism as relevant to international law. His work with the ambitious title *The Constitution of the International Legal Community* was published in 1926.[3] For him, global constitutionalism was a matter of the structure and subdivision of spheres of jurisdiction in the international community. His emphasis on

[3] Alfred Verdross, *Die Verfassung der Völkerrechtsgemeinschaft* (J. Springer, Wien 1926).

procedural constitutional rules differs from the current emphasis on substantive constitutional norms. Although Verdross was very influential, his vision of global constitutionalism can almost be regarded as utopian in consideration of the two World Wars that followed his publication. At the time, however, his concern appears to have been to promote an international rule of law organised in the League of Nations, as a means of countering the ideology of 'might is right' that later led to the First World War.[4] The debate over global constitutionalism re-sparked with Wolfgang Friedmann in 1964, who referred to international constitutional law as 'a new field of international law'.[5] Writing during the Cold War, Friedmann observed a dilemma between the sovereign nation States on the one hand and the identification of common needs and goals through international organisation on the other hand.[6] He notably wrote this in an epoch preoccupied with cooperation and institution-building, and amidst the last efforts of decolonisation. Verdross later returned to his ideas of global constitutionalism in the treatise co-authored with Bruno Simma in 1976.[7] This time, he referred to the United Nations Charter as the global constitution of the international community.[8]

While the preceding international lawyers initiated the debate, it is only in the past decade or so that global constitutionalism has moved to the centre of international legal discussions. Susan Breau describes it as 'one of the "hot topics" in international law research'.[9] In 2004, the first Chair for International Constitutional Law was created at the Amsterdam Center for International Law in the Netherlands, held by Erika de Wet. 2009 saw the publication of the book *The Constitutionalization of International Law* by three eminent participants to the debate, Jan Klabbers, Anne Peters, and Geir Ulfstein[10] and the book *Ruling the World? Constitutionalism, International Law and Global Governance*, edited by Jeffrey L. Dunoff and Joel P. Trachtman[11]. These explications are followed with a continuation of the debate in a symposium issue in the International Journal of Constitutional law. 2012 will see the launch of a new journal dedicated to and titled *Global Constitutionalism*. And yet, despite

[4] Bruno Simma, 'The Contribution of Alfred Verdross to the Theory of International Law' (1995) 6 EJIL 41.

[5] Wolfgang Friedmann, *The Changing Structure of International Law* (Stevens, London 1964) 152–159.

[6] *Ibid* 293.

[7] Alfred Verdross, Bruno Simma, *Universelles Völkerrecht* (3rd edn Duncker & Humboldt, Berlin 1984).

[8] *Ibid* Preface VII.

[9] Susan C. Breau, 'The Constitutionalization of the International Legal Order' (2008) 21 LJIL 560.

[10] Jan Klabbers, Anne Peters, Geir Ulfstein, *The Constitutionalization of International Law* (OUP, Oxford 2009).

[11] Jeffrey L. Dunoff and Joel P. Trachtman (eds), *Ruling the World? Constitutionalism, International Law, and Global Governance* (CUP, Cambridge 2009).

all these efforts, it is still not clear what is meant by global constitutionalism, at least when used in international legal circles. There has so far been no comprehensive categorisation of the issues, and nor has there been any sustained critical analysis of the claims involved. Nicholas Tsagourias, who edited *Transnational Constitutionalism: International and European Perspectives,* wrote in the introduction to this 2007 volume that, while the discourse on international constitutionalism is 'gaining momentum' it is still 'in its infancy and appears rather slippery'.[12] Bardo Fassbender, for his part, has characterised the notion of a global constitution as 'blurry'.[13] This book aims to get a grip on what has hitherto seemed so 'slippery', and to bring focus to the 'blurriness' that has afflicted international legal discussions of global constitutionalism to date.

[12] Nicholas Tsagourias, 'Introduction – Constitutionalism: a theoretical roadmap' in Nicholas Tsagourias (ed), *Transnational Constitutionalism, International and European Perspectives* (CUP, Cambridge 2007) 7.

[13] Bardo Fassbender, 'The Meaning of International Constitutional Law' in Ronald St. John Macdonald and Douglas M. Johnston (eds), *Towards World Constitutionalism – Issue in the Legal Ordering of the World Community* (Martinus Nijhoff, Leiden 2005) 840.

CHAPTER ONE

DIMENSIONS OF GLOBAL CONSTITUTIONALISM IN PUBLIC INTERNATIONAL LAW

A constitution should be short and obscure.[1]

Introduction

Many suggestions have been made as to what a global constitution could and should be composed of and which process supposedly amounts to constitutionalisation. While there is currently no one document or set of norms recognised as the global constitution, there are different but overlapping contemporary debates in international law regarding global constitutionalism. The aim of Chapter 1 is to categorise the variety of conceptions that are employed to describe global constitutionalism. In doing this, I attempt to extract the main constitutional themes that, according to the relevant author, makes their vision a global constitutional vision. The central focus of the various visions of global constitutionalism will determine how the contributions of largely contemporary academics are grouped. I call these groups the 'dimensions' of global constitutionalism.

At the outset, some relevant distinctions and some remarks regarding the methodology of this chapter must be made. The first issue that is to be clarified is the issue of selection: which contributions to the debate on global constitutionalism were selected as being part of public international law? Global constitutionalism is an interdisciplinary body of knowledge and research and is neither a coherent nor a comprehensive concept. As the issues concerning global constitutionalism involve questions of universal and particular concepts, of law and politics, of ideas and pragmatics, of values and participation, and many more such contested areas, global constitutionalism itself is a terrain of debate.[2] The interdisciplinary character makes it difficult to ascertain which contributions derive from which discipline, hence there is no clearcut delimitation of contributions to public international law. The following

---

[1] Napoleon Bonaparte (1769–1821).

[2] The term 'global constitutionalism' could be classified as a term that Walter Bryce Gallie referred to as an 'essentially contested concept'. Gallie's paper bearing the same name, which he presented at the Aristotelian Society, stated that it was impossible to define certain appraisive concepts; such concepts should rather be examined on how the concept has been used by different parties throughout history. (1956) 56 Proceedings of the Aristotelian Society 167–198.

contributions have been selected on the basis of their *legal* nature. All the selected ideas view global constitutionalism as based on a legal order in the international or transnational sphere, i.e. a normative system which transcends the national legal system. Since it is impossible to discuss all ideas on global constitutionalism, a selection of key ideas is presented.

The second methodological issue concerns the distinction between the claim that a global constitution already exists and the claim that a process is under way that will eventually lead to the existence of a global constitution. Suggestions for global constitutionalism include (a) a descriptive approach: such suggestions rely on a specific existing document or a specific set of norms, describing them as *the* global constitution; and (b) the normative approach: such suggestions focus on norms, documents, or principles that *could* one day harden to a global constitution. This approach mostly deals with constitutional*isation*, i.e. the process that leads to a global constitution.[3]

One possible approach for an examination of global constitutionalism would be to separate these two branches of thought. This approach has not been adopted in the following because of two concerns: impracticality and illogicality. It goes without saying that there is a significant overlap between the ideas on the existence of a global constitution and ideas on global constitutionalisation. Some scholars might refer to a certain set of norms as making up the global constitution, while others might refer to these same norms as an indicator for the process of constitutionalisation. Human rights norms are a prime example of this overlap. Some scholars, whose work is explored below, identify certain fundamental human rights norms that have reached peremptory status as *the* global constitution; others identify them as indicative and contributory to the *process* of global constitutionalisation. The following portrayal is therefore not divided into two separate parts, with one focusing on ideas of existing global constitutions and one focusing on ideas of emerging global constitutions because it would be impractical. A further reason (illogicality) for not making this distinction is because the increased number of characterisations of 'a global constitution' could indeed be viewed as a *trend* of constitutionalisation. The more contributions there are on the nature of a global constitution, the more symptomatic this is of a process of global constitutionalisation. A separation between assertions of the existence of a global constitution on the one hand and statements about the undergoing of a process of constitutionalisation on the other hand might then be regarded as illogical.

At this point, it seems necessary to refer to the categorisation of the dimensions of global constitutionalism. I suggest four dimensions of constitutionalism in public international law as one way of organising the ongoing debate on

---

[3] See for this distinction also Jan Klabbers, 'Setting the Scene' in Jan Klabbers, Anne Peters, Geir Ulfstein, *The Constitutionalization of International Law* (OUP, Oxford 2009) 4.

global constitutionalism. These four dimensions together make up the bulk of the discussion:

1) *Social Constitutionalism* (emphasising coexistence);
2) *Institutional Constitutionalism* (emphasising governance through institutions);
3) *Normative Constitutionalism* (emphasising specific fundamental norms); and finally
4) *Analogical Constitutionalism* (emphasising analogies to domestic and regional constitutionalism).[4]

These four dimensions reflect the primary focus of the contributors of public international law to the field of global constitutionalism. As with most categorisations of this kind, there are no clear delimitations but rather a strong overlap of views. For example, Jürgen Habermas speaks of the international community (at the centre of attention in Social Constitutionalism); he is in favour of a multilayered system (the centre of attention in some forms of Institutional Constitutionalism); he argues that global constitutionalism should include the protection of human rights (argued by exponents of Normative Constitutionalism); and finally he also uses the EU as a model of supranational power that he envisages for the international sphere (argued by some supporters of Analogical Constitutionalism). At the centre of this vision for global constitutionalism lies the idea of a multilayered system, which is why he has been grouped with the advocates of Institutional Constitutionalism here.[5] Although the following aims at portraying the main preoccupations of contributions on global constitutionalism, it is possible that some of the writers would categorise themselves differently.

A further methodological issue was how to characterise the split between views on the constitutionalisation of international *law* on the one hand and the constitutionalisation of the international *order* on the other hand. There are scholars, such as Jost Delbrück and Angelika Emmerich-Fritsche, whose visions are predicated on the distinction between the two in the sense of a 'world law' on the one hand and on international law on the other. Scholars of international relations and political theory also often subscribe to this view. However, from a *normative* perspective, all contributors to the debate on global constitutionalism are in fact on the same page: they all refer to the existence of a framework composed of norms that are applicable to the international

[4] Christine E. J. Schwöbel, 'Situating the Debate on Global Constitutionalism' (2010) 8 (3) International Journal of Constitutional Law *forthcoming*.

[5] See Jürgen Habermas, Ciaran Cronin (tr), 'Does the Constitutionalization of International Law Still Have a Chance?' in *The Divided West* (Polity, Cambridge 2006) 116ff.

legal community. In terms of the methodology, it therefore seems too strained to make a distinction between these views.

As a final methodological point it must be mentioned again that – so as to achieve as inclusive an account of global constitutionalism as possible – the terms 'global constitution' and 'global constitutionalism' are not predefined. The following contributions have been selected on the basis that they all invoke the concept of 'global constitutionalism', not because they fit a certain definition of 'global constitution'.

The chapter begins, in Section I, with visions of '*Social Constitutionalism*', a vision defined by the idea that the international sphere is an order of coexistence. Ideas of Social Constitutionalism, it will be found, centre political concerns of participation, often relying on liberal democracy as a model framework through which participation can be achieved. Section II undertakes to highlight visions that I have categorised as '*Institutional Constitutionalism*'. It is put forward that Institutional Constitutionalism places questions of accountability at the forefront of considerations of constitutionalism. In these contributions to the debate, the locus of power is identified first, and this is then underlined through a constitutional order. Section III is headed '*Normative Constitutionalism*' to categorise those views of global constitutionalism that centre on the importance of a common normative (value) system. This is distinct from the 'normative approach' described above in that the term here accentuates the use of *norms* themselves. Section IV discusses '*Analogical Constitutionalism*'. Analogical Constitutionalism is advocated by scholars that find certain patterns in the international sphere which are familiar to them from their own legal systems. They then apply the familiar concept to the international sphere. Chapter 2 concludes with a summary of the key themes of global constitutionalism that are the building blocks for the four dimensions I identified. The mapping of the debate reveals that the key themes are all associated with liberal democratic political theory. The question of whether this leads to limitations, and, if so, how, is the object of the chapter that follows.

Section I: Social Constitutionalism

The first dimension of global constitutionalism that will be analysed is the view that the basis for global constitutionalism lies in coexistence in an international social order. Proponents of this view believe that an international normative order exists that is applicable to certain subjects of this very order to regulate their coexistence. It is ascertained that the international sphere incorporates a global constitutional order formed on the basis of certain social relationships between subjects of this order. The first vision discussed is the view that the 'international community' is a constitutional order; the second the idea of a global civil society.

A. *The International Community School*

Writing in 1998 about the nature of the UN Charter (in a descriptive sense) as the global constitution, Bardo Fassbender coined the term 'the international community school'.[6] The emphasis of this school is the notion of a paradigm shift that has allegedly taken place in the international sphere. It is alleged that a shift has occurred away from a sovereignty-centred system to a value-oriented or individual-oriented system.[7] The idea of the international community as an integrated system is found in many visions of global constitutionalism. Indeed, the idea of an international community establishing an international legal order runs through most ideas of global constitutionalism like a red line.[8] The existence of a legal order is after all an important facilitating factor for constitutionalism. Proponents of the international community school centre their attention in terms of global constitutionalism on various points. Some are, for example in favour of a system that is based on the UN (such as Bardo Fassbender), while others are in favour of basing an international legal system on peremptory norms (such as Christian Tomuschat). These ideas of global constitutionalism will be discussed in more detail in the course of the Chapter. This sub-section will briefly look at the main scholars of 'the international community school' - who will also (re)appear in other sub-sections. As was mentioned above, a strict categorisation would be both over-inclusive and under-inclusive. In that sense, the categorising of the international community school is already an indication of the weaknesses of categorisation itself since this school of thought is not only part of Social Constitutionalism but also the remaining three dimensions. As the name suggests, the existence or establishment of a *community* is at the centre of attention, meaning it is best grouped with Social Constitutionalism. The thrust of 'international community' varies. It can mean an international community of States, a community of all the subjects of international law, or an international community of global citizens. The late Judge of the International Court of Justice Hermann Mosler is considered as an early subscriber to the view that international law has developed beyond a merely consensual organisation to become an international legal system. In his Hague Lectures in 1974, Mosler endeavoured to portray international society as a legal community; he aimed to illustrate that

---

[6] See Bardo Fassbender, 'The United Nations Charter As Constitution of the International Community' (1998) 36 Columbia Journal of Transnational Law 546ff.

[7] Christian Tomuschat, 'International Law: Ensuring the Survival of Mankind on the Eve of a New Century' General Course on Public International Law (1999) 281 Recueil des Cours de l'Académie de Droit International 237.

[8] The belief that the international sphere is an international legal order is a common assumption of contributors to the debate on global constitutionalism. This will be analysed in more depth in Chapter 3.

international society, consisting of States and (governmental) organisations, constitutes a community governed by a distinct law.[9]

Fassbender views global constitutional law as a sub-discipline of public international law. He believes that constitutional law of the international community has a separate existence to domestic constitutional law, although it may be influenced by constitutional ideas and practices developed in a national context.[10] In terms of the separate legal (and constitutional) order in the international sphere, Fassbender refers to the changes that have taken place in international law, commenting that the notion of constitutionalism seems to capture some of these changes.[11] He is a strong advocate of making such elements of a global constitution more concrete and therefore associating it with the UN Charter.[12] This aspect of his argument will be discussed in further detail below.[13] The vision of an international community, which has its separate legal existence in an international order, has become very popular among public international lawyers, particularly European ones. The term 'international community' is now firmly entrenched as part of the vocabulary of international law. Christian Tomuschat, a notable proponent of the vision of an integrated international community, sees the function of constitutional rules as the limitation of all forms of political power, international and municipal. In his view, this limitation is for the benefit of international peace, individual rights, and the rule of law.[14] He therefore particularly emphasises the first key theme of constitutionalism, the limitation of power. Tomuschat's view also rests strongly on the assumption that international law can direct and control social reality in general and political power in particular. He goes so far as to claim that States are the *instruments* of the international community.[15] The directing and controlling of social reality is a central tenet of governance (the institutionalisation of power), the second key theme of global constitutionalism.

B. *Global Civil Society*

Some contributors to the debate on global constitutionalism emphasise the indispensability of States in the international order, others are of the opinion

---

[9] Hermann Mosler, 'The International Society as a Legal Community' (1974) 140 Recueil des Cours de l'Académie de Droit International 1–320; revised version published as Hermann Mosler, *The International Society as a Legal Community* (Sijthoff & Noordhoff, Alphen aan den Rijn 1980).

[10] Bardo Fassbender, 'The Meaning of International Constitutional Law' in Ronald St. John Macdonald and Douglas M. Johnston (eds), *Towards World Constitutionalism* (Koninklijke Brill NV, Leiden 2005) 838.

[11] *Ibid* 840.

[12] *Ibid* 846 ff.

[13] See *Institutional Constitutionalism.*

[14] *Tomuschat, 1999* (n 7) 23.

[15] *Ibid* 95. Emphasis added.

that world law and global constitutionalism can be found in the idea of a civil world law which does away with the centrality of the State in the international order. Visions of a civil world law largely belong to the latter, emphasising the centrality of popular legitimacy. Gunther Teubner, Andreas Fischer-Lescano, and Philip Allott argue against a State-centred constitutionalism and promote the notion of a global constitutionalism of civil society instead.

Gunther Teubner advances his idea of global constitutionalism of civil society by way of portraying the existence of autonomous 'global civil constitutions'. In his view, these global civil constitutions express a 'constitutionalization of a multiplicity of autonomous subsystems of world society'.[16] Teubner expands on Niklas Luhmann's pioneering work on civil society.[17] He dismisses any attempts at applying the circumstances of the nation State uncritically to the world society because he believes that the decentralisation of politics in world society is not sufficiently taken into account in such visions.[18] Teubner premises his idea of constitutionalisation on three central trends of the 21st century: digitalisation, privatisation, and global networks.[19] In order for global constitutionalism to take into account these three trends and also the decentralisation of politics, constitutionalism is entirely disassociated from the State; instead Teubner argues in favour of a multiplicity of civil constitutions.[20] According to him, constitutionalisation is about the liberation of highly specialised dynamics through their societal institutionalisation. He believes that constitutionalisation is at the same time a form of institutionalisation of self-restraint mechanisms to prevent society-wide power expansionism.[21] While Teubner has an element of constitutionalist idealism because of his future-oriented vision, he also claims that such trends towards global civil constitutions are real and can be observed on a global scale.[22] Teubner's vision comprises participation-oriented and rights-oriented elements. The concerns about exclusion of segments of the population in processes of global communication are concerns of participation, as are the issues of disciplining social dynamics.[23] Moreover, civil constitutions also incorporate an element of rights-orientation. Teubner distinguishes between the organisational and the spontaneous part of a constitution. While the organisational part is concerned

[16] Gunther Teubner, 'Globale Zivilverfassungen: Alternativen zur staatszentrierten Verfassungstheorie' (2003) 63 Zeitschrift für ausländisches öffentliches Recht und Völkerrecht 6; see also Math Noortmann, *Enforcing International Law: From Self-Help to Self-Contained Regimes* (Aldershot, Ashate 2005).

[17] Niklas Luhmann, *Das Recht der Gesellschaft* (Suhrkamp, Frankfurt 1993) 582 ff.

[18] *Teubner* (n 16) 3–4.

[19] *Ibid* 2.

[20] *Ibid* 6.

[21] *Ibid* 10.

[22] *Ibid* 6.

[23] *Ibid* Summary 28.

with formal functions, the spontaneous part is concerned with value-oriented functions.[24] In respect of the latter, a comparison with basic rights is drawn. Teubner's view gives us an insight into further key themes of constitutionalism that can commonly be found in contemporary literature on global constitutionalism. In terms of the participatory and accountability elements, he refers to the *limitation of power* and the *institutionalisation of power* (identified as key themes of constitutionalism in the preceding part); regarding value-oriented elements, Teubner mentions *ideals* (a further key theme) and *individual rights* (the fourth key theme) as well as a *standard-setting capacity* (the final key theme) of constitutions. The main emphasis is on civil society and its participation in global processes.

Andreas Fischer-Lescano begins with the observation that a constitution is a special form of structural coupling of two different systems – the political and the legal. On the global sphere this coupling has put the international community as the decision-making unity into effect.[25] In his view, the circularity of politics (existing through the paradox of limited sovereignty) and the circularity of law (existing through the paradox that law defines law) are interrupted in the concept of a constitution.[26] According to him, the global legal system is divided into a centre and a periphery. The centre is visible in the courts (international and national courts deciding on global remedies) while the periphery is made up of all the areas of the legal system that are not courts, i.e. States, NGOs and other actors of civil society.[27] Besides engaging in their specific institutional functions, these courts engage in setting a standard for human rights law.[28] He divides 'the Global Constitution' into (1) Jurisdiction norms (global remedies rules), (2) *Jus Cogens* and (3) Norms about norms (Art. 38 ICJ Statute).[29] Similar to Teubner, Fischer-Lescano believes that global constitutionalism must primarily be understood as political global constitutionalism. He too believes that such a political global constitutionalism must go beyond public international law and its predominant limitation to States, to include civil society. Fischer-Lescano describes this body of law the *lex humana*, which is in contrast to (but has the capacity to be part of) the *ius gentium*.[30] He is, in contrast to Teubner, much more assertive about the aspect of rights-orientation within global constitutionalist thought. Specific reference is made to fundamental norms of global constitutionalism (identified as *jus cogens*), which include certain human rights, for example the rights to be

---

[24] *Ibid* 25–26.

[25] Andreas Fischer-Lescano, 'Die Emergenz der Globalverfassung' (2003) 63 Zeitschrift für ausländisches öffentliches Recht und Verwaltungsrecht (ZaöRV) 759.

[26] *Ibid.*

[27] *Ibid* 738.

[28] *Ibid* 741.

[29] *Ibid* 760.

[30] *Ibid* 750ff.

free from torture and genocide. He refers to them as the fundamental values of the international community (*Fundamentalwerte der Internationalen Gemeinschaft*).[31] Finally, norm-making norms, to be found in Article 38 of the ICJ Statute, are considered a necessary element of a global constitution.[32] This idea of norm-making norms as constitutional norms will be examined more closely below as 'meta-rules' in the section on 'Analogical Constitutionalism'. Although Fisher-Lescano touches on many of the established key themes of global constitutionalism, his main focus is on civil society and its participation in order to limit the single locus of power.

In *Eunomia*, Philip Allott suggested a vision for a new global order that could be described as purely directed towards the future. Although he does not endorse the view that such an order exists or is even in the process of coming into existence, indeed has more recently claimed that the constitutionalising of international society is 'more improbable than ever'[33], Allott's vision is nevertheless valuable in the context of global constitutionalism. He not only includes a vision for the reform of the fundamental conceptions of international law, but also goes beyond this to demand the change of fundamental conceptions of international society itself. A global constitution is at the heart of this vision. In the first edition of *Eunomia*, Allott declared that his ambitious project has the purpose of proposing a 'general theory of society and law which is potentially universal ... a theory capable of being the theory acted upon by all participants in international society'.[34] Allott believed that a change in the general theory of society (also, 'a new general international theory') would inevitably lead to a reform of the fundamental conceptions of international law into a comprehensive legal system:

> Given the scale and complexity of the events of international society, it is obvious that the law of that society must sooner rather than later, form itself into a legal system at least as rich and complex as the more advanced national legal systems.[35]

At the centre of his vision lies the ability of the whole of international society to define itself ('social self-constituting of humanity').[36] In his later book, *The Health of Nations*, Allott provides a practical theory for the ideas from *Eunomia*.[37] He maintains the idea of social international society in what he terms the development from the 'social animal' to the 'social species'.[38] Allott

[31] *Ibid* 745.
[32] *Ibid* 748.
[33] Philip Allott, 'The Emerging International Aristocracy' (2003) 35 New York University Journal of International Law and Politics 336.
[34] Philip Allott, *Eunomia: New Order for a New World* (OUP, Oxford 1990) *Preface* xix.
[35] *Ibid* xxii.
[36] *Ibid Preface* xi.
[37] Philip Allott, *The Health of Nations* (CUP, Cambridge 2002) xi.
[38] *Ibid* ix.

does not refer specifically to a paradigm shift, but his arguments are in the same vein. He begins *The Health of Nations* with the words: 'The landscape of the human world is changing.'[39] His observations of changes to international social society are put into relation with changes in the international and national sphere.

Allott's vision of the constitution of an international society, a global constitution, has been referenced many times. Such a constitution is 'the fruit of a society's contemplation of itself in time and space.'[40] This self-constituting has three faces – a legal constitution, a real constitution, and an ideal constitution.[41] In the legal constitution, society sees its past ('its total self as it has been, as necessity, as obligation'). In the real constitution, society sees its present ('its total self as it is, as actuality, as action'). In the ideal constitution society sees its future ('its total self as it might be, as potentiality, as desire.').[42] This last type of constitution is a reflection of the key theme of social idealism. Since this theme is a little more difficult to grasp, it merits explaining here. Constitutions often incorporate ideas of improving society for the future; this vision is presented in the language of ideals. In modern constitutions, ideals are often translated into the call for the recognition and respect of inherent rights. Social idealism is often key for the legitimacy of a constitution, since constitutions not only require a legitimate method of being constituted, but must also include a legitimate agenda; one which is directed to the good life of all that live in that society. This key theme can be difficult to distinguish from the key theme of standard-setting (used here synonymously with standardisation and systematisation). Standard-setting, although similar to ideals in that they are both directed towards a better future, takes up a space of its own. Constitutions are often believed to be a collection of guidelines, whether ideal or practical, for the functioning of the polity that they constitute. Adherence to these guidelines is believed to lead the people of the polity to greater development. Standard-setting, in contrast to ideals, is thus a concrete notion of progress presented by way of a fixed plan or system.

Allott understands the three faces, the three constitutions, as being in a constant process of integration, as ceaselessly changing perspectives of the constitution in question. In this sense, Allott's vision of constitutionalism is very different to the other visions of constitutionalism that prefer to consider more rigid models. It will be seen in the following chapters that such flexibility could be very welcome in order to prevent some limitations that are inherent in the prevailing rigid theories of constitutionalism.

---

[39] *Ibid.*

[40] *Ibid* (9.1) 132.

[41] *Ibid* (9.6–9.10); 134–136; Philip Allott, 'Reconstituting Humanity – New International Law' (1992) 3 EJIL 225 (11).

[42] *Allott, 1992* (n 41).

This idea of constitutionalism includes the key themes of constitutional standard-setting (the legal constitution, which has set a standard for the actual/real constitution), elements of the limitation of power and governance (in the actual constitution), and elements of social idealism (the ideal constitution). Although these key themes are included in Allott's vision, at the heart of his idea is civil society and therefore the idea of a participation-oriented constitution.

C. *Summary*

'Social Constitutionalism' emphasises a participation-oriented idea of constitutionalism in the global sphere. Central to this dimension of global constitutionalism are the concepts of participation, influence, and accountability. International law is believed to offer a forum for participation, which is seen as the ultimate form of the limitation of (absolute) power and thus a form of justifying power. The advocates of Social Constitutionalism believe a shift has occurred in terms of the legitimacy of international law in that it has changed from a State-centred law predicated on consent to a comprehensive legal order of coexistence. Within this order social relations have emerged that must be protected and promoted. A global constitution is considered as a framework for this new international order, which has the function to regulate social behaviour. Such regulation of social behaviour is believed to operate through participation of the subjects of the constitution. The international community school views the international community as the very forum in which participation can be exercised (whether by States, non-governmental organisations or individuals). Advocates of a global civil society argue that individuals can and must take part in the international forum. The political labels that provide such forms of participation with legitimacy are 'civil society' (Teubner and Fischer-Lescano) and 'international society' (Allott). In domestic legal orders, this notion of participatory constitutionalism for the purpose of legitimacy is commonly referred to as constitutional democracy. The key constitutional themes that make up the building blocks of Social Constitutionalism are (a) the key theme of the limitation of power (special emphasis is on this key theme), (b) the key theme of governance, (c) the key theme of individual rights, (d) the key theme of social idealism, and (d) the key theme of individual rights. These are at the same time the central premises of all visions of global constitutionalism portrayed as encapsulating the contemporary debate.

Section II: Institutional Constitutionalism

'Institutional Constitutionalism' looks to where power is situated in the international sphere and seeks to legitimise this power through its institutionalisation. Institutionalisation questions largely concern the accountability of decision-makers. It is thought that accountability on the international sphere is best provided for in the form of certain international institutions. Three types of Institutional Constitutionalism are described: First, the idea of a constitutional order of *global governance* will be described. This view of constitutionalism dismisses the notion of a separate and comprehensive global constitution but rather explains it as multilayered and multifaceted. The second view portrays the *United Nations (UN) Charter* as the global constitution. This popular view of global constitutionalism is predicated on the belief that UN law amounts to a global constitutional framework. It makes reference to the formal and substantive constitutional features as well as more superficial features such as its widespread applicability, and the clarity and certainty of the UN Charter. Finally, the law of the *World Trade Organisation* (WTO) and the law of the *International Labour Organisation* (ILO), referred to as microconstitutionalism becoming macroconstitutionalism, will be examined in terms of their alleged constitutionality. The law of these institutions is considered to be 'constitutionalising' in a way that reaches beyond the organisation itself to the international sphere. These visions of global constitutionalism place much emphasis on democratic notions of representation and accountability.

A. *Global Governance*

Resulting from increased global cooperation in issues that were formerly under the exclusive competence of State governments, global networks of governance have emerged. Governance is mostly understood as the overall process of regulating and ordering issues of public interest. In the international sphere, 'governance' pertains to the exercise of authority in exclusion of an overarching governmental authority, in other words, 'governance without a world government'.[43] Thus, governance in the international sphere is neither exercised by a specific international nor by a specific national government. Global governance themes have attracted much attention among international relations scholars – indeed were originally conceived by them.

A number of eminent scholars of both international relations and international law subscribe to some form of a multilayered and multifaceted vision of global constitutionalism that lacks central governance. Anne Peters describes a network of constitutions that traverses both the national and the international legal orders. She declares that State constitutions' original claim to form a complete basic order is defeated and that therefore State constitutions are no longer 'total constitutions'.[44] Peters asserts that the international sphere

[43] James N. Rosenau, 'Governance, Order, and Change in World Politics' in James N. Rosenau, Ernst Otto Czempiel (eds) *Governance without Government* (CUP, Cambridge 1992) 7.

[44] Anne Peters, 'Compensatory Constitutionalism: The Function and Potential of Fundamental International Norms and Structures' (2006) 19 LJIL 580.

includes some formal properties of constitutional law, that some constitutional functions are fulfilled, and that some universal values are identifiable.[45] However, there are 'gaps' that debar a complete and comprehensive constitutionalism. The gaps include the fact that the phenomena that are described as constitutionalisation could also be described as 'thicker legalisation'; moreover, certain anti-constitutional trends (such as US hegemony and fragmentation of international law) can be detected. One should therefore consider *compensatory* constitutionalisation on the international plane in the form of transnational democratic structures that together encompass a 'constitutional network'.[46] Peters argues that this structure of a network of constitutionalism on the global level has emerged through two elements: globalisation on the international level and de-constitutionalisation on the domestic level.[47] As a result, global entities have been entrusted with previously typically governmental functions, meaning that State constitutions can no longer regulate the totality of governance.[48] Peters' view on global constitutionalism is influenced by her interpretation of constitutionalism as defined by democratic functions. Her reference to the 'constitutional principle of democracy' illustrates the perceived deep link between political democratic functions and constitutionalism:

> The hollowing out of national constitutions affects not only the constitutional principle of democracy, but also the rule of law and the principle of social security. ... Only the various levels of governance, taken together, can provide full constitutional protection.[49]

In Peters' view, the 'hollowing out' of national constitutions will not lead to their complete disappearance. She believes that the influx of international legal obligations is leading to an insistence that States safeguard certain constitutional principles. This relationship between international and national law is thus a 'network' rather than a 'hierarchy' of rules.[50] Peters places much emphasis on the requirement and establishment of a legal order. She claims that the basic premise of the constitutionalist school is that the international community is a legal community.[51] Peters defines such a community as a community governed by rules and principles, not (only) by power.[52] The (re)construction of a network made up of international and national constitutional features

---

[45] Anne Peters, 'Global Constitutionalism in a Nutshell' in Liber amicorum Jost Delbrück, *Weltinnenrecht* (2005) 548.

[46] *Peters, 2005* (n 45) 537. Emphasis in the original; *Peters, 2006* (n 43) 579–610, particularly 592.

[47] *Peters, 2005* (n 45) 536–537.

[48] *Ibid*; *Peters, 2006* (n 44) 580.

[49] *Peters, 2005* (n 45) 537; *Peters, 2006* (n 43) 580.

[50] *Peters, 2005* (n 45) 542.

[51] *Ibid* 541.

[52] *Ibid.*

would help compensate for the national constitutional deficiencies.[53] Peters' view on global constitutionalism clearly favours the key theme of governance in the form of institutionalisation of power. By focusing on governance, she advances a democratic vision of global constitutionalism. This necessitates democratic structures in the international sphere.

One of the first visionaries of a multilayered and multifaceted interplay between the national and the international sphere was of course Anne-Marie Slaughter in *A New World Order*.[54] She describes a web of links between, what she terms, 'disaggregated' State institutions made up of government networks. By this she means that although States still exist in the new world order, they relate to each other, not only through the Foreign Office, but also through regulatory, judicial, and legislative channels.[55] She explains that global governance is caused by the process of 'citizens going global'.[56] She rejects the idea of a global constitution since she believes that such a constitution would require a formal global government.[57] She suggests an alternative to formal global government: an informal set of principles. Informal principles and norms should operate independently of formal codification, 'even as the actors and activities they would regulate form and reform in shifting patterns of governance'.[58] Slaughter's ideas have inspired many authors writing about global constitutionalism, although most international lawyers opt for a formal type of global constitutionalism, which nevertheless rejects the idea of a global government. Authors have taken inspiration from the idea of a global network of governance and describe this in terms of global constitutionalism.

Stefan Kadelbach and Thomas Kleinlein also describe a multilayered international legal system. They base their argument on the concept of general principles of law enshrined in Article 38 (1) (c) of the ICJ Statute.[59] Three distinct categories are described: first, principles that are generally recognised provisions of domestic law; second, general principles originating in international relations; and third, general principles applicable to all kinds of legal relations.[60] This method introduces principles of national constitutional law into public international law while at the same time upholding established consent. They attempt a 'reconstruction of the constitutional approach to

---

[53] *Ibid* 550.
[54] Anne-Marie Slaughter, *A New World Order* (Princeton University Press, Princeton 2004).
[55] *Ibid* 5.
[56] *Ibid* 17.
[57] *Ibid* 245.
[58] *Ibid.*
[59] Stefan Kadelbach and Thomas Kleinlein, 'International Law – a Constitution for Mankind? An Attempt at a Re-appraisal with an Analysis of Constitutional Principles' (2007) 50 GYIL 337ff.
[60] *Ibid* 339.

public international law as a theory of constitutional principles.'[61] This reconstruction, so they argue, must take place when there is a need to transfer principles of national constitutional law to international law. Such a need is evident where public international law is structurally equivalent to State constitutions but lacks adequate provisions of its own.[62] While one could argue that the described principles are secondary rules in the sense of H.L.A Hart or meta-rules in the sense of Tomuschat, they in fact concern the regulation of conduct and are thus primary (substantive) rules. Kadelbach and Kleinlein identify universal respect for human rights, democratic legitimacy or accountability, the rule of law and also the principle of respect for the environment as (national) constitutional principles that are (international) general principles of international law and thus international constitutional norms.[63] Kadelbach and Kleinlein regard principles as distinct from and immune to the shortcomings of values. While values and principles have an equivalent structure in legal argumentation, principles have the advantage of being dynamic rather than final. They claim that idealism is key for constitutionalism and principles are central elements for enabling idealism. Kadelbach and Kleinlein explain that a principle posits an 'ideal-ought'; they refer to this as an 'optimization requirement'.[64] According to them, this is what distinguishes principles from rules. Principles do not require a generalised decision of supremacy, but allow for balancing and flexibility and leave some leeway to the competent body.[65] This is similar to Allott's idea of the necessity of an ideal constitution. The rejection of predetermined values in favour of a more flexible approach is an important aspect of later suggestions for reconceptualising global constitutionalism and will be examined in greater depth in the following chapters.

One of the most eminent contemporary scholars of political philosophy, Jürgen Habermas, has also observed that the multilevel system of governance makes up a political constitution of a decentralized world society.[66] In his book, *The Divided West*, Habermas dedicates a chapter to the question: 'Does the Constitutionalization of International Law Still Have a Chance?'[67] He declares that the goals of international relations are peace, international security, the promotion of human rights and democracy throughout the world. The question is whether law has a role to play in achieving these goals. There are two possibilities: either by way of legal procedures in the framework of

[61] *Ibid* 338.
[62] *Ibid* 342.
[63] Stefan Kadelbach and Thomas Kleinlein, 'Überstaatliches Verfassungsrecht: Zur Konstitutionalisierung im Völkerrecht' (2006) 44 AVR 235, 254.
[64] *Kadelbach, Kleinlein, 2007* (n 59) 345.
[65] *Ibid* 346.
[66] *Habermas* (n 5).
[67] *Ibid* Chapter 8.

world organisation, or by the unilateral decision-making of 'a well-meaning hegemon'.[68] Habermas believes that a world organisation constituted through international law could address the goals of international relations if it were in a multilayered form. There should be a *supranational* level, which would have the capacity of ensuring functions pertaining to securing peace and promoting human rights and there should be a *transnational* level, which would concern the problems of global domestic politics (he suggests regional or continental regimes modelled on the EU).[69] Similar to Anne Peters and echoing Anne-Marie Slaughter, Habermas notes that 'States are losing their autonomy in part as they become increasingly enmeshed in the horizontal networks of a global society.'[70] Habermas observes that the current 'post-national constellation' of international affairs is supportive of the constitutionalisation of public international law.[71] In his view, the United Nations with its Charter as its core, are achievements on the (arduous) way to a political constitution of world society.[72] In his view, the UN would play a significant role at the *supranational* level.[73] Visions of global constitutionalism that are wholly based on viewing the UN Charter at 'the global constitution' will be discussed below.

Miguel Poiares Maduro is a further scholar arguing in favour of a constitutional approach to global governance.[74] Similarly to Peters, Maduro claims that global constitutionalism has not made national constitutions redundant but rather that there are different instances of applicability.[75] Unlike Peters, who identifies the constitutional value of global governance on the basis of the constitutional function of governance itself, Maduro emphasises the requirement of legitimising power in constitutional terms.[76] He illustrates that the form and locus of power have changed from what was traditionally a State monopoly. Traditionally, the form of power – the constitution of a nation State – and power itself coincided in the same locus, the State. Global governance, however, has caused a shift of power to global sites. The form of power, i.e. the mechanisms that determine the exercise of such power, has also changed.[77] Crucially, in some instances such power can no longer be traced back and legitimated through the State constitution.[78] Thus, reasons Maduro,

[68] *Ibid* 116.
[69] *Ibid* 136.
[70] *Ibid* 115, 116.
[71] *Ibid* 115.
[72] *Ibid* 173ff.
[73] *Ibid* 136.
[74] Miguel Poiares Maduro 'From Constitutions to Constitutionalism: A Constitutional Approach for Global Governance' in Douglas Lewis (ed) *Global Governance and the Quest for Justice* vol I (Hart Publishing, Oxford and Portland, Oregan 2006) 227ff.
[75] *Ibid* 251–252.
[76] *Ibid* particularly 251.
[77] *Ibid* 229.
[78] *Ibid*.

since States cannot constitutionally control global governance, there must be a structure that can.[79] Maduro does not refer to the constitution of a *legal order*, rather (consistently with his emphasis on political constitutionalism) the constitution of a *polity*:

> The polity is the basic assumption of a Constitution. [...] The Constitution both defines and presupposes a polity of political community whose member are bound by such constitution.[80]

Maduro distinguishes between national constitutions and constitutionalism, claiming that national constitutions include a long-term political contract, which is supported by or with a polity, a political community. He asserts that constitutionalism, in contrast, is broader. Constitutionalism is defined as a normative theory that allocates, disciplines, and governs power in order to maximise the constitutional ideals of freedom and full participation and representation.[81] Such a theory is applicable beyond the nation State: 'It is and ought to be applicable to any institution that exercises power.'[82] Finally, the argument is applied to global governance. According to him, global governance allocates, disciplines, and governs power in the international sphere. It is evident that the key theme of global constitutionalism that Maduro bases his argument on is (political) governance, particularly the legitimising (and therewith accountability) of governance through constitutionalism.

Although mostly emerging from the field of international relations, *cosmopolitan* visions of global constitutionalism can also be regarded as part of international law contributions. The cosmopolitan view is based on the requirement of a global normative order and hence fulfils the above criterion for it to be considered as pertaining to public international law. The ideal is the *cosmopolis* created through a global civil society. Emphasis is placed on the establishment of a global political community, which is constituted of and by a society of free and equal individuals. The notion of cosmopolitanism can be described as political constitutionalism aiming to constitute global democracy. Cosmopolitan constitutionalism is closely related to the aforementioned global governance idea of global constitutionalism in that it envisions democratic processes on an international scale. It can be distinguished from the global governance view in that cosmopolitanism seeks to achieve a comprehensive global order, while global governance ideas are typically much more sectional. Cosmopolitan constitutionalism generally assumes 'that an essential core of the concept of democracy can be disembedded from the notion and institutions of the constitutional nation state and re-planted within transnational

[79] *Ibid* 233.
[80] *Ibid* 235.
[81] *Ibid* 251.
[82] *Ibid*.

governance systems …'[83] David Held claims that the 'cosmopolitan model of democracy' is a necessary instrument to ensure the accountability of the related and interconnected power systems of the world. Held describes these power systems as a series of overlapping local, regional and global processes requiring three things: first, that the territorial boundaries of the systems of accountability be recast to show that there is not one power hub; second, that the role and place of regulatory and functional agencies be rethought to include those agencies that are not 'centralised'; and third, that the articulation of political institutions be reformed to include the participation of key groups in the democratic process. These key groups are agencies, associations and organisations of the economy as well as national and international civil society.[84] Constitutionalism therefore becomes an instrument for institutionalising democratic procedures in the international sphere in order to obtain accountability for power processes. In other words, constitutionalism is designated as a means of achieving worldwide democracy.

Another form of global governance in international law, concerning regulation and administration, is found in the growing area of *global administrative law*. Global administrative law proponents regard the blurring of the domestic and the international, the performing of administrative functions of different officials and institutions at different levels, and the general increase of public power in the administrative realm as a 'growing trend towards administrative-law type mechanisms' on the global scale.[85] Nico Krisch and Benedict Kingsbury are among the most eminent scholars researching in this area. Krisch and Kingsbury explain that there are widely varying forms and institutions exercising administrative and regulatory functions, and that these forms and institutions are distinctly administrative in that they concern 'the setting and application of rules by bodies that are not legislative or primarily adjudicative in character'.[86] Krisch and Kingsbury consider constitutional forms only for the domestic scale and generally reject constitutionalisation of power structures.[87] According to the above definition that all contributions that regard themselves as part of the 'global constitutional' debate also qualify as such, the concept of global administrative law is therefore, prima facie,

[83] Claire Methven O'Brian, 'Reframing Deliberative Cosmopolitanism: Perspectives of Transnationalisation and Post-national Democracy from Labour Law – Part I/II' (2008) 9 German Law Journal 1008.

[84] David Held, *Democracy and the Global Order: From the Modern State to Cosmopolitan Governance* (Stanford University Press, Stanford 1995) 267ff.

[85] Nico Krisch and Benedict Kingsbury, 'Introduction: Global Governance and Global Administrative Law in the International Legal Order' (2006) 17 EJIL 1, 2.

[86] *Ibid* 3.

[87] Krisch states: 'In the circumstances of global governance, attempts at "constitutionalizing" the political order by forcing it into a coherent, unified framework are problematic as they tend to downplay the extent of legitimate diversity in the global polity'. Nico Krisch, 'The Pluralism of Global Administrative Law' (2006) 17 EJIL 248.

a distinct debate.[88] However, it can certainly be noted that the impetus for the growth of interest in global administrative law and global constitutionalism is rooted in similar thoughts on changes in international law and the international sphere in general. Global constitutionalism and global administrative law both attempt to explain the shifting power and legal structures that have accompanied the growth in international decision-making bodies, they also both address concerns of legitimacy and participation.[89]

B. *The United Nations*

Institutional Constitutionalism can refer to a single institution and its institutional law. In international legal discourse, the word 'constitution' is also used for the characterisation of foundational treaties of international organisations. In the cases of international organisations that have a large number of members States, it has therefore been suggested that the foundational treaty should span beyond the organisation itself to also include the member States. The first and foremost such international organisation is the UN and its foundational treaty, the UN Charter. The assertion that the Charter of the UN is a global constitution is one which has been the object of much academic thought and has been an inspiration for many publications. The analysis of scholars is based on the thesis that the UN Charter is not only the constitution of the UN organisation, but goes beyond this to be a constitution for the world.

As with other suggestions for a global constitution, the extent to which the UN Charter is believed to *be* a global constitution or instead to initiate a process of constitutionalisation varies. As is familiar from the above discourses, the variations depend on which definition for constitution the author opts for. Ronald St. John Macdonald and Bardo Fassbender are among the most assertive proponents of granting the UN Charter the label 'the global constitution'. Macdonald claims boldly that

> [i]t is apparent … that the material content of the Charter of United Nations is indeed constitutional and that we are fully justified in treating the Charter as the constitution of the international community.[90]

There are various methods by which the constitutional character of the Charter of the United Nations is demonstrated. The writers that advocate the global constitutional nature of the UN Charter commonly refer to a distinction

---

[88] A further analysis of this would go beyond the scope of this book, but is an intriguing question that offers much room for further research.

[89] Krisch, Kingsbury (n 85), Krisch (n 87); for a further analysis of the *appeal* of the global constitutionalist debate, see below, Chapter 4.

[90] Ronald St. John Macdonald, 'The International Community as a Legal Community' in Ronald St. John Macdonald and Douglas M. Johnston (eds), *Towards World Constitutionalism – Issues in the Legal Ordering of the World Community* (Brill, Leiden 2005) 879.

between the formal (institutional) and the material (substantive) element of a constitution.[91] The following illustrations of arguments are therefore also divided into the institutional content on the one hand and the normative content on the other hand.

Frequent reference is made to the various organs of the United Nations, which have functions comparable to organs of power in the national sphere. Macdonald expresses the view that the provisions for the establishment of the organs (the General Assembly, Security Council, and others set forth in Chapter III UN Charter) are a reflection of the formal constitutional authority by which power is delegated from the people to their respective government representatives.[92] In his article from 1998, Fassbender begins by observing that every constitutional instrument must provide for the performance of basic functions of governance. He explains that the Charter fulfils this requirement through the express provisions relating to legislation, application of law, and adjudication.[93] Macdonald refers to Allott's definition of constitutions for qualifying the limitation of power in the UN Charter as a constitutional aspect. As discussed above, Allott's 'constitution of a society' includes three constitutions in one – the legal, the real, and the ideal.[94] To paraphrase Macdonald, the limitations on the exercise of a power of the UN Security Council reflects the trichotomous balance between the legal, the real (which he calls 'actual') and the ideal.[95]

Besides the assertion of institutional/formal constitutional aspects of the UN, substantive aspects are also claimed to be constitutional. Although the UN Charter does not have an extensive catalogue of individual norms, included are nevertheless a set of norms that are aimed at governing the behaviour of member States. The main substantive principles are identified as the maintenance of peace and security as set out in Article 1 (1) UN Charter; the prohibition of the use of force laid down in Article 2 (4) UN Charter; the peaceful settlement of disputes (Arts. 1(1), 2 (3) and 33); the principle of equal rights and self-determination of peoples (Art. 1 (2)); the principle of cooperation (Art. 1 (3)); the promotion of respect for human rights and fundamental freedoms without any form of discrimination (Art. 1 (3)); and the respect of the sovereign equality of all its Members (Art. 2 (1)).[96] These substantive norms are regarded as constitutional norms due to their content. It is furthermore observed that this supremacy in content is secured through a formal

---

[91] See particularly Pierre-Marie Dupuy 'The Constitutional Dimension of the Charter of the United Nations Revisited' (1997) 1 Max Planck Yearbook of United Nations Law 3.
[92] *Macdonald* (n 90) 863.
[93] Eg *Fassbender, 1998* (n 6) 574.
[94] *Allott, 1990* (n 34) 134.
[95] *Macdonald* (n 90) 863.
[96] *Dupuy* (n 91) 3.

supremacy of the norms, attributed to Article 103 of the UN Charter. Macdonald describes Article 103 of the Charter of the UN as 'one of the most persuasive arguments in favour of the view that the Charter is in fact a constitution.'[97]

The majority of contributors to this debate identify the formal and substantive requirements of a constitution and then move on to describe why the UN Charter may be described as the constitution of the world in a more cosmetic sense. This includes ideas of consent, clarity, and the necessities of today's world. Since the United Nations is the only organisation that boasts near-universal membership and is thus considered as the primary institutional representative of the international community, it is explained as fulfilling the requirement of universality that a global constitution demands.[98] Jürgen Habermas refers to the inclusiveness of the United Nations and the universality of UN law as one of the three 'normative innovations' which make it possible to interpret the Charter as a global constitution. The other two are the explicit link between the goal for achieving peace with the politics of human rights and the link between the prohibition to use force and the threat of criminal action and sanctions.[99] According to Stefan Kadelbach and Thomas Kleinlein the universality of the Charter satisfies the requirement of consent: States have consented to being members of the United Nations and all law emanating from the organisation is then consensus-based. According to Kadelbach and Kleinlein, it is this consent (in the form of 'general consensus' to the UN and all its laws) that defines the Charter as the constitution of the international community.[100] Fassbender additionally makes the point that the designation of the UN Charter as the global constitution would provide for clarity 'to get out of the fog of the indistinct constitutional rhetoric'.[101] Taking stock of his ten years of thinking and writing about global constitutionalism, Fassbender still maintains his belief that the UN Charter should be viewed as the global constitution. Indeed, he believes that history will corroborate this, claiming boldly that: 'the Charter of the United Nations will be acknowledged as the twentieth century's most important contribution to a constitutional history of the world.'[102]

The idea that the UN Charter constitutes a global constitution embraces all of the key themes of global constitutionalism that were determined above

[97] *Macdonald* (n 90) 862.

[98] *Fassbender, 1998* (n 6) 567.

[99] *Habermas* (n 5) 160ff.

[100] *Kadelbach, Kleinlein, 2007* (n 59) 318.

[101] *Fassbender, 2005* (n 10) 848.

[102] Bardo Fassbender, 'Rediscovering a Forgotten Constitution' in Jeffrey L. Dunoff and Joel P. Trachtman (eds), *Ruling the World: Constitutionalism, International Law, and Global Governance* (CUP, Cambridge 2009) 147.

(which possibly explains the popularity of this vision). It is proposed that the Charter limits the power of States, institutionalises the authority of the United Nations Charter, protects individual rights, and has a standard-setting capacity. The reference to the function of the UN to 'protect and safeguard international peace and security' also brings the idealising element of the constitution to the fore.

C. *Microconstitutionalism becoming Macroconstitutionalism*

The constitutionalisation of international organisations is an area of research that analyses certain structures within organisations (for example the decision-making functions of particular organs) and questions whether these structures amount to 'constitutional' functions. If the debate regards exclusively the organisation (Anne Peters refers to this as 'microconstitutionalism'[103]), then it is distinct to considerations regarding global constitutionalism.[104] However, constitutionalisation of international organisations can concern global constitutionalism if the constitutional functions are thought to extend beyond the specific institution and the particular area of law that it regulates to a form of 'macroconstitutionalism'.

According to the above definition, microconstitutionalism is founded on the notion that the foundational treaties of international organisations may be qualified as the constitution of the relevant organisations. Since such visions are not visions of *global* constitutionalism, they will only be mentioned briefly. Although this idea does not pertain to a global order, it nevertheless supports the notion that a constitutional order can exist in the international sphere beyond the nation State. The founding treaties are often also titled 'constitutions', which indicates that they could be seen as reference documents for a specialised legal order. Such notions of constitutionalism do not try to explain or construct an international legal order, but rather one that is confined to the specific organisation. The constitutionalist visions within organisations sometimes feed into a global vision of constitutionalism as a multilayered and multifaceted system as seen above. A number of fragmented and specialised subsystems of international law exist and thus a 'constitution' for each such

[103] See eg Anne Peters, 'The Merits of Global Constitutionalism' (2009) 16 Indiana Journal of Global Legal Studies 408.

[104] Such specialised constitutionalism does not necessarily have to be connected to a specific institution, as seen with respect to debates on environmental constitutionalism, for example. Environmental constitutionalism is specialised in terms of its subject-matter (meaning it would possibly qualify as 'microconstitutionalism'), but is global in terms of its ambit – the environment as a whole (meaning it would qualify as 'macroconstitutionalism' in this respect). See Daniel M. Bodansky, 'Is there an International Environmental Constitution?' (2009) 16 Indiana Journal of Global Legal Studies 565ff. Bodansky, although coming to the conclusion that there is no environmental constitution per se, claims that environmental treaty regimes have a constitutional dimension in that they establish ongoing systems of governance. (*Ibid* 574f.)

subsystem could exist. Since the activities of international organisations go beyond the specific organisation, a constitutional approach concerns issues that may affect any subjects within the scope of the organisations' decision-making radius. Anne Peters states:

> A constitutionalist approach to the law of International Organizations provides the justification for legal constraints on the increasing and hence potentially intrusive or even abusive activities of those organizations.[105]

The WTO has been the particular object of study in terms of microconstitutionalism and macroconstitutionalism. Certain legal aspects are considered as 'constitutionalising' the WTO: the restriction of self-interests of both private individuals and government officials; the compulsory dispute settlement system that makes decisions enforceable; and the international priority of treaty law over derived legislation.[106] Part of the parlance of global constitutionalism is the reference to 'a constitutional economic order'. Ernst-Ulrich Petersmann is an eminent advocate of the notion that WTO law creates global constitutional law (macroconstitutionalism). He observes that, since WTO law 'protects freedom and non-discrimination across frontiers…[and] promotes rule of law more effectively than any other worldwide treaty system', it already serves a (global) constitutional function.[107] Moreover, he notes that constitutional functions are also served through the fact that the WTO Agreement asserts legal supremacy and provides a legal framework for the periodic negotiation of new WTO Agreements.[108] According to him, this constitutional function should be supplemented with human rights for additional constitutional safeguards.[109] Petersmann's view on global constitutionalism is therefore also a compendium of the key themes of constitutionalism noted above. Not only does he refer to the political functions of a constitution, but also to the value-oriented content of a constitutional order. In his earlier work, Petersmann centres his vision of global constitutionalism on the former; however, in his most recent work he suggests that the protection of human rights lies at the heart of constitutionalism.[110]

The ILO has also been subject to discussions of constitutionalisation trends. Stefan Kadelbach and Thomas Kleinlein claim that the ILO resembles a constitutionalised subsystem in a system of constitutionalisation on the international plane. According to them, the ILO meets the requirements of a

---

105 *Peters, 2005* (n 45) 538.

106 Deborah Cass, *The Constitutionalization of the World Trade Organization* (OUP, Oxford 2005).

107 Ernst-Ulrich Petersmann, 'The WTO Constitution and Human Rights' (2000) 3 Journal of International Economic Law 20.

108 *Ibid* 20.

109 *Ibid* 21.

110 Jeffrey L. Dunoff 'Why Constitutionalism *Now*? Text, Context and Historical Contingency of Ideas' (2005) 1 Journal of International Law & International Relations 195.

constitutional subsystem. Three characteristics define the requirements for a constitutionalised subsystem: first, a hierarchy of norms; second, legitimacy of governance through institutionalisation; and third, the promotion of (value-oriented) principles.[111] The first characteristic, the hierarchy of norms, is identified as existing between the ILO Constitution, the ILO Conventions, and soft law. The second characteristic of a constitutionalised subsystem – the legitimacy of governance through institutionalisation – is identified in the participation and regulation of civil society. Kadelbach and Kleinlein believe the ILO is 'legitimate' because it has developed an institutionalised process of participation of civil society; besides, the representatives in the ILO institutions are both composed of (member) State delegates and members of workers' and employers' organisations (the so-called tripartite system). Additionally, unions and associations participate in the supervision of labour standards and, as is set out in Article 24 and 26 ILO Constitution, may submit a representation or complaint against States which are in breach of these. Kadelbach and Kleinlein interpret this cooperation with interested groups as 'a special standard of legitimacy'.[112] The third characteristic of value-orientation is believed to be visible in the promotion of constitutional principles 'such as human rights and the participation of associations in the working-out of labour standards within the member states.'[113] Debates on constitutionalism *within* organisations are growing as international organisations achieve greater influence on the international plane and their decisions have an impact on domestic legal orders.[114]

D. *Summary*

The main concerns of those advocating Institutional Constitutionalism are questions of the limitation and accountability of power through participation and representation. In the case of the latter, accountability and legitimacy are considered necessary hallmarks of a constitutional order. Central to the concerns of participation and accountability (in other words the allocation of power) are ideas of the institutionalisation of such power. It is often believed that participation and accountability can best be achieved through the establishment of institutions. The aforementioned authors all view these concerns as addressed in democratic systems and therefore adhere to a vision of global constitutionalism in a democratic order. The key themes of global constitutionalism that this dimension focuses on are the limitation of power (the first key theme) on the one hand and the institutionalisation of power (the second key theme) on the other hand.

---

[111] *Kadelbach, Kleinlein, 2007* (n 59) 325–327.
[112] *Ibid* 327.
[113] *Ibid.*
[114] See Jan Klabbers, *An Introduction to International Institutional Law*, (2nd edn CUP, Cambridge 2009) 314–316.

Section III: Normative Constitutionalism

Some authors of international law identify specific norms as global constitutional norms, which they believe provide the framework for a global constitutional order. Distinct from Institutional Constitutionalism, these visions do not necessarily have an institutional element; rather, their legitimacy is derived from their inherent (moral) value. Public international lawyers mostly postulate the normative emphasis of global constitutionalism in that they set out a number of values that consider a constitution as it should be.

Firstly, visions of world law will be discussed. This vision is predicated on the belief that there are certain norms which must be treated differently to other norms because of their inherent value to society. This is followed by the vision of global constitutionalism which identifies certain norms as constituting a hierarchy within international legal norms – a property that makes them constitutional. From a hierarchy of norms, the examination turns to the closely related concept of fundamental norms of international law. In the course of the portrayal of Normative Constitutionalism, it emerges that these visions strongly rely on a rights-oriented approach. An objective value-order is at the centre of these ideas – a concept that is predominantly associated with liberalism.

A. *World Law*

Global constitutionalism as a framework for a distinct world law is a vision that encompasses a universal legal and political order, often thought to overarch or be detached from international law itself. It is concerned with questions of both participation and fundamental rights. Drawing on the cosmopolitan theories of Kant, Angelika Emmerich-Fritsche makes her case for a world law concept. In her view, world law can be realised through a global constitution. World law is comprised of global contracts, treaties, and universal international law.[115] What she refers to as the currently imperfect, fragmentary constitutions of the global order such as the constitution of the European Union or the Charter of the United Nations can be connected to embody a global constitution:

> There are possibilities to complete the fragmented global constitution, in particular to democratize it, to implement the rule of law (especially legal protection) and to connect the constitutions of ILO and WTO in form and/or content. The partially imbalanced processes of constitutionalisation can be unified within the framework of the United Nations to a coherent constitution of the world.[116]

---

[115] Angelika Emmerich-Fritsche, *Vom Völkerrecht zum Weltrecht* (Duncker & Humboldt, Berlin 2007) 'Short-Summary' 1072–1073.

[116] *Ibid* 1073.

Emmerich-Fritsche puts the evolution of world law down to what is now a familiar argument for change on the international sphere: a paradigm shift. This shift is evident in a number of changes taking place in the international sphere. A shift has taken place from the sovereignty of States towards legal subjectivity of individuals. Moreover, it is to be found in the supremacy of the rule of law over the principles of sovereignty, reciprocity, and efficiency.[117] Significantly, Emmerich-Fritsche makes a distinction between world law and international law: World law is defined by its higher level of legally binding provisions that have emerged through processes of institutionalisation and constitutionalisation. International law can achieve the rank of world law if it loses its former feature of inter-State law and instead takes on features of world law.[118] Emmerich-Fritsche echoes the thoughts of Jost Delbrück who speaks of world (internal) law, *Weltinnenrecht*. This is perceived as the law that transcends inter-State law.[119] They both claim that international law should be referred to as world law when it has reached this transcending stage.[120] Since globalisation entails a paradigm shift for international law, globalisation could thus not only signify an end of the nation State, but also an end of international law.[121] A distinction between world law and global governance is also made. Global governance concerns mostly processes of the setting, interpretation, and execution of rules; it therewith refers to a system of operations and ordering, and not to the concept of law itself.[122] Emmerich-Fritsche adds an additional dimension to the requirements for a global constitution: the requirement of an *ordre public*. She argues that it is necessary for the international community to be a legal community in order for it to be referred to as an international *ordre public*. One can speak of an international *ordre public* when there is more to the international order than merely the sum of bilateral and multilateral legal relations. Like Anne Peters, Emmerich-Fritsche requires the legal community to be based on superior common principles of its members and not merely on strategic power relations.[123] The existence of an international *ordre public* in turn is, according to Emmerich-Fritsche, a requirement for the existence of a global constitution.[124] In her view (and contrary to the

---

[117] *Ibid* 1072.

[118] *Ibid* 1072.

[119] Jost Delbrück, 'Wirksameres Völkerrecht oder neues "Weltinnenrecht"? Perspektiven der Völkerrechtsentwicklung in einem sich wandelnden internationalen System' in Klaus Dicke et al (eds) *Die Konstitution des Friedens als Rechtsordnung* (Duncker & Humboldt, Berlin 1996); Jost Delbrück, 'Perspektiven für ein "Weltinnenrecht"?' in Gedächtnisschrift für Jürgen Sonnenschein (De Gruyter Recht, Berlin 2003) 793.

[120] *Emmerich-Fritsche* (n 115) 192; *Delbrück, 1996* (n 118) 346f.

[121] *Emmerich-Fritsche* (n 115) 193, Stephan Hobe 'Völkerrecht im Zeitalter der Globalisierung' (2003) 41 AVR 453ff.

[122] *Emmerich-Fritsche* (n 115) 192.

[123] *Ibid* 708.

[124] *Ibid* 707–708, with reference to Günther Jaenicke, 'Zur Frage des internationalen Ordre public' (1967) 7 Berichte der Deutschen Gesellschaft für Völkerrecht 80.

view of global civil law), such a global constitution would be one constituted by States, rather one constituted by global citizens.[125]

In regard to the key themes of global constitutionalism that were discussed above, the idea of a world law reflects all five. The limitation of power is dealt with (the identification of the restraint of power through law); governance through institutionalisation of authority is considered (the identification of different levels of acting in the public interest and its accountability through democratic processes); the concept of a global constitution contains the element of social idealism (visions of the future world order); the global constitution is without doubt considered as providing a standard-setting capacity (the systematisation of 'world law' itself); and the protection of individual rights is thought an inherent part of a global constitution.

B. *The Hierarchical Order*

Brun-Otto Bryde claims that it is the hierarchy of norms of public international law that determines the existence of a constitutional order of international law.[126] He claims that the purpose of a constitution is to restrict the lawmaker's omnipotence, now a familiar theme of constitutionalism. In international law, States and international organisations adopt the role of the lawmaker and these 'lawmakers' are bound by a set of higher norms – this process is regarded to be global constitutionalism.[127] Bryde, like many German scholars of constitutionalism, emphasises the distinction between the procedural constitutional rules of lawmaking and adjudication on the one hand and substantive constitutional principles on the other hand.[128] He contrasts the Westphalian model of international law – in his words, a 'well-ordered anarchy of States' – with the constitutionalist system of international law. He defines the constitutionalist system as:

> not horizontal but verticalised. It recognises a source of legitimacy that is higher than the individual states, a hierarchy of norms in which ordinary legal rules have to be reviewed against constitutional principles, and it employs constitutionalist methods of interpretation.[129]

Bryde emphasises that the core of constitutional international law is the general acceptance of a common interest of mankind.[130] All States have agreed to

[125] *Emmerich-Fritsche* (n 115) 708. See Gunther Teubner for the view of global constitutionalism constituted by global citizens (n 16).

[126] Brun-Otto Bryde, 'Konstitutionalisierung des Völkerrechts und Internationalisierung des Verfassungsrechts' (2003) 42 Der Staat 61f; Brun-Otto Bryde, 'International Democratic Constitutionalism' in Ronald St. John Macdonald and Douglas M. Johnston (eds) *Towards World Constitutionalism: Issues in the Legal Ordering of the World Community* (Martinus Nijhoff Publishers, Leiden 2005) 104ff.

[127] *Bryde, 2005* (n 134).

[128] *Ibid* 104.

[129] *Ibid.*

[130] *Ibid* 107.

submit to the supremacy of these common interests (such as environmental protection, or human rights law). Bryde explains that the verticalisation of international law has also taken place in a normative sense through the 'higher law' norms such as *jus cogens*, which protect the common interest of mankind against violation.[131] While some weakness of constitutionalisation is identified in the incomplete institutional constitutionalisation of international law, he believes that institutions must follow the normative and conceptual lead. He believes that a regressive adjustment is no longer possible and that 'development' is therefore inevitable.[132] Bryde further advocates the necessity of the creation of an international democratic civil society (something that has, according to him, already begun) and consequently a 'transnational democratic organisation.' This is, according to Bryde, necessary in order to legitimise the institutionalisation of the constitutional order.[133]

Although not explicitly referring to the 'hierarchy of norms', Luigi Ferrajoli describes it in his illustration of the normative effect of the UN Charter and the Universal Declaration of the Rights of Man of 1948.[134] He argues that from the moment of the signatory States' submission to fundamental norms 'sovereignty became a logically inconsistent concept'.[135] Ferrajoli invites his readers to 'take seriously' the existing international legal framework. This means recognising the global constitution in embryo that already exists in the UN Charter and the various international conventions and declarations of human rights.[136] Although still lacking any institutional guarantees, he believes that global constitutionalism has already been formally established.[137] He also refers to the paradigm shift that has taken place in international law, explaining that international law has changed from a contractual system, in which sovereignty (in its external dimension) was the paradigm, to 'a true legal order of a supra-State kind.'[138] He does not only refer to *de facto* formal global constitutionalism (the descriptive approach), but also to the *requirement* of constitutionalism as a method of making supra-national agencies accountable for their decision-making (the normative approach).[139] The agencies that have caused a shift in decision-making away from nation States (to themselves) need to be controlled through constitutional guarantees of peace and human

[131] *Ibid* 108.
[132] *Ibid* 110.
[133] *Ibid* 115ff.
[134] Luigi Ferrajoli, 'Beyond Sovereignty and Citizenship: a Global Constitutionalism' in Richard Bellamy (ed) *Constitutionalism, Democracy and Sovereignty: American and European Perspectives* (Avebury, Aldershot 1997) 154.
[135] *Ibid* 154.
[136] *Ibid* 155.
[137] *Ibid.*
[138] *Ibid* 154.
[139] *Ibid* 157.

rights; he demands their political accountability.[140] These demands stress the idea of governance through the institutionalisation of power as a key theme of global constitutionalism. In his essay *Beyond Sovereignty and Citizenship: A Global Constitutionalism*, Ferrajoli finally takes the idealistic theme of (global) constitutionalism to the maximum:

> [T]he legal project at the basis of global constitutionalism is, in the long term, the only realistic alternative to war, destruction, the rise of a variety of fundamentalisms, ethnic conflicts, terrorism, an increase in famines and general misery.[141]

This quote in fact sums up Normative Constitutionalism: While democratic features such as the restriction and institutionalisation of power are believed to be significant, it is the value-oriented aspect of constitutionalism that is at the heart of this dimension.

C. *Fundamental Norms*

A further related variant of Normative Constitutionalism is the idea that certain fundamental norms incorporate such central values of international society that they constitute a framework for the rest of international (and domestic) law. In their entirety, the norms are then referred to as the global constitution. These norms are considered to have an objective existence, although their source is neither in norms of international organisations nor in other bilateral or multilateral State agreements. The label 'fundamental norms' is believed to signify that they apply to all members of the international community, irrespective of questions of sovereignty or, for that matter, consent. Fundamental norms are mostly described as those which set basic or minimum standards or morals; they can therefore often be traced back to humanitarian impulses of the nineteenth century, where the individual became the central focus of thought. Two examples of fundamental norms are *jus cogens* norms and norms applying *erga omnes*. *Jus cogens* norms are often described as constitutional norms of the international order. Advocates of the international community school, such as Christian Tomuschat, and advocates of other visions of constitutionalism refer to these norms, if not as constituting the global constitution themselves, then at least as constituting a part of the global constitution. There is no universally recognised definition for the content of *jus cogens* norms and there is no exhaustive catalogue. To gain a better understanding of the norms, *jus cogens* are contrasted with *jus dispositivum*, which has a non-imperative, yielding nature.[142] Some examples of norms that have been regarded as *jus cogens* are the prohibition of the use of force, the crime of genocide and other

---

[140] *Ibid.*

[141] *Ibid* 159.

[142] Alfred Verdross, '*Jus Dispositivum* and *Jus Cogens* in International Law' (1966) 60 AJIL 58.

grave human rights violations, and core guarantees of international humanitarian law.[143] Although they are undefined in terms of their *content*, they are codified in a major multilateral treaty of public international law, the Vienna Convention on the Law of Treaties (VCLT), as having an extraordinary *effect* in international law – the effect of overriding what is traditionally the very basis of public international law: State consent. Article 53 VCLT prescribes the effect of peremptory norms on treaties of international law: they have the effect of voiding a treaty contrary to the peremptory nature of a *jus cogens* norm, meaning they have the ability to constrain the contractual capacity of legal persons. The concept of *jus cogens* is believed to have created a space for norms that are above State consent, therewith producing a hierarchy in an area of law that is traditionally considered horizontal rather than vertical. Juan Carrillo Salcedo observed:

> We can no longer defend an exclusively voluntarist conception of international law … since the existence of norms of international *jus cogens* … show that it has to an extent been transcended … The notion of *jus cogens* has introduced a hierarchy into contemporary international law.[144]

Thus, it is believed that the VCLT establishes a normative hierarchy in treaty law, with *jus cogens* norms as superior law.[145] This capacity to trump other norms is regarded as a constitutional feature. According to Michael Byers, the constitutional character of *jus cogens* norms is indeed 'obvious'. Byers believes that nowhere else in the international legal system is the ability of some rules to limit the State ability of norm-developing, -maintaining, or -changing so clear.[146] Such ability is, for him, indicative of their constitutional character.

Erika de Wet describes a constitutional order composed of fundamental norms with *jus cogens* norms as its core. In contrast to the aforesaid, she ascribes them this constitutional character on the basis of their *value* not on the basis of their effect.[147] Thus, de Wet is according *jus cogens* norms with content, a content that justifies their effect. Emphasis is placed on human

---

[143] Lauri Hannikainen, *Peremptory Norms (Jus Cogens) in International Law: Historical Development, Criteria, Present Status* (Lakimiesliiton Kustannus: Finnish lawyer's Publishing Co, Helsinki 1989).

[144] Juan Antonio Carrillo Salcedo, 'Reflections on the Existence of a Hierarchy of Norms in International Law' (1997) 8 EJIL 583.

[145] In strong opposition to a hierarchy, *see* Prosper Weil, 'Towards Relative Normativity in International Law? (1983) 77 AJIL 413; Georg Schwarzenberger, 'International *Jus Cogens*?' (1965) 43 Texas Law Review 455. Regarding the compatibility of a hierarchy and the interdependence and indivisibility of human rights, *see* Teraya Koji, 'Emerging Hierarchy in International Human Rights and Beyond' (2001) 12 EJIL 924.

[146] Michael Byers, 'Conceptualising the Relationship between *Jus Cogens* and *Erga Omnes* Rules' (1997) 66 NordicJIntlL 220.

[147] Erika de Wet, 'The Emergence of International and Regional Value Systems as a Manifestation of the Emerging International Constitutional Order' (2006) 19 LJIL 611–632; *idem*, 'The International Constitutional Order' (2006) 55 ICLQ 51–76.

rights as the common value in the international society. De Wet defines the global constitution as an

> embryonic constitutional order in which the different national, regional and functional (sectoral) regimes form the building blocks of the international community ("international polity") that is underpinned by a core value system common to all communities and embedded in a variety of legal structures for its enforcement.[148]

For de Wet, the international value system concerns norms with a strong ethical underpinning that have acquired a special hierarchical standing through State practice.[149] International values are, according to her, a layering of universal *jus cogens* norms and *erga omnes* obligations.[150] De Wet explains that the first layer is constituted by *jus cogens* norms, which have by definition an *erga omnes* effect. The second layer consists of *erga omnes* norms that have 'not yet' evolved into *jus cogens* norms.[151] International organisations, particularly those arising from the UN Charter system, have assisted in shaping these international values (mostly, but not exclusively, human rights) by way of concretisation.[152] Thus, de Wet's key constitutional themes are concerns for social idealism (visions for perfecting the future) as well as the protection of individual rights. She believes that substantive superiority consequently awards certain norms with superiority in a formal sense. The constitutional idea of idealistic values with ethical and moral foundations is a theme that has been part of global constitutional thought since the Stoics of Antiquity.[153] Normative hierarchy in turn – as the consequence of idealism – has been an aspect of constitutionalism since the modern era of the West and the rise of positivism.

Erga omnes norms are attributed a role in a global constitutional order due to their supposedly universal application. It was the International Court of Justice (ICJ) that drew particular attention to the concept of *erga omnes* norms. In its famous *obiter dictum* in the *Barcelona Traction* case of 1970, the ICJ first made the distinction between the obligations of a State towards the international community as a whole and obligations arising towards other individual States. In this case, the ICJ stated that the former are the concerns of all States; all States have a legal interest in their protection and therefore apply *erga omnes*.[154] The content of norms with *erga omnes* character is considered to be

---

148 *Ibid* 613.
149 *Ibid* 613–614.
150 *Ibid* 614.
151 *Ibid* 616.
152 *Ibid* 615–616.
153 See Chapter 2.
154 ICJ *Case Concerning the Barcelona Traction, Light and Power Company, Limited (second phase) (Belgium v Spain)* [1970] ICJ Rep 3 para 33. See also *Legal Consequences of the Construction of a Wall in the Occupied Palestinian Territory*, Advisory Opinion (9 July 2004) para 155.

largely identical to that of *jus cogens* norms.[155] Jost Delbrück, who was mentioned above as advocating for a *Weltinnenrecht*, argues that *erga omnes* norms exist alongside *jus cogens* norms, and constitute a category of norms in their own right. He believes they are a new element in the hierarchy of international law and thereby attest to the ongoing process of constitutionalisation of international law.[156] The existence of *erga omnes* norms articulates basic interests and needs as well as fundamental values of the international community as a whole; in short, the public interest.[157]

Geir Ulfstein proposes an institutional slant on the above ideas concerning fundamental rights by suggesting the establishment of a World Court of Human Rights.[158] Ulfstein envisions that the intention of such a court would be to empower an international judicial organ, which ensures a growth in the respect for 'core values in the international community'.[159] Such an institution could be regarded as a 'facet' of the constitutionalisation of international law.[160]

As mentioned above, the visions of global constitutionalism based on fundamental norms are all value-oriented ideas of an overarching common interest or common moral basis among participants of international society. Although some *jus cogens* and some *erga omnes* norms can be associated with questions of participation, the main focus of authors determining the content of these norms is on individual rights, specifically human rights. The political aspect of Normative Constitutionalism is mostly concerned with the restriction and institution of political power for the purpose of the protection of individual rights.

D. *Summary*

Normative Constitutionalism incorporates all of the key themes of global constitutionalism that were listed above: a) Limitation of power; b) Institutionalisation of power (largely for the purpose of restraining it); c) Idealism; d) Standard-setting; and e) Protection of individual rights. The particular emphasis of these approaches to global constitutionalism centre the protection of rights-oriented dimensions of constitutionalism. The supreme key theme of this type of global constitutionalism is the limitation of government

---

155 *Kadelbach, Kleinlein, 2007* (n 59) 316.

156 Jost Delbrück, 'Laws in the Public Interest – Some Observations on the Foundations and Identification of *erga omnes* Norms in International Law' in Volkmar Götz (eds) *Liber amicorum Günther Jaenicke – zum 85. Geburtstag* (Springer, Berlin 1999) 17–36 (particularly 35).

157 *Ibid* 18.

158 Geir Ulfstein, 'Do We Need a World Court of Human Rights?' in Ola Engdahl and Pål Wrange (eds), *The Law as it Was and the Law as it Should Be* (Brill, Leiden 2008).

159 *Ibid* 271.

160 *Ibid.*

through the protection of individual rights. Maduro described the motivation for this type of constitutionalism (which he calls Rights Constitutionalism) by arguing: 'The fundamental fear is that of the many. The fundamental suspicion lies over the political process.'[161] Consequently, power is transferred to alternative institutions (courts, international organisations, the market), which are idealised, a notion which mirrors the idealism of the norms that are to be protected.

The view that is advocated by all proponents of Normative Constitutionalism is that an international legal order exists with certain superior (constitutional) norms. International law is seen as having moved away from its preoccupation with State interest and State will towards a relativity of rights and duties.[162] This shift is often claimed to be due to a paradigm shift in international law.[163] It is submitted that public international law has changed from an area of law in which law was made through consent to a law that is determined in large part through certain (global) values. The values that come to the fore in the above descriptions of global constitutionalism differ depending on the focus of the author, but they all refer to universal norms such as 'public interest norms', 'fundamental norms' or as 'international community norms'.

Section IV: Analogical Constitutionalism

The final vision of global constitutionalism discussed here draws analogies between features of the international sphere and features of domestic and regional constitutional orders. Scholars contributing to this dimension of global constitutionalism identify constitutional principles of certain legal orders (national or regional) and describe parallel principles in the international sphere.

A. *Meta-Rules Constitutionalism*

A popular, and possibly one of the oldest visions of global constitutionalism in (Westphalian) public international law is the idea that meta-rules are constitutional principles of the international sphere. In 1926, Alfred Verdross published a book titled *The Constitution of the International Legal Community*.[164] For those days certainly an ambitious title. Verdross described such a constitution as being: 'those norms which deal with the structure and subdivision of,

---

161 *Maduro* (n 74) 242.

162 *Emmerich-Fritsche* (n 115) 703.

163 Ernst-Ulrich Petersmann, *Europäisches und weltweites Integrations-, und Verfassungs- und Weltbürgerrecht* in: Liber amicorum Thomas Oppermann (2001) 367f.

164 Alfred Verdross, *Die Verfassung der Völkerrechtsgemeinschaft* (J. Springer, Vienna 1926).

and the distribution of spheres of jurisdiction in, a community'.[165] Verdross is best known for his work on general principles as a source of international law,[166] and it is in this vein that he refers to a presupposed legal validity of positive norms (based on consent).[167] Christian Tomuschat echoed Verdross' view in 1993. In his lectures in The Hague, Tomuschat referred to constitutional norms as 'meta-rules'. He described meta-rules as:

> rules on how the bulk of other rules are produced, how they enter into force, how they are implemented and who, in case of differences over their interpretation and application, is empowered to settle an ensuing dispute.[168]

Alfred Verdross' definition of a constitution and Tomuschat's definition of meta-rules are of course a nod towards H.L.A. Hart's secondary rules.[169] Tomuschat confusingly explained that meta-rules can be either formal in nature (the rules that define the sources of international law, for example), or substantive (such as the rules of sovereign equality of States, or the ban of the use of force).[170] By making this distinction between formal and substantive meta-rules, he is no longer adhering either to his original definition or to the generally accepted division of primary and secondary rules made by Hart. In Tomuschat's view, meta-rules of international law include Article 2 (1) of the UN Charter, which appertains to the principle of the sovereign equality of States; Article 38 (1) of the Statute of the International Court of Justice, which is considered as referring to the sources of international law; and Article 26 of the Vienna Convention on the Law of Treaties, which declares that every treaty in force is binding on the parties to it and must be performed in good faith.[171] He explained that this framework of basic rules applies to States 'with or without their will [to constitute] the constitution of the international community'.[172]

Both Verdross and Tomuschat have since departed from their original views on global constitutionalism. In 1976, Verdross and his co-author Bruno Simma

---

[165] *Ibid* v.

[166] See Bruno Simma, 'The Contribution of Alfred Verdross to the Theory of International Law' (1995) 6 EJIL 1–54.

[167] Alfred Verdross, *Völkerrecht* (5th edn Springer, Vienna 1964) 22.

[168] Christian Tomuschat, 'Obligations Arising for States Without or Against Their Will' (1993) 241 Recueil des Cours de l'Académie de Droit International 216.

[169] Bardo Fassbender states that it is 'clearly' influenced by Hart in 'The Meaning of International Constitutional Law' in Nicholas Tsagourias (ed), *Transnational Constitutionalism: International and European Perspectives* (CUP, Cambridge 2007) 315; HLA Hart *The Concept of Law* (OUP, Oxford 1981) 92: 'Primary rules are concerned with the actions that individuals must or must not do, secondary rules are all concerned with the primary rules themselves. They specify the ways in which the primary rules may be conclusively ascertained, introduced, eliminated, varied, and the fact of their violation conclusively determined.'

[170] *Fassbender, 2005* (n 10) 843.

[171] *Tomuschat, 1993* (n 168) 211–212.

[172] *Ibid* 211.

published a new edition of Verdross' original treatise. In the book, now titled *Universal International Law: Theory and Practice*, Verdross claims that constitutional law of the universal community is today embedded in the UN Charter.[173] Tomuschat's idea of constitutionalism has developed into a more value-oriented notion. In 1999, Tomuschat stated that protection is afforded by the international community to certain basic *values*. Protection, according to Tomuschat, is afforded even against the will of individual States.[174]

Since Meta-Rules Constitutionalism is, for the largest part, not concerned with substantive rules in the sense of basic legal values, idealism and the protection of individual rights are not considered. Furthermore, Meta-Rules Constitutionalism does also not concern the political aspects of constitutionalism, although it must be noted that the envisaged norms do concern the limitation of power, institutionalisation, and governance to a certain extent. These political elements are, however, not relevant to concerns of participation; rather they are relevant to the concern of standardisation. Meta-Rules Constitutionalism is concerned with the development of society according to a fixed plan or system that is standardised in a procedural sense.

B. *The Domestic Constitutional Order*

Robert Uerpmann discusses global constitutionalism in international law with the help of analogies to national constitutional systems, in particular his own (German) constitutional system. His focus is the attempt to argue in favour of a comprehensive international constitutional system of international law, which mirrors national constitutions. While he dismisses the existence of an inclusive global constitution (as of yet), he identifies certain constitutional elements in public international law.[175] Uerpmann therefore bases his argument on a number of assumptions. First, he claims that a constitution must constitute at least one main subject or organ.[176] Despite its weaknesses, the UN is thought to be a main subject of international law. Second, international constitutional law must provide for certain procedural rules.[177] He asserts that despite the lack of a centralised legislature in the international community, international law has specific rules on legislation through its doctrines of the sources of international law. The VCLT is compared to a law of contract, which - as a contract itself - has no constitutional status in a formal sense. But, since the VCLT is antecedent to any other treaty of international law, it can be

[173] Alfred Verdross, Bruno Simma, *Universelles Völkerrecht: Theorie und Praxis* (3rd edn Duncker & Humboldt, Berlin 1984) 69f.

[174] *Tomuschat, 1999* (n 7). Emphasis added.

[175] Robert Uerpmann, 'Internationales Verfassungsrecht' (2001) 56 Juristen Zeitung 565–572.

[176] *Ibid* 566.

[177] *Ibid* 565, 567.

understood as constitutional law.[178] Uerpmann then discusses the requirement of an executive branch. While there is no executive authority in international law, there is also no requirement for an executive organ in the international sphere. Rather, international law is a law of coordination rather than subordination, in comparison to civil law, where the parties to a contract agree on their own methods of dispute settlement.[179] Regarding the judicative branch of power, Uerpmann discusses the jurisdiction of the ICJ and its lack of obligatory jurisdiction.[180]

Subsequent to discussing the procedural aspects of a constitutional order, he discusses substantive (material) constitutional law. Uerpmann identifies human rights norms and international economic rules as constitutional norms in a material sense (they specify which rights individuals have vis-à-vis States and are therefore in terms of their content worthy of being constitutional – *Verfassungswürdig*).[181] He then analyses whether the requirement of the existence of constitutional norms in a formal sense (law that is superior to other laws) can be satisfied. In this context, *jus cogens* norms are mentioned. The prohibition of the use of force, the prohibition of genocide, and certain core human rights norms are observed as being *jus cogens*. The compelling character of *jus cogens* norms codified in Article 53 VCLT signifies their global constitutional law character in a formal sense.[182] *Erga omnes* norms are also thought to be constitutional law in a formal sense. Uerpmann believes that *jus cogens* norms are part of an emerging global constitution, which has not fully been consolidated but is in the process of consolidation. While he claims that *erga omnes* rules are also constitutional law in a formal sense, he assigns them a lesser priority. *Erga omnes* norms can (only) designate obligations consequential upon the performance of an act as contrary to international law; *jus cogens* norms, however, can make an act void.[183] It is significant that, in his doctrinal approach – in which he scans a considerable amount of sources of international law in a whirlwind fashion – Uerpmann touches on all the key themes of constitutionalism determined above.

---

[178] Constitutional law in a formal and material (*formell* and *materiell*) sense is legal terminology in German constitutional law. Constitutional norms in a formal (*formell*) sense refers to norms that have been given constitutional character through a specific democratic procedure. The written constitution is the typical constitutional law in a formal sense. Constitutional law in a material (*materiell*) sense refers to the substantive law, meaning the specific contents of the norms that give them constitutional character.

[179] *Uerpmann* (n 175) 568.

[180] *Ibid* 569.

[181] *Ibid* 569–571.

[182] *Ibid* 571.

[183] *Ibid* 572.

C. *European Constitutionalism*

A reference must also briefly be made to the views on constitutional trends in Europe. Europe can be considered as a forerunner in terms of constitutionalism beyond a single nation State. The status of the European Court of Human Rights as a constitutional court (meaning the constitutionality of the European Convention on Human Rights and Fundamental Freedoms) has been advanced by the former Presidents of the Court Luzius Wildhaber and Rolv Ryssdall, as well as by the former Registrar Paul Mahoney.[184] Furthermore, many writers on global constitutionalism consider the EU in its political form and the constitution of the EU in its legal form to be models for constitutionalism on a global level. Many of the above scholars consider the EU as a model for international law – at least to some extent – including Habermas, MacDonald, and Petersmann.[185] In 2004, Mattias Kumm examined in how far international law can be awarded with legitimacy from a constitutional perspective by making analogies between international law and EU law.[186] He suggested a constitutionalist framework for international law that draws on ideas of EU law. One such suggestion required the international legal principle of 'sovereignty' to be understood as being replaced with the European legal principle of 'subsidiarity'.[187] Kumm explains that subsidiarity was also used to guide the drafting of the European Constitutional Treaty.

But, politically the constitutional framework for the EU has been less successful. On 29 October 2004, the Heads of State or Government of the EU member States signed the *Draft Treaty Establishing a Constitution for Europe.*[188] The text of the Constitution was based on certain elements: the inclusion of a Charter of Fundamental Rights, the attribution of powers (between the Union and the Member States), the introduction of a mechanism to ensure respect for the principle of subsidiarity, and the inclusion of procedures which can facilitate citizens' right of legislative initiative.[189] The Treaty had to be approved and ratified in the form of referendums in some countries and parliamentary

---

[184] Steven C. Greer, *The European Convention on Human Rights* (CUP, Cambridge 2006) 169 f, referencing *inter alia* Luzius Wildhaber, 'A Constitutional Future for the European Court of Human Rights?' (2002) 23 Human Rights Law Journal 161; E. A. Alkema 'The European Convention as a Constitution and its Court as a Constitutional Court' in Paul Mahoney, Franz Matscher, Herbert Petzold and others (eds), *Protecting Human Rights: The European Perspective – Studies in Memory of Rolv Ryssdall* (Carl Heymans, Cologne 2000) 41–63.

[185] *Habermas* (n 5) 136; *Macdonald* (n 90) 853ff; *Petersmann, 2001* (n 163).

[186] Mattias Kumm, 'The Legitimacy of International Law: A Constitutionalist Framework of Analysis' (2004) 15 EJIL 907.

[187] *Ibid* 921.

[188] European Convention Doc. 850/03; 18 July 2003.

[189] See, eg J. H. H. Weiler and Marlene Wind (eds), *European Constitutionalism Beyond the State* (CUP, Cambridge 2003).

approval in others before it could enter into force. The Constitutional Treaty of 2004 was rejected in two referenda, in France and the Netherlands; other EU Member States abandoned their ratification processes as a response. After the failure of the Constitutional treaty, the European Council decided on a Reform Treaty, known as the Lisbon Treaty, in its stead. This treaty, also called into question by many Europeans, finally came into force on 1 December 2009. Despite the rejection of the formal Constitutional Treaty, the opinion has been voiced many times that the EU possesses a constitution in a material sense regardless of its ratification.[190] While it has been difficult to achieve the notion of an exclusive European Constitution (both politically and in legal theory), the model of a multilevel constitution in which powers are shared between the Union level and the nation State level has become more popular.[191] Kadelbach and Kleinlein summarise this opinion: 'The theory of multilevel constitutionalism resting on the assumption of shared competencies does not depend on the political success of the Constitutional Treaty.'[192] Authors writing about public international law have adopted a similar idea of multilevel constitutionalism.[193]

D. *Summary*

Advocates of 'Analogical Constitutionalism' find familiar patterns in domestic and regional legal systems to extrapolate them to the international sphere. To understand the key themes of constitutionalism that these scholars apply, one would therefore do well to look at the domestic or regional constitution that they themselves are familiar with. One key theme stands out in particular: that of the standard-setting capacity of constitutions. Analogical Constitutionalism places much emphasis on the idea of law as a system. It should be mentioned that all of the above visions are to a certain extent analogous to domestic constitutionalism, not just those pertaining specifically to Analogical Constitutionalism.

Conclusion

The above descriptions have revealed that global constitutionalism in international legal perspective is a complex and multi-dimensional area of debate. Despite this complexity, it has emerged that in all dimensions global constitutionalism takes its bearings from the same key themes and certain central

190 For an overview over EU constitutionalism see Armin von Bogdandy and Jürgen Bast (eds), *Principles of European Constitutional Law: Modern Studies in European Law* (Hart Publishing, Oxford 2005).

191 Stefan Oeter, 'Federalism and Democracy' in Armin von Bogdandy and Jürgen Bast (eds) *Principles of European Constitutional Law* (2005) 53ff.

192 *Kadelbach, Kleinlein, 2007* (n 59) 322.

193 *Peters, 2005* (n 45) 541.

ideas. These key themes are, so to say, the building blocks of the contemporary debate on global constitutionalism. One form of grouping the central ideas has been suggested in the four dimensions of global constitutionalism.

The above has categorised four dimensions of global constitutionalism: 'Social Constitutionalism', 'Institutional Constitutionalism', 'Normative Constitutionalism' and 'Analogical Constitutionalism'. While the five key themes established in Chapter 1 can be found in various combinations in the four dimensions of global constitutionalism, certain key themes are emphasised more in certain dimensions:

1) 'Social Constitutionalism' emphasises the key theme of a limitation of the single locus of power through participation.
2) 'Institutional Constitutionalism' emphasises the key themes of governance through institutionalisation of power.
3) 'Normative Constitutionalism' emphasises a common value system through the protection of individual rights and idealism.
4) And finally, 'Analogical Constitutionalism' includes the key themes that are seen as being incorporated in the respective domestic and regional constitutional orders. As was concluded, this dimension includes all key themes of constitutionalism, emphasising the systematisation of law (the fourth key theme).

The analysis of the dimensions of constitutionalism and the respective key themes reveals certain patterns, which enable further categorisations – either more specific or more general. One more general categorisation of the four visions of global constitutionalism is to ascertain which main stream of political theory they follow: 'Social Constitutionalism' and 'Institutional Constitutionalism' focus on participation-oriented forms of constitutional models. The goal of participatory constitutionalism is believed to be achieved by means of *democratic* processes. 'Normative Constitutionalism' and 'Analogical Constitutionalism' on the other hand focus on rights-oriented forms of constitutional models. Although tainted by over-simplification, this normative value-oriented model could be dubbed a *liberal* model.[194] Chapter 3 will focus on a closer analysis of the meaning of 'democratic' and 'liberal' and 'liberal democratic' in this context. To sum up the key themes of global constitutionalism on the one hand and the four dimensions of constitutionalism reviewed on the other hand: there are two main models of global constitutionalism, a democratic one and a liberal one, although each has also features of the other. The next chapter will focus on these building blocks of global constitutionalism; it will be considered where the key themes find their origins and why international lawyers apply them to global constitutionalism.

---

[194] *Schwöbel, Situating* (n 4).

CHAPTER TWO

A HISTORICAL ANALYSIS OF KEY THEMES OF GLOBAL CONSTITUTIONALISM

What's past is prologue.[1]

Introduction

For centuries, thinkers have been fascinated by ideas we would today refer to as having a bearing on global constitutionalism. As seen in the previous chapter, global constitutionalism is not a comprehensive concept but rather an amalgamation of ideas (key themes), with some thinkers stressing certain features and some thinkers stressing other features of what they believe would be constitutive of a global constitution. Chapter 2 takes a closer look at the key themes that have been considered as the defining features of a global constitution. The chapter aims to answer the following questions: What are the origins of the five key themes of global constitutionalism? How do the ideas at the same time reflect the preoccupations of the thinkers of that day and age? How is it that these five themes are considered to be the building blocks of contemporary global constitutionalism by *all* participants to the debated (albeit with varied emphases)?

In order to address these questions, a number of assumptions had to be made. First, I made the assumption that the five key themes have their origin in Western thought and therefore began with European history pertaining to certain legal frameworks that encircle society. This is unfortunately a somewhat circular undertaking, as any historical or epistemological approach is: In order to unravel conceptions one must make a choice as to where to begin, which in a sense predetermines part of the outcome. Affected by the foregoing limitations, I made the second assumption that, although there is a general consensus that modern constitutions have their roots in 17th and 18th century Europe, the ideas of constitutionalism (broken down into their key themes) did not appear at this time from oblivion, but rather have their roots in European Antiquity. Why then Antiquity? This is more of a practical issue: simply because of a lack of available sources that predate Western Antiquity. This prompts the third assumption. I was of course not only examining the history of constitutionalism, but also the history of public

[1] William Shakespeare, *The Tempest* (Courier Dover Publications, London 1999) 27.

international law; after all, my work concerned global constitutionalism from an international legal perspective. I made the assumption that there are deep connections between global constitutionalism and public international law, with their respective ideas overlapping, shaping, and stimulating each other. Of course, there are scholars that believe that public international law only emerged with the idea of sovereignty and the Treaty of Westphalia, but I made the (informed) assumption that public international law also did not emerge from a nothingness and that its ideas also begin (meaning they were first recorded) in Antiquity. These observations are closely connected to the fourth and final assumption. Based on the findings particularly from Analogical Constitutionalism, it must be assumed that the five key themes of global constitutionalism are at the same time key themes of some systems of (Western, specifically European) national constitutionalism. Thus, the historical analysis follows the origins of domestic constitutionalism as it does the origins of global constitutionalism. Particular to the latter are the three common premises that constitutions exist beyond the nation State, that there is a certain unity or homogeneity in the international sphere and that the idea of global constitutionalism itself is universal. These premises, or common assumptions, of all participants to the debate on global constitutionalism will be analysed in more depth in the next chapter. In this chapter, the history of these premises runs alongside the history of constitutionalism to form what we today understand as global constitutionalism.

The chapter has been split into five sections, each pertaining to a certain time in history. The common division of Classical Antiquity, the (European) Middle Ages, the (Western) Modern Era, the time of Colonialism and Imperialism and Post-Modernity/the present-day has been adhered to. This division has been undertaken both for practical reasons of clarity and familiarity. It must be stressed here that this is a division of Western, predominantly European, history. This fact and its implications will be dealt with in more depth in later chapters. In terms of methodology it may have made sense to divide this chapter into the five key themes and then to identify the roots of the themes. However, the key themes, as will be seen, have developed in an overlapping manner, making this an almost impossible task. For example, the first key theme, the restriction of power, can be understood both in a participatory-democratic sense as in Ancient Greece or in an individual rights sense (the State must refrain from violating individual rights of its citizens).

While the descriptions attempt to be as wide-ranging as possible, the literature that has been used necessarily causes the description to be selective and restricted. It has already been mentioned that an epistemological approach is in a sense always a subjective undertaking. While an attempt has been made to use original sources, there was needless to say a process of selection involved in which sources to rely on. This is all the more evident for later literature (from the Enlightenment onwards) since the number of sources naturally increases the closer to the present day one ventures. Since this is a study of international law contributions to the debate on global constitutionalism, there is a large increase in literature from the traditional roots of international law onwards, often associated with the Treaty of Westphalia of 1648. Where there was a larger choice of literature, the critical literature rather than the purely descriptive literature was opted for. This was done as a way of introducing a critical analysis of the current trajectories of global constitutionalism. The in-depth critical analysis will be undertaken in Chapter 3.

The first recorded ideas of global constitutionalism begin around the 5th century BCE in Ancient Greece and Ancient Rome, a time that is commonly referred to as Classical Antiquity. Whereas in those days there were no written constitutions as we know them today, many modern views on constitutionalism have their roots in the writings of philosophers of Classical Antiquity. This chapter therefore begins with an examination of the works of Ancient Greek philosophers that were most influential in shaping what can be understood as 'global constitutionalism' today. Most importantly, this is when ideas of *universality* of law – in the form of natural law – were first formed. The natural law concept, although sometimes more and sometimes less pronounced, accompanies ideas on global constitutionalism beyond Antiquity through to current views. Throughout European history, the concept of natural law underwent significant changes and followed certain trends. In Antiquity it changed from being understood as a law of nature in a physical sense, to being a 'superior' moral law that could act as a corrective to positive law. This introduces the *first* key theme of constitutionalism: the limitation of power through legal rules. The *second* key theme of constitutionalism is determined soon after, in the writings of Aristotle: governance and the institutionalisation of power. While Aristotle speaks of a natural law, this is in truth limited to the *polis* – the city-State. Diogenes' philosophy, as the origin of cosmopolitanism, is an important signpost for the development of global constitutional debates. The chapter moves on to discuss Stoicism and the beginnings of thoughts on the concept of universal morals and ethics. These are the origins of the *third* key theme of constitutionalism: its social idealism. As another great influence on the development of law, the Romans are discussed next. It will be demonstrated how the field of law came to be understood as a more practical rather than philosophical field and the idea of setting a certain standard through law emerged. This standard-setting capacity is classified as the *fourth* key theme of global constitutionalism. The discussion on the Romans sees the beginnings of the influence of Christianity on legal thought. The notions of global constitutionalism in the Middle Ages of the West are discussed next, beginning with the Western Roman Emperor Gratian. This section looks at the main discourses and preoccupations of scholars of the Middle Ages, namely Christian discourses on God and a divine law, those of ethics and morals, and those of the individual and his or her rights. Some of the key themes that were extracted in the philosophical writings of the scholars of Antiquity will be revisited and the origins of the *fifth* and final key theme of constitutionalism – the protection of individual rights – is explored. It will be determined how this Christian concept of individual rights was increasingly severed from its religious roots in the writings of Grotius and Pufendorf and transformed to a secular theory. Scholars such as Hobbes and Locke expanded on the theories of innate rights in the Enlightenment – a time which was to mark the beginning of the Modern Era of the West. This era, beginning in the 17th century, will be examined in the third section. The reader's attention will be directed to the growing recognition for the concept of State sovereignty in international law. It will be clarified how this led to the decline – or at least the receding – of grand theories of universality in law and at the same time to the rise of written constitutions. I examine how thoughts on a universal/natural law were kept alive in constitutionalism despite the rise of the nation State as the sole source of law. The era of colonisation and imperialism of the non-Europeans by the Europeans from the 16th to the 20th century is discussed next. It is identified how international law and constitutionalism served as tools of the Europeans in their civilising mission. Reference is made to the work of writers such as Anghie and Anaya, who illustrate that the language of law was (mis)used and altered to justify the territorial and culture domination over non-Europeans. The view then shifts to today's post World War II constitutional landscape. It is discussed how 'the international' or 'the global sphere' is once more of immediate significance and demanding attention, in an economic, social, political and legal sense. The emergence of global issues has led to (renewed and revamped) discussions of global constitutionalism in many disciplines.

The following spans no less than 2,400 years and thus criticisms of over-compression are of course justified. The thoughts fly through the centuries in a manner that does in no way pay credit to the rich history. As noted earlier, I have made very limited selections of what I consider to be the defining thoughts of a particular time to *exemplify* rather than *exhaust* them. The length of the sections mirrors the key themes that are explored. The section on Antiquity is therefore the longest since the first four (of the total five) key themes are framed in this time.

Section I: Antiquity

A. *The Greeks*[2]

Ancient Greece is credited with being the birthplace of democracy. Democracy of that time was based on the premise of the limitation of power, the first key

[2] European classical antiquity is commonly considered as beginning with the works of the poet Homer. His works are the earliest recorded Greek poetry from around the 8th to 7th century BCE.

theme of constitutionalism, and to a certain extent the institutionalisation of power, the second key theme. The notion that power of decision-makers within a given society must be limited and that decision-makers must be held accountable was in this time closely linked to thoughts on natural law. Natural law is significant in two ways, one regarding the limitation of power and the other since natural law is believed to derive its validity from ideas of universality. What is meant by the use of the term 'natural law' has varied strongly throughout the centuries. It has been observed that 'few terms in the history of law have had such a variety of meanings as the "law of nature" or "natural law"'.[3] The use of the terminology is bewildering because authors of the same period employ the term differently and indeed the same writers also often employ the term with varying connotations.[4] The universality of natural law was rooted in varying concepts which provide the term with its different meanings; these being, *inter alia*, human nature, a universal rationality, the laws of nature, ancient customs, or a divine law.[5]

The early thinkers of Ancient Greece predominantly considered natural law as a phenomenon that was in accordance with nature in the physical sense, 'similar to the laws of the natural sciences in modern terminology'.[6] The Sophists, a group of intellectuals of the 5th century BCE, radically altered concepts of natural law by directing attention away from the physical universe toward the State and its relations to individuals.[7] The Sophists employed rhetoric as an art of illustration and persuasion, claiming they could find an answer to everything by way of systematic argumentation. The poets preceding the Sophists (such as Homer, for example) had tied all issues of the legitimacy of notions such as 'virtue' and overall conceptions of 'nature' and the 'universe' into ideas on the roles of deities. The Sophists called such terminology into question.[8] Hippias (around 460 BCE-399 BCE), a Sophist, was, according to Plato, the first to discuss the distinction between *nomos* and *dikaion* as the distinction between man-made (positive) laws and universal laws emanating

[3] Charles Grove Haines, *The Revival of Natural Law Concepts* (Harvard University Press (HUP), Cambridge MA 1930) 4.

[4] *Ibid.*

[5] Benjamin F. Wright Jr. compiled a list of meanings pertaining to 'natural' in natural law, particularly as used in American political theory: 'American Interpretations of Natural Law' (1926) 20 American Political Science Review 542, 543: 1) Divine law or the law of God. 2) Rational or reasonable. 3) In accordance with human nature. 4) In accordance with ancient law or custom. 5) Pertaining to the physical system of the universe. 6) The just or equitable. 7) The ideal as differentiated from or opposed to the actual. 8) Principle pertaining to the moral nature of man. 9) The original as distinguished from the conventional. 10) Pertaining to the state of nature. 11) The appropriate of fitting. 11) In harmony with the conditions of growth or existence.

[6] *Haines* (n 3) 24.

[7] *Haines* (n 3) 5.

[8] For an introduction to the Sophist teachings, see Michael Gagarin, Paul Woodruff (eds), *Early Greek Political Thought from Homer to the Sophists* (CUP, New York 1995) xxii–xxxi.

from the gods.[9] He illustrated that *nomos*, as manmade law, could be utilised for tyranny to reign but that this utilisation of law was contrary to nature.[10] He therewith challenged the former terminology of the *nomos basileus* (of law as a gift of the gods), which made unjust law impossible because self-contradictory.[11] *Dikaion* was to be understood as the counterpart to *nomos*, as an original natural order, according to which all people are equal by nature and are only made unequal by *nomos*. Hippias chose to illustrate the opposition between *nomos* and *dikaion* as an opposition between politics and nature. This illustration was to be the beginning of the notion of natural law as a corrective of positive law.[12] Philosophers henceforth occupy the role of critics of lawmakers and judges.[13] The purpose of the natural law, of an overarching law, was criticism of the ruling authority. From today's perspective, such a view seems to foreshadow the revolutionary thoughts and actions that took place many years later in (predominantly France of) the 18th century CE. Natural law as a corrective for positive law appears to be the origin of the first key theme of constitutionalism: that of the *limitation of power* – in this case, the restraint of State power through higher law. While the concept of a written constitution, drafted on the basis of the sovereignty of the people, only came into being many centuries later, the Ancient Greeks already felt the need for a check on political decisions in a source higher than the decision-maker himself – a central tenet of liberalism today.

Aristotle (384 BCE-322 BCE) expanded on the idea of natural law, according him the label of 'father of natural law'. He laid the foundations for the philosophical thought of a dualism between the customary, natural, and universal law on the one hand, and the local, conventional, and ordinary enacted manmade law on the other hand.[14] Whilst Aristotle postulated the existence of a natural order of mankind, he believed that the nature of humans could only be

---

[9] Benjamin Jowett (tr), Plato, *Protagoras*, 337c-d, The Internet Classics Archive.

[10] *Ibid.*

[11] The tradition of a sacral justice was dominated by the poets Homer, Hesiod, the Orphics and Theognis. Braithwaite clarifies: 'the poems of Homer and Hesiod, and the plays by the three great tragedians, were the texts by which the Greeks transmitted their beliefs about the gods, the ordering of divine and human affairs, and their moral teachings about how men should live. This literature served them as drama, theology, and moral philosophy combined.' William T Braithwaite 'An Introduction for Judges and Lawyers to Plato's *Apology of Socrates*' (1994) 25 Loyola University Chicago Law Journal 525.

[12] Sophocles illustrates his notion of a higher law in his tragedy *Antigone*. In the play, Antigone attempts to wilfully disobey the orders of the King, her father, in order to secure a respectable burial for her brother who was a traitor to the King. She muses on the existence of a law that overrides the law of the King: 'They [the gods that make higher law] are alive, not just today or yesterday: they live forever, from the first of time, and no one knows when they first saw the light.' Sophocles, Robert Fagles (tr), *The Three Theban Plays – Antigone, Oedipus the King, Oedipus at Colonus* (Penguin Books, Harmondsworth 1982) (verses 506–508) 82.

[13] Erik Wolf, *Griechisches Rechtsdenken* Vol 2 (Vittorio Klostermann, Frankfurt am Main 1952) 84.

[14] *Haines* (n 3) 6.

realised in the *polis*. Ancient Greece was split into (mostly autonomous) city-States, which were referred to as *poleis*. *Polis* also refers to belonging to this (political) entity by way of citizenship. To paraphrase Mogens Herman Hansen, for Aristotle, the citizen-body was the *matter* of the *polis*, while the constitution was the *form* of the *polis*.[15] Aristotle claimed that law only applied to the relations between persons and since a human could only be a person within the *polis*, *polis* law was the only law.[16] Outside of the *polis*, a different variety of 'law' existed: law in a metaphorical sense. Whoever lives outside the *polis* loses the characteristics of humanity, of the ability to think rationally, speak, and act; those living outside the *polis* are either gods ('being higher than man') or animals ('a poor sort of being').[17] The person is referred to as a *zoon politikon*, a social creature that lives within and constitutes a political community. Citizens acquire their natural perfection only in the company of others – in the 'place of assembly' within the *polis*, the *agora*. According to Aristotle, *polis* law is divided into natural law and enacted (positive) law. Natural law is described as having 'absolute (universal) validity'.[18] He thereby identified two key features of natural law, universality and validity. Ever since Aristotle, natural law is believed to be a law that combines and equates its validity with its source. While positive law is dependent on a valid source for it to be valid itself, natural law has no such requirement. The link between natural law and constitutionalism has often been based on this postulation of validity. Today, many constitutions draw their validity from natural law ideas that are believed to be pre-political, meaning no further justificatory basis is required. Although scholars succeeding Aristotle base their thoughts of validity on Aristotle's view of natural law, Aristotle in fact had rather a different understanding of natural law. Since Aristotle linked natural law inextricably to the *polis*, he placed issues of political justice at the forefront of discussions on nature. Rather than basing the validity of natural law on natural law itself (as was done with reference to Aristotle henceforth), he saw the basis and validity of natural law as rooted in the *polis*. Thus, as circumstances in the *polis* change, so must natural law. Natural law is consequently not immutable in Aristotle's view. The link to the *polis* of both positive law and natural law means that they are coequal. Aristotle's 'natural law' was therefore not universal to the world nor was it a law that pre-existed the State. Later pronouncements on natural law that see natural law as something pre-existing the State and political structures, and

---

[15] Mogens Herman Hansen, *Polis: An Introduction to the Ancient Greek City-State* (OUP, Oxford 2006) 110.

[16] Aristotle, D A Rees (ed), H H Joachim (tr), *The Nicomachean Ethics* (Clarendon Press, Oxford 1951) (1134a23–1136a9) 153, 154.

[17] Aristotle, Ernest Barker (tr), *The Politics of Aristotle* (Clarendon Press, Oxford 1948) (1253a 9) 5.

[18] *Aristotle, Ethics* (n 16) 155.

which can be employed as a corrective to positive law, can thus not necessarily rely on Aristotle.[19]

Aristotle was not only preoccupied with the limitation of political power as Hippias before him, but also focused on the *institutionalisation of power*. According to Aristotle, not all people are born equal, rather, some people are born to rule, and others are born to be ruled.[20] These circumstances are predetermined by nature. The power of those who reign must be exercised for the common good. Today, the importance of the process of regulating and ordering issues of public interest is recognised as a principle, commonly termed 'governance'.[21] According to Aristotle, governance can only be practised if the ruling class is able to represent the serving class and political power is justly distributed.[22] Such representation and power-distribution requires institutionalisation of power and therewith accountability for actions of power, a theme that has been at the centre of discourse on constitutionalism ever since.

The philosophical school succeeding Aristotle marked a significant change, occurring through a new interpretation of the political. While the identification of the person as a *zoon politikon* remained, the interpretation of the nature of the political changed.[23] The concept of the political sphere was adjusted in accordance with the geo-political circumstances. As the influence of the great Greek city-States gave way to the expanding influence of a large Roman empire, so the understanding of the political expanded from the city-State to a larger, global, scale. Stefan Lippert names the Greek philosopher Diogenes (approximately 412/404 BCE-323 BCE) as the embodiment of this change.[24] Diogenes was a beggar who declined any form of social life established through institutions; although living within the city, he did not live in the *polis*. He took on the life of an animal, comparing himself to a dog, praising the virtues of such creatures. Nevertheless, he still saw himself as a social being although his *polis* was not the city but rather the world.[25] In his lost works about the Politea, Diogenes is believed to have identified the cosmic constitution, constituted by natural law, as the only correct constitution.[26] Through the expansion of the regional norm system to a world system, the idea of cosmopolitanism was born.

---

[19] Stefan Lippert, *Recht und Gerechtigkeit bei Thomas von Aquin: Eine Rationale Rekonstruktion im Kontext der Summa Theologiae* (N.G. Elwert Verlag Marburger Theologische Studien, Marburg 2000) 53.

[20] *Aristotle, Politics* (n 17) 35ff.

[21] James N. Rosenau 'Governance, Order, and Change in World Politics' in James N. Rosenau, Ernst-Otto Czempiel (eds) *Governance Without Government* (CUP, Cambridge 1992).

[22] *Aristotle, Politics* (n 17) 116ff.

[23] *Lippert* (n 19) 55.

[24] *Ibid.*

[25] *Ibid.*

[26] It has been observed that Diogenes' cosmopolitanism was 'negative' since it rested in a rejection of the *polis*; see Ryan Krieger Balot, *Greek Political Thought* (Blackwell Publishing, Malden MA 2006) 284.

Ancient Stoicism, a philosophical school of thought of Ancient Greece first founded in the 3rd century BCE, elaborated on the term and notion of cosmopolitanism. *Cosmos* literally means 'order' and is also referred to as world order. While many ideas of Aristotle's political philosophy remain intact in Stoicism (particularly the limitation and the institutionalisation of power), the Stoics added an additional (third) dimension: the cosmos as the world as a whole, characterised as the community of gods and humans. The cosmos was thought to be a 'quasi-civic and political entity'.[27] Thomas Aquinas, whose influence will be discussed below, later explained the three dimensions of Stoicism as *lex aeterna* (eternal law), *lex naturalis* (natural law), and *lex humana* (human law).[28] The *lex aeterna* is universal reason, fate, and as Chrysippus[29] stated according to Cicero (106 BCE-43 BCE): 'the universal existence in which all things are contained.'[30] The corresponding normative order to this (mostly philosophical) order was understood as a world law or cosmic law: One must live in harmony with the divine order of the universe.[31] While world law refers to the cosmos in the physical sense, *lex naturalis* concerns human nature. The normative order of human nature is one of universal reason (*logos*), which can be obtained through self-control and fortitude. *Lex naturalis* is understood as the 'true law', unalterable for humans, in accord with nature:

> There will not be a different law at Rome and at Athens, or a different law now and in the future, but one law, everlasting and immutable, will hold good for all peoples and at all times. And there will be one master and ruler for us all in common, God, who is the founder of this law, its promulgator and its judge.[32]

Notably, the central aspect here is virtue. Stoicism taught that it was virtuous to maintain a will (and actions following from this will) in accordance with nature. The third dimension, the *lex humana*, or manmade law, is only binding on individuals so long as it is in accordance with natural law, which itself is god-given. These distinctions lead to a 'trinity' of god, nature, and reason. God creates humans as naturally rational beings that live in a community (*animal*

---

[27] A. A. Long, 'Law and Nature in Greek Thought' in Michael Gagarin, David Cohen (eds), *The Cambridge Companion to Ancient Greek Law* (CUP, Cambridge 2005) 424.

[28] Thomas Aquinas, Alessandro Passerin D'Entrèves (ed), J. G. Dawson (tr), (*Summa Theologiae* I), *Aquinas Selected Political Writings* (Blackwell, Oxford 1948) (Question 91, Art. 1–3) 113–115. Aquinas believed that there was an additional dimension in divine law (Question 91, Art. 4), this will be discussed further below.

[29] Chrysippus (280–207 BCE) was one of the most influential Stoic philosophers. He was a follower and successor of Zeno, the founder of Stoicism.

[30] Marcus Tullius Cicero, C. D. Yonge (tr, ed), *De Natura Deorum*, *The Treatises of M. T. Cicero* (George Bell and Sons, London 1878) 15. Cicero, a Roman statesman and philosopher, introduced the Stoic school of thought to the Romans in his books on philosophy.

[31] *Lippert* (n 19) 55.

[32] Marcus Tullius Cicero, Clinton W. Keyes (tr), *De Re Republica, De Legibus* (HUP, Cambridge MA 1948) (III 22, II 4, 10) 211.

rationale et sociale). Consequently, humans should share the law and make it a common good.[33] Stoicism is not based on monotheistic religious conceptions of god; rather, god is often equated with nature and with reason. Thus, there is no clear-cut trinity as it may at first seem. The ethical dimension of the law is regarded as the source of its universality, meaning nature can be utilised as a value measure of laws. Thus emerges a different type of understanding of global law to Aristotle's *polis* understanding. According to Stoicism, a global law for all humans is an ethical dimension, which acts as a guidance to leading a virtuous life. The idea of the universal shifted from the political (relations between the individual and the State) towards the individual and his self. Natural law therewith adopted an ethical, or more precisely, an idealist theme.[34] Social idealism in constitutions is generally the designating of an ideal for the future society that has not been actualised in the present society – and may never in fact be actualised in this way, but is regarded as 'the good life'. *Social idealism* is the third key theme of global constitutionalism. For the Stoics, the idea of an ideal law was linked to *self*-improvement. It was thought one could improve oneself through the practice of *ataraxia* (imperturbability), a supreme duty of self-control over passions and irrationality.[35] The idea of an ethical/ideal dimension of a higher law is later entrenched in many constitutions alongside the political dimension of the limitation and allocation of power. Constitutional idealism today is to be understood in the sense of a normative ideal for the future based on societal values. Such value-laden idealism is commonly found in the form of human rights. Although the concept of the individual and his or her free will was later to be connected to the limitation of political power that was mentioned above, this development did not take place until the Enlightenment. For the Stoics, ideals were also directed towards a future, a better future, but they were much more abstract than the normative idealism in today's constitutions. They can be best understood as general principles of how to achieve a good life. These universal and immutable principles of natural law were regarded as superior to any other law – a notion that was later to lead to the concept of formal superiority of certain ethical principles in the form of a normative hierarchy. While Aristotle's interest was for the political and thus State/city constitutions, the Stoics were more interested in moral universality.

No matter which function the law took up in Ancient Greece – whether ethical, as a limitation on power, or as a means to institutionalise power – it was always considered a serious matter of public concern. The idea of the all-encompassing power of law and its sovereignty was one of the fundamental

---

33 *Cicero, De Natura* (n 30) 412.
34 *Haines* (n 3) 7.
35 This attribute has influenced the present-day use of the term 'stoic'.

principles of Greek thought.[36] This thought tradition has prevailed in many theories of law to this day and many constitutions' legitimacy relies on the assumption of the all-encompassing power of the law.[37]

B. *The Romans*

The expanding Roman Empire, which was to lead to the Roman conquest of Greece in 146 BCE, incorporated much of the Greek philosophical thought into Roman culture, but with a new twist. Law was applied in a practical rather than a theoretical manner, according it more resemblance to what we understand as the profession of law and distancing it from what we consider as philosophy. The Romans made particular use of the theories of natural law for political and legal purposes. As in the Greek philosophical tradition, the terminology of natural law described a global law. The Romans relied on the Greek notions of universality and society while developing their idea of normativity further.

The Romans developed a comprehensive legal system, introducing the distinction between *jus civile* (civil law) as the law of the Roman citizens, and the *jus gentium* as the law of peoples.[38] The *jus gentium* (law of peoples) was deemed as a law that transcended State boundaries; it was viewed as an ideal law, often equated with or used synonymously with *jus naturale* (natural law).[39] For the Romans, *jus gentium* meant a set of universal principles of common law recurring among different peoples – an understanding that was to lead to later concepts of public international law and has been retained in the German word for public international law *Völkerrecht*, meaning law of peoples. The significance of *jus gentium* grew as the Roman empire expanded and with it the necessity to settle legal relations with other peoples.

Contemporaneously with the rise of the Roman Empire came the rapid expansion of Christianity in the Mediterranean region. Christian theologians, a new group of thinkers, appropriated much of the Graeco-Roman concepts into their own theology. These theologians, learning of the theories of natural law, argued in favour of an additional global law: a divine law. In line with the rather nebulous history of natural law up to this point, natural law concepts and divine law concepts were sometimes thought to be synonymous, were sometimes thought to have some overlap, and were at other times considered

---

[36] *Haines* (n 3) 7.

[37] An understanding of the appeal of this idea – the power of law to regulate social reality – is developed in regard to contemporary visions of global constitutionalism in more depth in Chapter 4.

[38] Ulpian, Alan Watson (ed, tr), *The Digest of Justinian* (University of Pennsylvania Press, Pennsylvania 1998) para 1.

[39] *Lippert* (n 19) 70. Lippert emphasises that *jus naturale* was not necessarily on the same level as *jus civile* and *jus gentium* since nature itself was understood as a norm-constituting factor.

as being completely separate. But natural law and divine law were both always regarded as 'higher law'. The *jus gentium*, on the other hand, remained the law of the peoples, not enjoying such elevated status.

Augustine (354–430 CE), a philosopher and theologian from North Africa assumed the tripartite division of the law of the *Stoa*. Augustine referred to the *lex temporalis* (positive law that is valid so long as it is not contrary to *lex aeterna*), the *lex naturalis* (a natural law commanding humans to be just), and *lex aeterna* (unchangeable law in accordance with the rationality and will of God to conserve creation).[40] Augustine thus interpreted the impersonal 'cosmic reason' of the Stoics as grounded in a purely (mono-)theistic foundation. He consequently argued that the necessity as well as reason of all that exists rests in the personal will of God.[41] This reasoning was to prevail for most of Europe of the Middle Ages, a time that was heavily influenced by confessional theories.

In 529 CE, the Christian Emperor Justinian ordered the closing down of the philosophical schools in Athens by imperial decree since he felt that the polytheistic and pagan undercurrents of the schools were not compatible with his religious belief.[42] At this time, the concept of *jus naturale* was believed to mean a body of ideal principles. These principles could be rationally apprehended by humans and included the perfect standards of right conduct and justice.[43] The rational apprehension of ideas was a thought that re-emerged in the period of Enlightenment of the Western philosophy and culture of the 18th century. It is notable that, in contrast to the 18th century, the standard of right conduct and justice was not linked with the concept of individual rights. The legal significance of a natural *right* was therefore not part of the theory of a natural law. The growing 'sophistication' of the legal system and the closing of the philosophical schools prompted a separation of the principles of natural law and natural justice from philosophical thought. From there on, the terms found their expression in the hands of the judge and administrator.[44] The *application* of natural global law by the judges highlighted a new capacity of a higher law: that of setting a standard. If a judge relied on natural law to rule on a specific case, he thus set a standard for that legal system. Such standardisation was crucial for a belief in the development of the law. This *standard-setting*

---

[40] St. Augustine, W. M. Green (ed), *De Libero Arbitrio* in *Corpus Christianorum: Series Latina*, vol. 29 (Brepols, Tunhout 1970) (I 15, 31); Karsten Friis Johansen, Henrik Rosenmeier (tr), *A History of Ancient Philosophy: From the Beginnings to Augustine* (Routledge, New York 1998) 623.

[41] Anton-Hermann Chroust, 'The Philosophy of Law of St. Augustine' (1944) 53 The Philosophical Review 195.

[42] Edward Grant, *A History of Natural Philosophy: From the Ancient World to the Nineteenth Century* (CUP, Cambridge 2007) 61.

[43] *Haines* (n 3) 11.

[44] *Haines* (n 3) 8.

capacity of natural law is analogous to the standard-setting provisions of most modern constitutions. Modern constitutions commonly include provisions which are viewed as guidelines for the development of law and society, encompassing visions of progress. Standardisation is the fourth key theme of global constitutionalism.

C. *Summary*

In sum, the above analysis of the philosophers' preoccupations of Antiquity identifies that four of the five key themes of global constitutionalism have their roots in the writings and traditions of Greek and Roman thinkers of Antiquity. Since this period knew neither sovereign States nor written constitutions as we know them today, the idea of a higher global law and ideas of constitutional character were often united. The four themes of global constitutionalism situated in Western legal and philosophical history so far are:

1) The belief that such a law has the ability to limit power,
2) The belief of the capacity of such a law to legitimise governance through the institutionalisation of power,
3) The notion that there exists a higher order, which is ideal in terms of the future society, and
4) The idea that a constitution has the ability to systematise the law as a future reference for society

These four themes all emerged from thoughts on natural law. All of the above four themes will be encountered again in the below; this indicates the importance and eminence of the intellectual origins of Western Antiquity for contemporary views on global constitutionalism.

Section II: The European Middle Ages

A. *The Rise of Divine Law*

The jurists and theologians of the Middle Ages were predominantly preoccupied with three ideas: divine law, ethics, and individual rights. These three occupations were to have a significant impact on the key themes mentioned above, particularly in how far they shaped ideas of emerging *national* constitutions. Divine law was of prime importance to the jurists and theologians of the Western world. The distinction between a superior law and an inferior (man-made) law was a notion carried over from Antiquity. Superior law was increasingly equated with a universal law of God. Natural law theories often merged with divine law theories in this period. There was a general consensus between the scholars that natural law theory, as transmitted from Stoicism to the Middle Ages through both the *Corpus Juris* of Justinian and the expatiations of the Church Fathers, concerned certain fundamental principles of right and justice rooted in the very nature of the world. There was also consensus that man, since he is rational, is capable of knowing these principles and shaping his life according to them. The scholars also shared the view that positive laws and institutions can only claim validity so long as they are in accordance with the prescriptions of natural law.[45] There was much disagreement however on the content of natural law. Natural law was still regularly equated with what is today understood as natural science meaning that questions such as the natural instincts of animals were often intertwined with normative concepts. Gratian (359–383 CE), a Christian Roman Emperor, introduced to canon law the distinction between divine law and human law,[46] and introduced the interpretation of *jus naturale* as divine law distinct from animal instincts. *Jus naturale* represented the immutable general moral principles that God implanted in human nature. According to the ecclesiastic historian Alexander James Carlyle, the Church Fathers believed that 'there was a law written by nature in men's hearts which is the true rule of human life and conduct' and that the 'law of God is in the heart of the just man. … not the written law but the natural law.'[47] Despite these efforts by Gratian, there remained many different interpretations of natural law and divine law. In the 13th century, Thomas Aquinas (1225–1274 CE) undertook to systematically disentangle, harmonise, and define the views and terminology of theology and law. He did this in his treatise, the *Summa Theologica*.[48] Referencing and expanding on Aristotelian philosophy, Aquinas categorised four branches of law: First, *eternal law*, which is God's plan for the governing of the universe by divine reason.[49] Second, *natural law*, which is participation in eternal law by rational creatures, and is enshrined in the form of precepts;[50] Third, *human law*, which is the detailed application of natural law principles by man to specific circumstances;[51] And fourth, *divine law*, which is to be understood as a supplement to natural law and is known through revelation rather than reason. It is composed of the principles appropriate to man's search for direction in his actions with respect

[45] Ewart Lewis, 'Natural Law and Expediency in Medieval Political Theory' (1940) 50 Ethics 145.

[46] The law of the Church was codified in canon law; eg James A. Coriden, *An Introduction to Canon Law* (2nd edn Paulist Press, New York 2004).

[47] Alexander James Carlyle, *A History of Medieval Political Theory in the West* (New York and London, 1903) vol 1, 104, 105.

[48] This synthesis of Greek philosophy and Christian doctrine was the height of what is referred to 'Scholasticism', the system of the 12th to 14th century which undertook to reconcile the theology of the Church Fathers with Greek, particularly Aristotelian, philosophy. See eg Joseph Rickaby, *Scholasticism* (Constable, London 1911).

[49] *Aquinas*, (n 28) (Question 91, Art. 1) 113.

[50] *Ibid* (Question 91, Art. 2) 115.

[51] *Ibid* (Question 91, Art. 3) 115.

to his final end (an end of eternal blessedness).[52] The specifically Aristotelian aspect of Aquinas' classifications is the definition of natural law as *not* being immutable, thus being able to change in accordance with the changing circumstances of life.[53] The other significant dimension of Aquinas' work is the attempt to understand morality in the *legalistic* terms of a natural law. Although it had been attempted before, Aquinas' work was to become paradigmatic for this undertaking.[54] Importantly, moral standards of natural law had become a structure of norms in Aquinas' system, albeit in the form of legal precepts rather than specific rights or duties.[55] Such a notion of the normative force of morals was an adaptation from Antiquity, particularly from the Stoics.[56]

Although Aquinas had four categories, the jurists of the Middle Ages generally adopted the Roman thinkers' division of law into natural law (*jus naturale*), law of nations (*jus gentium*), and civil law (*jus civile*). The *jus gentium* was considered as a set of customs (of civil law) applicable to all peoples and *jus civile* was understood as the set of customs of a particular community. *Jus naturale* was viewed as a body of principles. In order for customs (*jus civile*) to be valid, it was believed that they had to be reasonable and in accordance with natural law. The conception of the standard-setting capacity of natural law was thus kept alive as one of the key themes of a global constitution. This has been translated into constitutions today in the form of principles – take the German *Rechtsstaatsprinzip* (rule of law) for example. It is regarded as crucial that all other legal rules must be in harmony with this constitutional standard. Standard-setting is to be understood as the systematisation of law, namely the idea that society should progress and develop according to a fixed plan or system enshrined in constitutionalism.

Emphasis should be placed on the fact that natural law of the European Middle Ages was mostly believed to emanate from God. Both the king and the pope, as the bearers of political and religious power, were thought only to be answerable to God for justification of their acts of power. Spurred by thinkers such as Aquinas, the demand for kings to rule justly and according to law grew. It was, however, not until after the Reformation of the Church that thinkers detached natural law theories from God to instead find their source in human reason.[57] The precursors of these detachments were the Spanish jurists, who, although believing in the law of nature as an inflexible code willed by God, fostered a belief in the natural *rights* of man. The Jesuit Francis Suárez (1548–1617) made a clear distinction between natural law and natural rights.

---

[52] *Ibid* (Question 91, Art. 4) 115, 117.
[53] *Ibid* (Question 91, Art. 2, Question 94, Art. 2, 4) 115, 123.
[54] Knud Haakonssen, *Natural Law and Moral Philosophy* (CUP, Cambridge 1996) 15.
[55] *Lewis* (n 45) 148.
[56] *Lippert* (n 19) 61.
[57] *Haines* (n 3) 17.

Natural law was understood as a law that 'embraces all precepts or moral principles.'[58] Natural rights, according to Suárez, are means to the realisation of the goals set by the natural law.[59] The latter corresponded with the Christian thought of individual personality; a thought that had become a feature of Christian scholarship throughout the Middle Ages and had spilled over to the anti-clericals: 'To ecclesiastical thinkers men were equal in the eyes of God; to the anti-clericals they were equal in the eyes of man.'[60] Christians place much emphasis on the individual and his or her personal salvation. Although Suárez made no distinction between natural law and religion – he saw natural law as contained in the Ten Commandments of the Old Testament – he introduced a notion that has since found acceptance in the vast majority of modern constitutions: the notion of the necessity of the *protection of individual rights* by the State. Many national constitutions today include a Bill of Rights, enshrined to protect the individual from arbitrary State acts. The protection of certain fundamental rights is commonly also a feature required of visions of global constitutionalism and is the fifth and final key theme of global constitutionalism.

Two principal influences were to mark the beginning of what is often referred to as the Early Modern Period: the disappearance of religious unity among Christians after the Reformation, and the beginnings of European overseas expansion. The thinkers of that time had to adapt their theories to these changes. Thus, an increasing number of voices declared that the principle of the inviolable dignity of the individual person entailed freedom of conscience for all, regardless of faith. This tied into criticism of scholastic natural law theory, which also had to adjust to the changing world of growing European power structures. It was a natural step to question a so-called 'natural' law that was not applicable outside of the Christian world, i.e. in the new colonies. For how could a law apply to non-Christians that was dependent on both believing in God and the 'knowledge' of God as the creator of the world? Furthermore, in view of this newly discovered diversity, how was it possible to provide a theoretically coherent account of religious and moral notions?

Francisco de Vitoria (circa 1492–1546), a Spanish theologian and jurist, wrote two famous lectures in which he posed these questions and attempted to find answers regarding the relationship between the colonisers and the colonised. The lectures, *De Indis Noviter Inventis* ('On the Newly Discovered Indians'), and *De Jure Bellis Hispanorum in Barbaros* ('On the Law of War of the Spanish on the Barbarians') are concerned with the colonial efforts by the Spanish in South America.[61] Antony Anghie contends that Vitoria

---

[58] Francisco Suárez, 'Tractatus de Legibus ac Deo Legislatore' in *Selection from Three Works*, Classics of International Law (Clarendon Press, Oxford 1944) (II ch 17) 210.

[59] *Ibid* 326.

[60] *Haines* (n 3) 19.

[61] Anthony Pagden and Jeremy Lawrence (eds), *Francisco de Vitoria: Political Writings* (CUP, Cambridge 1991) 233.

reconceptualised existing juridical doctrines and invented new ones in order to deal with the novel challenge of the Indians that emerged through colonialism.[62] This is where international law – its inception, its precepts and its utilisation – comes into the picture. Anghie explains that there was no preceding international law that could be applied to the newly discovered territories, therefore certain concepts had to be *created* in order to regulate the relationship.[63] In this quest of creativity, Vitoria reformulates the relationship between divine, natural and human law.[64] Vitoria places questions of ownership in the sphere of natural law and includes the (non-believing) Indians in this sphere.[65] He thereby detaches natural law from belief and creates a secular system administered by a secular sovereign (rather than the previous divine law articulated by the Pope). Furthermore, Vitoria reengages *jus gentium* as a law of peoples by bringing the Indians into the scope of this law. Anghie has illustrated how this reasoning was a means of justifying Spanish intervention. According to Anghie, Vitoria set out in his work that the cultural practices of the Indians were at variance with universal norms – norms that in effect were Spanish practices – and that this discrepancy required the civilising mission of the Spaniards.[66] In his second lecture on the war between the Spanish and the Indians, Vitoria declares that the transformation of the Indians (in terms of a civilising operation) is to be achieved by the waging of war. Crucially, Vitoria states that only sovereigns have the right to wage war. Vitoria then reintroduces divine law (which he has previously rejected in favour of a secular natural law) to the law of nations by claiming that only Christians can wage a just war – therewith only Christians are sovereign.[67] The Indians, when fighting the Christians, are hence perpetually violating the law of nations. He therefore rationalised a dualism between the global (secular) natural law and a sophisticated (Christian) law of nations. The law of nations as it was then had no response to the new challenges that occurred through colonisation. New concepts were created to suit the political expediency of the powerful European States while simultaneously supplying a legal justification for the politics.

B. *The Secularisation of Law*

Protestant natural law, with Hugo Grotius (1583–1645 CE) as the pre-eminent advocate, responded to the growing scepticism regarding justifications through divine law. The novelty was in the objection to the presupposition of a moral

---

62 Antony Anghie, *Imperialism, Sovereignty and the Making of International Law* (CUP, Cambridge 2007) Ch 1, in particular 15.
63 *Ibid.*
64 *Ibid* 18.
65 *Ibid.*
66 *Ibid* 22.
67 *Ibid* 23–28.

continuity and interdependence between God and humanity.[68] Grotius, now often referred to as the 'father of international law', drew on notions of universality, law, and society and applied them to the relations between States. In these themes, he was very much influenced by the thinkers of Antiquity. Almost the entirety of this textual authority for his seminal work *De Jure Belli ac Pacis* comes from Antiquity.[69] Nevertheless, Grotius did not entirely abandon the religious vocabulary. Indeed, the sources from Antiquity can, according to David J. Bederman, be equally divided between biblical quotes and the writings of classical authors.[70] The Protestant distinction between the *rationality* of the relationship between God and humans on the one hand and *faith* in this relationship on the other hand was central to Grotius' work. This in turn facilitated the idea that only faith could bridge the gulf between humanity and its Creator.[71] As Grotius' work exemplifies, thinkers were no longer predominantly occupied with God and divine law but were increasingly occupied with thoughts on the individual and human laws, prompted by growing interest in law applicable to equals. This also led to a shift away from universal superior law to law applicable to equals. Grotius, while not daring to break completely with the significance of God as the source of a divine law,[72] was very influential in preparing the ground for notions of morals which were independent of religion.[73] In his work, he responded to the political requirements of his time and country: to find not only a legal but also a moral justification for war and intervention.[74] And indeed much of Grotius' theories on war but also particularly on natural rights 'originated in his attempt to justify the claims of Dutch traders to operate in the colonies of Spain'.[75] As the focus on the individual grew, so did the question of the individual's role in society. The idea surfaced that the moral obligation of individuals rests in the protection of society and humanity. This notion paved the way for a justification for going to war on sound moral grounds, independent of religion. It also paved the way for the idea that 'individuals with natural rights are the units of which all social organization is made'.[76] The belief in society of individuals was to be central to

---

[68] *Haakonssen* (n 54) 25.

[69] David J. Bederman, 'Reception of the Classical Tradition in International Law: Grotius' *De Jure Belli ac Pacis*' (1996) 10 Emory International Law Review 3.

[70] *Ibid.*

[71] *Ibid.*

[72] Hugo Grotius, Walter Schätzel (tr), *Hugo Grotius: De Jure Belli ac Pacis – Libri Tres* (Mohr Siebeck, Tübingen 1950) (I 1 XV) 54.

[73] For a concise account of Grotius' life and events that influenced his works, see the foreword in Walter Schätzel, *ibid.*

[74] Hugo Grotius (1583–1645) lived at a time that the Dutch refer to as the Golden Age. The Dutch dominated world trade in the 17th century, thus becoming a rich country, able to invest in the furthering of arts, literature, and science. The Dutch fought bloody wars over the pre-eminence of the sea and trade power. See eg Maarten Roy Prak, Diane Webb (tr), *The Dutch Republic in the Seventeenth Century* (CUP, Cambridge 2005).

[75] *Ibid* 29.

[76] *Haakonssen* (n 54) 28.

the thinkers that were to draft the first modern constitutions in the newly independent United States of America and in France. Grotius made use of the theory of natural law in order to refer to a law of sovereign States as well as to refer to a law of individuals. Much of Grotius' argument is based on the analogy between individuals and sovereign States. He argued that the natural state of man was morally similar to the situation of States with respect to each other.

The Mediaevals believed that natural rights (as the source of the equality of all men) arose from an original and primitive state of nature. To many scholars – theologians and jurists – this state of nature corresponded to the condition of men before the origin of sin.[77] The development of the theologians' and jurists' concept of inherent and inalienable rights prompted a need for calling the powers of the State into question and provided fertile ground for demands for the limitation of State power. To both theologians and jurists, there was a law – divine for the former and natural for the latter – that was superior to positive (man-made) laws; a law that man-made laws had to correspond with in order for them to be granted with validity. As discussed above, this theme of the limitation of power through a higher law was one of the themes that had occupied their predecessors of Antiquity.

While the voices demanding the limitation of State power on the basis of a higher law grew louder, a theory was being developed, which was to cause the concept of natural law to recede: Jean Bodin developed the theory of sovereignty. Bodin (1530–1596 CE) defined sovereignty in the Six Books of the Commonwealth as 'the absolute and perpetual power … of commanding in a State',[78] the *potestas legibus soluta*: the power that is independent of the law. The concept of sovereignty Bodin was referencing was attached to the sovereign – in Bodin's country of origin the French monarch. Bodin followed arguments formulated by Machiavelli (1469–1527), who had suggested in his work *Il Principe*, Princes were bound by superior laws of morality and religion (alone) and were accountable only to God for any breaches thereof.[79] According to Bodin 'there is nothing on earth greater than a sovereign prince, save God alone.'[80] Thus, political and legal thought had caught up with political reality.[81] The theory of sovereignty paved the way for an understanding of the State as the sole source of law, countering the concept of natural law as a source of law. It bears emphasis that natural law of the late Middle Ages/early Modern Era was (still) mostly believed to emanate from God. Despite the observations of

---

[77] *Haines* (n 3) 26.

[78] Jean Bodin, *Six Books of the Commonwealth*, quoted in W. T. Jones, *Masters of Political Thought*, vol II (London 1947) 57.

[79] Niccolo Machiavelli, George Anthony Bull, Anthony Grafton (tr), (*Il Principe*) *The Prince*, (Penguin Classics, London 2003).

[80] *Bodin, Jones* (n 78) 58.

[81] Francis Stephen Ruddy, *International Law in the Enlightenment – The Background of Emmerich de Vattel's Le Droit des Gens* (Oceana Publications, New York 1975) 13.

Protestant scholars that natural law was a secular body of law, the clasps of the church and the sovereign were still strong on the consciousness of the people. The belief that natural law, which determined the validity of civil law, emanated from God and the almost universal idea that political power also had divine origin, meant that civilians generally accepted political power and law. Christian rulers regularly invoked Romans 13 of the New Testament as evidence of divine political power in order to maintain such power. Romans 13:1–7 reads:

> Let every person be subject to the governing authorities; *for there is no authority except from God, and those authorities that exist have been instituted by God. Therefore whoever resists authority resists what God has appointed*, and those who resist will incur judgment. For rulers are not a terror to good conduct, but to bad. Do you wish to have no fear of the authority? Then do what is good, and you will receive its approval; *for it is God's servant for your good. But if you do what is wrong, you should be afraid, for the authority does not bear the sword in vain!* It is the servant of God to execute wrath on the wrongdoer. Therefore one must be subject, not only because of wrath but also because of conscience.[82]

The force of a belief in divine law cannot be underestimated. The link between compulsion by law *and* by religion was used as a means to legitimise political absolutism (of monarchs) as well as religious absolutism (of the church).

C. *Summary*

While, many of the preoccupations of intellectuals of the Middle Ages in Western Europe were the same as those of antiquity, a definite shift took place: With the rise of the importance of the individual and the State came the decrease in the importance of a global universal law. Questions of individuals within the State borders took centre stage in concerns of the people; issues of a *universal* law however became increasingly peripheral. It must be noted that although the concept of a universal/global law was preparing to take a back seat, the concept of public international law (as an inter-State law across the world) was becoming 'progressively sophisticated'. The key themes that were at the forefront of this time in Western history were the limitation of power, which was to be achieved through the fifth key theme identified: individual rights protection.

Section III: The Modern Era of the West

A. *The Centrality of the Nation State*

The Modern Era of Europe and the 'young' USA was defined by a sharp rise in the significance of law and the nation State. It would be too simplistic to state

[82] New Revised Standard Version; Emphases added.

that this brought with it the decline of visions of a universal law. Although positive law and written State constitutions were to reign supreme in Western Europe in its so-called Modern Era, the paradigms of this time had a very strong influence on later visions of global constitutionalism. It is therefore worth tracing the preoccupations of thinkers of this time and the trends in political and legal thought that followed them.

Thomas Hobbes (1588–1679 CE) postulated the idea of the State as the sole source of law. While Hobbes' state of nature referred to a universal concept, the law became detached from this sociological idea. Hobbes claimed that the world is presented to humanity for unlimited use; everyone is provided with a right to everything.[83] Individuals exercise this right to everything as their *jus naturale* whose prime concern is self-preservation. Since everyone has his or her own interests at heart, pursuit of self-preservation would lead to a war of everyone against everyone.[84] In order to prevent this self-defeating 'self-preservation', individuals should follow certain precepts, which limit their natural liberty and rights. Interestingly, Hobbes continued to place his theory within a doctrine of natural law:

> The right of nature, which writers commonly call *jus naturale*, is the liberty each man hath, to use his own power, as he will himself, for the preservation of his own nature; that is to say, of his own life;[85]

The law of nature may, according to Hobbes, be ascertained by reason. The recognition of an obligation to the laws of nature will lead to the establishment of contractual foundations – his famous social contract – through matching rights and obligations, which are considered as the basis of civil society.[86] When conceiving this theory, Hobbes seems to have 'secularised' morals entirely, thus taking Grotius' ideas a step further. Morals seem no longer to be inextricably linked to God, but are rather entrenched in society as a means to maintain this society. Although Hobbes did in fact maintain a theistic interpretation of morals through situating his theory in a natural law of divine commands, the secular aspect has been entrenched in many modern constitutions in the sections dealing with individual rights – commonly in a Bill of Rights.

Hobbes saw the laws of nature as an adequate code of conduct, enabling a peaceful social existence. However, since the 'state of nature' knows no terms such as right and wrong, justice and injustice, only war, we can have no security that laws will be obeyed. What is therefore needed to secure obedience to the laws of nature is a transfiguration into commands issued by an authority

---

[83] *Thomas Hobbes: Leviathan*, J. C. Gaskin (tr), (OUP, Oxford 1998) (ch 14) 87.
[84] *Ibid* 84.
[85] *Ibid* 86.
[86] *Ibid* 89.

possessing rightful claims to obedience. In Hobbes' view, only a sovereign with 'unlimited power' can provide for obedience and law and order.[87] In political terms this means an absolute sovereign. If society's inclination to self-preservation is to be balanced, the force determining the balance (the law of nature) must be institutionalised. Hobbes thus argued that a peaceful society that limits its concern for self-preservation for the good of society is only possible when the law of nature has become the sovereign's law. Hobbes, as Aristotle before him, therefore also places much weight on the necessity of institutionalising power. It is notable that his reasoning empties natural law of its meaning – natural law is henceforth linked and dependable on the sovereign power. The same problem arises as with Aristotle, who entrenched natural law in the *polis*: So long as natural law is not pre-political, it loses much of its persuasive force. This recognition added to the decrease in respect for universal rights and the growing respect for State rights.

The 'secularisation' of morals was continued in the works of Samuel Pufendorf who further developed Grotius' and Hobbes' thoughts on the scientific (rather than theistic) character of natural law.[88] Many written constitutions today emphasise the importance of pre-political rights, often in the form of inalienable human rights. Pufendorf (1632–1694 CE) saw the possibility of developing natural law as a complete 'science of morals', distinct from moral theology and analogous to the new deductive science.[89] This understanding of natural law furthered the idea of natural rights independent of society and the State. So while Hobbes believed that all rights have their source in the State, they are again freed from the State in Pufendorf's account. This concept of rights independent of the (pre-political) State was to lead to the strong emphasis on individual rights in the French declaration of 1789 and the constitutions that followed it.[90] John Locke (1632–1704 CE) was also interested in pre-political rights. He identified natural law as constituted by three natural rights – life, liberty, and property – as rights belonging to man in a pre-political state.[91] In contrast to Hobbes, Locke perceived natural law as existing in the state of nature. Pre-political natural law could, in Locke's view, be known and interpreted by reason. This law of nature, according to Locke, bound legislature and government; equality is its fundamental condition. Such findings were in accordance with the social and political needs of those times. Natural law thus developed from an ideal law in the early Middle Ages to a series of rational concepts by the beginning of the Early Modern Period. Locke's ideas

---

[87] *Ibid* (ch 21) 138 .

[88] Baron Pufendorf, Basil Kennet (tr), *The Law of Nature and Nations: Or, A General System of the Most Important Principles of Morality, Jurisprudence, and Politics in Eight Books* (5th edn J and J Bonwicke, London 1749).

[89] *Ibid* Ch II.

[90] *Haines* (n 3) 22.

[91] John Locke, *Two Treatise of Government* ed. (C. and J. Rivington, London 1824) (book II Ch VII sec 87) 179.

famously found their impact in American legal thinking.[92] They completed the dualism that had started with Aristotle: on the one hand there existed a universal and superior law common to all men and on the other hand there were man-made positive enactments, which were particular to the society and the contingencies of the moment. From this dualism between a superior (natural) law and positive enactments developed the need for superior laws to be set out in a positive form. Such positive form makes superior law controllable as a standard-setting mechanism for the positive enactments. Such ambitions provided fertile ground for the drafting of national constitutions as we understand them today.

B. *The First Written Constitutions*

Although national constitutions are not at the centre of the focus of this book, the examination of their key themes is crucial for the debate on global constitutionalism – as is of course most evident through Analogical Constitutionalism, which draws on ideas of domestic and regional constitutional orders. This same reasoning applies to the framers of the new written constitutions, who were very much influenced by their intellectual forefathers. Bederman explains that the framers of the Constitution were 'as much influenced by the political values and experiences of Classical Antiquity as they were by Enlightenment liberal philosophy and the exigencies of the struggle against Great Britain'.[93]

The first constitution of modern times is often traced back to Great Britain: The English Bill of Rights 1689 was the first document which was to bear similarity with later constitutions in that it referred to citizens' rights. The document was the consequence of the English Glorious Revolution of 1688, in the wake of which England had declared itself a constitutional monarchy.[94] The Bill of Rights was an Act of Parliament, which assumed the rights of a subject in a constitutional monarchy. It differed from later bills of rights in that it did not place emphasis on the individual's rights vis-à-vis the State as such, but rather was a list of privileges of the people as represented by parliament. For example, the Bill of Rights includes such rights as the freedom from taxation by royal prerogative without agreement by Parliament. The English Bill of Rights was particularly influential in terms of its link between citizens' rights and democracy. Although the notion of a constitution established through democracy had existed in Europe since the days of Ancient Greece,[95] it was

---

[92] *Haines* (n 3) 23.

[93] David J. Bederman, 'The Classical Constitution: Roman Republican Origins of the Habeas Suspension Clause' (2007–2008) 17 Southern Californian Interdisciplinary Law Journal 405.

[94] Michael J. Allen and Brian Thompson, *Cases and Materials on Constitutional & Administrative Law* (7th edn OUP, Oxford 2002) 64–65.

[95] Thucydides' famous quote 'Our Constitution … is called a democracy because power is in the hands not of a minority but of the greatest number' opens the Preamble of the *Draft Treaty Establishing a Constitution for Europe* (European Convention Doc. 850/03; 18 July 2003).

now to take on the specific form of a document symbolising the sovereignty of the people. It is widely believed today that a constitution of a nation State derives its legitimacy from an act initiated by or at least attributed to the people. By this act, the people attribute political capacity and its institutionalisation to themselves. The idea of democracy, as a tradition of participation, was therewith born from the traditions of limiting State powers and accountability, themselves born from the liberal traditions of autonomy and equality. Thus the commonly held opinion that a true constitution can only exist in a democracy in which the people have the political capacity. The link between the people and the constitutional document has become a pivotal aspect of the limitation of power and the institutionalisation of it.

The United States Constitution was adopted by the Constitution Convention in Philadelphia, Pennsylvania, in September 1787. It was drafted as a result of the U.S. Declaration of Independence from the British Empire (1776). The Constitution is the recognised framework for the allocation and institutionalisation of power in the United States. Although this constitution emerged from ideas of independence and change, the underlying ideas were, as previously mentioned, very much influenced by the intellectual trends in antiquity, the religious trends in the Middle Ages, and the notions of individuality and statehood of the Modern Era of the West and even from the period of colonialism and imperialism. The Constitution defines the three branches of government and their respective powers: the legislative branch (Congress), the executive branch (the President), and the judicial branch (headed by the Supreme Court). Belief in the need for a framework for power allocations is famously influenced by the French political thinker Montesquieu (1689–1755 CE). In his treatise 'The Spirit of the Laws', first published in 1748, Montesquieu advocates the need for a constitution which separates the power in a State:

> In every government there are three sorts of power: the legislative; the executive … [and] the judiciary power. …When the legislative and executive powers are united in the same person, or in the same body of magistrates, there can be no liberty, … Again there is no liberty, if the power of judging be not separated from the legislative and executive powers ….[96]

Montesquieu's separation of powers was compounded with Madison's idea of creating a mechanism of checks and balances.[97] This concept combines the constitutional key theme of the limiting of power and the constitutional key theme of the institutionalisation of power and is today considered a central tenet of the liberal tradition.

---

[96] Charles de Secondat, Baron de Montesquieu, *The Spirit of Law* (Francis Douglass and William Murray, Aberdeen 1756) (vol I book XI ch VI) 164, 165.

[97] John R Vile, *The Constitutional Convention 1787: A Comprehensive Encyclopaedia of America's Founding* (ABC-CLIO Press, Santa Barbara CA 2005) 83.

In 1791, the Ten Amendments, the United States Bill of Rights, were added to the U.S. Constitution. Although heavily influenced by the English Bill of Rights, the U.S. Bill of Rights differed from its English predecessor by clearly designating a limitation on the rights of government. Its content was a direct consequence of the discourses of the age of Enlightenment, particularly Locke's ideas on the freedom and equality of all people in the state of nature.[98]

The Declaration of the Rights of Man and of the Citizen, adopted in August 1789, was to be the first French constitution.[99] It was adopted during the French Revolution (1789–1799), the upheaval which led to the fall of the absolute monarch and the birth of the French Republic. Popular sovereignty – emanating from the equality of all citizens – was given particular attention, thus eliminating the special rights of the nobility and clergy. Drafting of written constitutions has since marked the political turn of countries, often a political turn from autocracy to popular sovereignty. From there on, constitutions have not only been a means of the restraint of individual power, but have moreover been a form of *self*-restraint which the people impose on themselves.[100] Additionally, statements of ideals such as the French *liberté, egalité, fraternité* have become a popular component of constitutions and constitutional thought.

The emergence of the nation State caused the concept of a global law to lose some of its significance as the State became the sole legitimate source of power and rights. Positivism as black-letter law grew and largely replaced natural law concepts. Constitutions were generally understood as written documents, which marked the constructivist/positivist attitude to the regulation of human affairs in contrast to the naturalist.[101] The age of rationality and enlightenment largely displaced concepts such as natural law, which had had religious connotations, and only man-made law was viewed as real law. A strict rule of sovereignty in all matters concerning the State was continually gaining importance. Internally, a State was free to choose its power structures itself, could be democratic or authoritarian, could have a monarch or an elected head of State; externally, a State could enter into international agreements or not.[102] Within this setting, there was little room for a transnational or even international law.

---

[98] Neil H. Cogan (ed), *The Complete Bill of Rights – The Drafts, Debates, Sources and Origins* (OUP, New York 1997).

[99] Maurice Duverger (ed), *Constitutions et documents politiques* (Presses Universitaires de France, Paris 1996) 17–18.

[100] John H Hallowell, *The Moral Foundation of Democracy* (Chicago 1954) 63–64.

[101] Dario Castiglione 'The Political Theory of the Constitution' in Richard Paul Bellamy, Richard Bellamy, Dario Castiglione (eds) *Constitutionalism in Transformation: European and Theoretical Perspectives* (Blackwell Publishers, Oxford 1996) 7.

[102] Antonio Cassese, *International Law in a Divided World* (Clarendon Press, Oxford 1986) 24.

It must be mentioned that constitutions occupied a special role in this age of the pre-eminence of man-made law. Notions of pre-political rights, which were thought to originate from natural law, and thoughts on human dignity, which could not be conferred on man by man, nevertheless found their place in constitutions and constitutional thought. The French Declaration of 1789 referred to universal and innate rights, which are to be valid in all times and places. For example, the first Article states: 'Men are born and remain free and equal in rights. Social distinctions may be founded only upon the general good.'[103] James Madison, when introducing the Ten Amendments to the Constitution (the Bill of Rights) to the 1st Congress emphasised the concept of natural rights inherent in all individuals.[104] It has thus been commented that the idea of natural law showed 'a remarkable persistence in American constitutionalism despite the decline of the intellectual prestige of natural law ideas.'[105] In the United Kingdom as in the United States, Judges were often to refer to natural law when it came to constitutional issues. In his famous speech denouncing taxation without representation, Lord Camden declared this type of taxation as

> Illegal, absolutely illegal, contrary to the fundamental laws of nature, contrary to the fundamental laws of this constitution … a constitution grounded on the eternal and immutable laws of nature.[106]

It is interesting to note that although sovereignty largely displaced musings on a universal law, the notion of universality was nevertheless maintained in constitutionalism. This in turn was utilised for strengthening the validity of the foundations of the nation State – often of course the constitution itself. The concept of a normative hierarchy – the formal supremacy of certain norms vis-à-vis ordinary norms – was thus a crucial aspect of constitutionalist thinking in the 'age of positivism.'

Despite the axiomatic nature of sovereignty and the nation State in the field of law, the cosmopolitan dream remained extant in the field of philosophy. The most eminent scholar concerned with cosmopolitanism of this time was Immanuel Kant (1724–1804 CE). In *Perpetual Peace,* Kant applied his social and political philosophy to a global scale.[107] He developed analogies between

---

[103] *Les homes naissent et demerent libres et égaux en droits. Les distinctions socials ne peuvent être fordeés que sur l'utilité commune.* Maurice Duverger (ed), *Constitutions et documents politiques* (Presses Universitaires de France, Paris 1996) 17.

[104] James Madison, 'Notes for Speech in Congress' June 8 1789 in Charles F. Hobson et al (ed) *Papers of James Madison,* (University Press of Virginia, Charlottesville 1979) (vol 12) 194.

[105] Thomas C Grey, 'Constitutionalism: An Analytic Framework' in J Roland Pennock and John W Chapman (eds), *Constitutionalism* (New York University Press, New York 1979) 203.

[106] William Cobbett, *The Parliamentary History of England, from the Earliest Period to the Year 1803,* vol XVI (T. C. Hansard, London 1813) 178.

[107] Immanuel Kant, Lewis White Beck (tr), (*Zum Ewigen Frieden*) *Perpetual Peace* (Bobbs-Merrill, Indianapolis 1957).

individuals and States to highlight that relations within a nation State can apply analogously to the international sphere (the approach taken in Analogical Constitutionalism). Kant argued that the state of nature was one of war – even if the hostilities do not take place perpetually, there is nevertheless a perpetual threat of war. Peace must therefore be made and this, according to Kant, is only possible through law. The same applies to States, they must be considered as in a state of war with each other. Like individuals, States must leave this state of nature to form a union under a social contract.[108] In *Perpetual Peace*, Kant begins with a description of a set of 'preliminary articles' aimed at reducing the likelihood of war.[109] They are negative in the sense that States are prohibited from a certain conduct with the purpose of causing a state of non-war.[110] The preliminary articles are complemented by 'definitive articles', whose purpose is to lead to the state of peace. The first definitive article sets out that every State should have a republican civil constitution, which would enable peace among civilians (*Bürger*) as well as peoples (*Völker*).[111] By 'republican', he means 'separation of the executive power (the government) from the legislative power'.[112] Kant reasons that since the people carry the burden of war (it is they that must go into battle and pay for warfare through taxes), States would be unlikely to go to war with one another. The second definitive article is that all States should be part of a federalism of States federated for the purpose of ensuring and maintaining peace (*Friedensbund*).[113] The third definitive article argues in favour of a cosmopolitan right of universal hospitality.[114] When discussing this, he refers to a global civil constitution (*Weltbürgerliche Verfassung*),[115] seemingly the first ever explicit reference to a global constitution. In Kant's vision, the civil constitution is a non-institutional constitution. Since the earth only provides for a limited amount of living space, there must have been a sense of sharing space in the past and there should also be one in the future. In the *Metaphysics of Morals*, which was published two years later, Kant considers that an organisation of States on a global scale would have to be a voluntary (*willkürliche*) coalition rather than a federation that can be dissolved at any time.[116] He reconsiders the idea of a model by which States subject themselves to public coercive laws (as he had envisioned in *Perpetual Peace*), now stating that it may be unrealistic.[117]

---

108 *Ibid* (8:346) 9.
109 *Ibid* (8:343–347) 6–11.
110 Udo Kern, *Was Ist und was Sein Soll* (Walter de Gruyter, Berlin 2007) 326.
111 *Kant, Perpetual Peace* (n 107) (8:351) 11–15.
112 *Ibid* (8:352) 11–15.
113 *Ibid* (8:354) 11–15.
114 *Ibid* (8:357) 11–15.
115 *Ibid* (8:357) 15.
116 Immanuel Kant, Mary J Gregor (tr, ed), (*Metaphysik der Sitten*) Metaphysics *of Morals*, (CUP, Cambridge 1998) (6:351) 120.
117 'Kant's Social and Political Philosophy' Stanford Encyclopedia of Philosophy http://plato.stanford.edu/entries/kant-social-political/. Patrick Capps asserts that the vision in *Perpetual*

Regardless of the fact that Kant seems to have changed his viewpoint, his visions of constitutionalism have been extremely influential for modern visions of global constitutionalism.[118] While Kant may have departed from his federalist vision, he certainly had a large impact on the key theme of the limitation of power.

C. *Summary*

The Modern Era of the West brought with it a growing importance of the nation State as the sole source of power. This worked in favour of ideas of national rather than global constitutionalism. Modern constitutionalism was developed in this era, prompted by the codifications of the French and U.S. national constitutions. Towards the end of this time, Kant reintroduced the idea of global constitutionalism. The Modern Era of the West saw the amalgamation of the key themes of constitutionalism in one single source of law: Political power was limited through the different branches of power; such power was institutionalised in State institutions; a codified constitution was increasingly viewed as the mechanism for both limiting as well as attributing power in the State. Since constitutions were born out or revolution, they very much embodied an ideal for the future society; this ideal was thought to rest on certain pillars which set the standard for the entire national society. It was in this time that individuals rights gained a central position in the demands of the people for the limitation of political power.

Section IV: Colonialism and Imperialism

A. *Colonialism*

The beginnings of colonialism of European States and the response of international law have already been touched upon in the above illustration on the European Middle Ages. The following section on imperialism will briefly outline the height of European colonial rule in the 19th century to the 1940s, from when on the colonised non-European societies acquired political independence. While the terms colonialism and imperialism are often employed synonymously, some authors refer to the territorial aspect of colonialism (the expansion and settling of territories) and the subordination aspect of

---

Peace could itself be 'surrogate' of a universal State, Patrick Capps, 'The Rejection of the Universal State' in Nicholas Tsagourias (ed) *Transnational Constitutionalism: International and European Models* (CUP, Cambridge 2007) 41.

[118] Patrick Capps, 'The Kantian Project in Modern International Legal Theory' (2001) 12 EJIL 1003; see the contributions in Chapter 2, particularly those referred to as 'World Law' contributions, 90–93. See also the Special Issue: The Kantian Project of International Law (2009) 10 German Law Journal.

imperialism (where one State controls the political sovereignty of another) to distinguish the two.[119] This distinction will be applied in the following. The section draws the attention of the reader back (from the first written constitutions) to international law. As was mentioned above, sovereignty and positive law reigned (almost) supreme in the 19th century. Ideas on global concepts of law were brought into disrepute as natural law ideas were rejected. Rather than recognising the existence of a truly universal law, the Europeans of the 19th century saw it as their (civilising mission) to bring European concepts of law to non-European societies. The Europeans did, however, use the vocabulary of their naturalist predecessors to justify their economic exploitation and cultural and political domination in non-European States. The discussion on the imperialism of the 19th century must therefore begin with the lawyers of colonialism in the 16th century.

According to Anghie and S. James Anaya, international law took up a central position in colonialism and imperialism as many concepts of international law were forged out of the attempt to create a legal system that considered and regulated the relations between the European and non-European worlds in the colonial confrontation.[120] European legal concepts of the 16th century were described as universal and civilised and non-European ways were regarded as particular and uncivilised.[121] On the basis of this, international law developed to facilitate colonial patterns promoted by European States. As discussed above, Francisco de Vitoria based his arguments of a universal law on natural law in the 16th century.[122] Anghie illustrates that the Indians were viewed by Vitoria as ontologically 'universal' for demonstrating the facility of reason but were considered socially and historically 'particular'. The Spanish social and cultural practices were – unsurprisingly – declared by Vitoria to be in harmony with the requirements of universal norms. This rationale granted the Spanish a powerful right of intervention to act in a way that would liberate the Indians from their particular rituals.[123] Vitoria's successors of the 19th century, although characterising themselves as positivists and therefore radically different from their naturalist predecessors, used the vocabulary of natural lawyers in order to argue in favour of the 'civilising mission'. While the naturalist international lawyers, although supporting the colonial mission, regarded international law as derived from reason and therefore applicable to all peoples, positivist international law centralised the sovereign and therefore distinguished between civilised States and non-civilised States, with international

119 *Anghie* (n 62) 11.

120 *Ibid.* S. James Anaya, *Indigenous Peoples in International Law* (OUP, 2nd ed Oxford 2004).

121 *Anghie* (n 62) 22.

122 *Pagden, Lawrence* (n 61).

123 *Anghie* (n 62) 22.

law only applying to the civilised States.[124] Following the Peace of Westphalia in 1648, the (civilised) world according to Europeans was divided into nation States. The concept of the nation State, based on European models of political and social organisation, became the building block of the political and social world. The defining characteristics of exclusivity of territorial domain and hierarchical, centralised authority were at odds with many of the decentralised political structures and overlapping territorial domains of much of the non-European world.[125]

B. *Imperialism*

Once the colonies had been established, the next challenge for the European powers was to uphold this power; and, again, international law provided a potent tool for this endeavour. In the mid-19th century, recognition of States in international law was conditioned upon certain forms of governance, this was of course the form of governance known to the European powers.[126] Not only was State sovereignty dependent on the forms of governance, acceptance into the society of civilised States was too.[127] While the rationale behind colonialism was predominantly economic profit, the 'Age of Empire' was all about the political domination of the foreign territories.[128] By 1914, virtually all the territories of Asia, Africa and the Pacific were under the control of a major European State; as a consequence, people in non-European countries were required to assimilate to a system of law that – since it derived from European thought and experience, can be described as fundamentally European.[129] With this assimilation came the import (or rather imposition) of certain values, values that were still very young in Europe at that time. Although the codification of constitutional values was regarded as a feature of sovereign States, the European constitutional values that had recently been drafted in the first constitutions were imposed on non-European States.[130] Immanuel Kant for example, despite rejecting the notion of an Empire, projected his European vision of a sovereign State onto the colonies. A true colony, according to Kant, was what he termed a *civitas hybrida*, 'a nation which has its own constitution, legislation and territory, and all members of any other state are no more than

[124] *Ibid* 35.
[125] *Anaya* (n 120) 22.
[126] Catherine Turner, 'Delivering Lasting Peace, Democracy and Human Rights in Times of Transition: The Role of International Law' (2008) 2 The IntlJ of Transnational Justice 127.
[127] *Anghie* (n 62) Chapter 2.
[128] See for example Eric Hobsbawm, *The Age of Empire, 1875–1914* (Pantheon Books, New Your 1987).
[129] *Anghie* (n 62) 33.
[130] Anthony Pagden, 'Stoicism, Cosmopolitanism, and the Legacy of European Imperialism' (2000) 7 Constellations 19.

foreigners on its soil' – including those of the 'mother state'. A true colony is *ruled* by the mother State but *governs* itself.[131] Anthony Pagden states it is 'difficult to conceive of Kant's image of a "republic" in any other context but that of the history – and in particular the history of republicanism – of western Europe.'[132]

The use of the concept of a constitution and constitutional elements is significant in the history of the United States. First, the Europeans extended their idea of constitutionalism to their colonies in order to establish and legitimise rule over the country. Then, the newly settled Americans utilised the idea of constitutionalism when fighting for independence from European rule. Interestingly, the former then employed the *same* concept to establish and justify sovereignty over the aboriginal peoples.[133] Notably, it was the key themes of constitutionalism that were imported into the non-European territories. There appears an uncanny parallel with the contemporary project of global constitutionalism – this will be the object of further analysis in the next chapter.

C. *Summary*

In the time of colonialism and later imperialism, there were very few discourses on global constitutionalism, rather constitutions were regarded as specifically European civilised concepts that were part and parcel of sovereign States. International law was viewed as a law between sovereign States that applied to the 'family of nations'.[134] Such rigorous views on the sovereign equality of States and the connected non-intervention in internal matters of other States were facilitating factors for a lack of legal mechanisms with which to prevent the First World War.

The League of Nations was an orchestrated effort following the Treaty of Versailles to establish an international legal organisation in response to the First World War. This association of States, set up in order to restrict political individual expansionist enterprises of States, was the first seed for renewed theories of a common (global) law. For the first time in post-Westphalian international law, a document was termed the global constitution. In 1932, Hersch Lauterpacht described the League Covenant as the 'fundamental charter of the international society'.[135] Later, he expanded this idea in his

[131] *Kant, Metaphysics* (n 116) 159.

[132] *Pagden* (n 130).

[133] James Tully, *Strange Multiplicity: Constitutionalism in an Age of Diversity* (CUP, Cambridge 1995) 42. Such use of the 'constitutional language' will be examined in more depth in Chapter 3.

[134] See for example Thomas Joseph Lawrence, *The Principles of International Law* (D.C. Heath & Co, Boston 1910) 58.

[135] Hersch Lauterpacht, 'Japan and the Covenant' (1932) 3 Political Quarterly 175.

article 'The Covenant as the Higher Law' in which he referred to the formal primacy of the Covenant to underline this thought.[136]

The formation of the United Nations as a response to the Second World War saw a growing number of voices in favour of a common global constitution, believed by some to be the UN Charter. The era of colonialism and imperialism saw the growing importance of international law as an inter-State law across the European and Europeanised world. Both domestic constitutional law and international law were employed as powerful legal and moral tools of legitimising imperialism.

Section V: Post-Modernity/The Present

Our present-day social, political, economic and legal orders are determined through the receding of the national and the growing importance of the international and transnational. The receding of the national has been described as the 'death of the nation State' or as the 'total crisis of the nation State'.[137] While some regard these formulations as over-stated, many consider that there has been a 'paradigm shift'.[138] The rise of the international and transnational is often described by use of the word 'globalisation'. National economies have given up their State-enforced restrictions in favour of international trade and investments, which has brought with it vast international capital flows. This process is being serviced through the spread of technology, which has itself required international participation. The growing participation in global, de-territorialised issues has prompted the emergence of global networks and institutions. In sociology and politics, international theory has experienced a return to the notion of cosmopolitanism. Cosmopolitanism is commonly based on the assumption that all people belong to a universal moral community. Ulrich Beck, in his book 'Cosmopolitan Vision' proclaims: 'The important fact now is that the human condition has itself become cosmopolitan'.[139] In terms of international law, these changes are reflected in a preoccupation with, and a repeated reference to, the 'international community'. International cooperation has also been the ground for the emergence of international networks and institutions, which act on behalf of the international community, and take up previously typically State governmental functions. The point of

---

136 Hersch Lauterpacht, 'The Covenant as the Higher Law' (1936) XVII British Yearbook of International Law 55.

137 Luigi Ferrajoli, 'Beyond Sovereignty and Citizenship: a Global Constitutionalism' in Richard Bellamy (ed) *Constitutionalism, Democracy and Sovereignty: American and European Perspectives* (Avebury, Aldershot 1997) 151.

138 The term was first coined by Thomas Kuhn in 1962 with his seminal work *The Structure of Scientific Revolution* (University of Chicago Press, Chicago 1962).

139 Ulrich Beck, *Cosmopolitan Vision* (Polity, Cambridge 2006) 2.

time in which the change towards 'internationalisation' began could possibly be brought back to the period after the First World War. Since then, the previously somewhat *laissez-faire* attitude towards internal and external legal affairs of a State has become increasingly restricted. The previous near-absolute sovereignty of States, which included the principle of non-intervention into internal affairs, has given way to cooperation and participation between States in their affairs. The number of bilateral and particularly multilateral treaties has expanded dramatically since the First World War. The number has increased even more since 1945, after the end of the Second World War, since human rights (which transcend borders) have become more and more significant. Additionally, the number of the subjects and actors of international law have increased (greatly legitimised by the doctrine of human rights). As international organisations, inter-governmental and non-governmental, as well as individuals have increasingly become actors and subjects of international law, the perception of the global community has shifted: there has been a shift from a community of States to a so-called international community.[140] The idea of an international community was augmented with the end of the Cold War in the late 1980s, early 1990s. Famously a 'new world order' was proclaimed.[141] Since the First, Second, and Third Worlds no longer existed, notions such as 'international community' became even stronger. In the early 21st century, most States in the world are tied into economic, political, social, and legal treaties with other States and organisations. The significance of international connectivity has not only increased the number of treaties, but also the number of organisations, subjects, and norms, of public international law. This has caused a renewed increase and interest in universal principles. The receding of the nation State in favour of a seeming international 'order' in conjunction with the rising importance of human rights has once more prompted calls for a common link between all. One of the ways in which the common link has been expressed is through the (re)introduction of discussions pertaining to a global constitution. Michael Byers summarised the significance of the international community, universality and constitutionalism by stating: 'international society is today more and more defining itself as universal, at least in terms of its fundamental, constitutional rules'.[142]

---

[140] See references to the 'international community as a whole' ICJ *Case Concerning the Barcelona Traction, Light and Power Company, Limited (second phase) (Belgium v Spain)* [1970] ICJ Rep 3 para 33; Preamble of the ICC-Statute (*Rome Statute of the International Criminal Court*, ICC-ASP/2/Res. 3; 12 September 2003), and Art. 42(b) of the ILC Articles on State Responsibility (*ILC Articles on Responsibility of States for Internationally Wrongful Acts*, UNGA Res. 56/83; 28 January 2002).

[141] See the former President George H.W. Bush at the end of the Gulf War: <http://bushlibrary.tamu.edu/research/public_papers.php?id=2217&year=1990&month=9>.

[142] Michael Byers 'Conceptualising the Relationship between *Jus Cogens* and *Erga Omnes* Rules' (1997) 66 NordicJIntlL 236.

But not only in the global sphere has constitutionalism been the recent focus of scholarly and political attention, in the national and regional spheres there has also been much debate about constitutionalism. On the national level, debates on constitutionalism have been central in the post-independence countries of Eastern Europe. Having the rejection of the previous regimes as a priority, post-Socialist states have favoured the Western liberal-democratic constitutional models. Constitutional democracy is often considered the sole legitimate structure for ensuring political freedom, with human rights as the central means to guarantee the freedom of the individual. Constitutions are today largely regarded as necessary for stabilising an unstable State (Iraq and Afghanistan are recent and evocative examples). On the regional level, discussions about a constitution for the European Union have flared up once more. In short, discourses on constitutionalism are widespread and with debates on universalism increasing, global constitutionalism is a growing area of discourse.

Conclusion

In conclusion, this chapter has shown that, although it was stated in the introduction to this book that the discourse on global constitutionalism is 'in its infancy', it belongs with a long tradition. Thinkers have been preoccupied with key themes of constitutionalism in a global sphere for many centuries. These themes have, although going through different trends and emphases, recurred in the Western historical discourse of constitutionalism. The previous chapter identified five key themes of global constitutionalism in the contemporary debate; this chapter has examined the intellectual origins of these key themes. The first section of the chapter outlined the beginnings of such notions in Antiquity. It was found that there was much emphasis on the philosophical meaning of a higher law – one that was mostly defined as a natural law. These thoughts on a higher law had their focus on universality and were completely independent of the nation State. The journey of the development of the key themes of global constitutionalism then took the reader through the Middle Ages, where notions of morality – often connected to religious ideas – were given a prominent role. It was then determined how notions of universality decreased through the rise of positivism in the Modern Era and how meanwhile theories of constitutionalism in the national sphere became increasingly 'sophisticated'. The idea of individual rights and the idea of sovereignty were central to this development. The discussion continued with a brief outline on the paradoxes of international law and the 'dark side' of global concepts throughout the time of imperialism.

In German legal constitutional tradition, a differentiation is made between substantive and formal features of constitutional norms.[143] It is worth giving thought to this distinction in terms of global constitutionalism and its key themes. The substantive themes point to the identification of a superior law. In a formal sense, this superiority mostly leads to a supremacy vis-à-vis ordinary law. This aspect of global constitutionalism has recurred as a key theme since European Antiquity, beginning with Hippias who identified natural law as a *corrective* to man-made law. The feature of acting as a *corrective* points to the substantive superiority on the one hand and the formal supremacy on the other. The five themes of global constitutionalism in a *substantive* sense are:

1) *limitation of power* (largely through legal rules and institutions, based on the assumption of law as a corrective),
2) governance through the *institutionalisation of power* (and therewith the constitution of a legal or political order),
3) *social idealism* in the sense of an ideal for the future based on societal values,
4) *Standard-setting* in terms of a systematisation of law, by which society is thought to progress according to a fixed plan or system enshrined in constitutionalism,
5) *Protection of individual rights* (not just as a means of restraining State power, but also as a State duty).

In a *formal* sense, the key theme of global constitutionalism is its supremacy vis-à-vis 'normal' rules. This supremacy could lie in the form of a 'trumping' of normal rules or in the form of a criterion in respect of the validity of other sources of the law. Importantly, the said key themes can also be qualified as some of the key themes of constitutionalism in general. They are not necessarily linked either to *global* constitutionalism or to national constitutionalism. There appears to be a historical crossroads between national constitutionalism and global constitutionalism: the Treaty of Westphalia in 1648. With the Treaty of Westphalia, the concept of sovereignty and therewith the idea of nation States was born. From this time onwards, there are two strands of constitutionalism, albeit strongly overlapping, interdependent, and at times indistinguishable. The idea of the 'global' constitution continues on its path, heavily influenced by the new nation State legal order, but distinct from it. And a new idea of constitutionalism is born: the idea of a constitution of the nation State. While the latter is of interest to this work in terms of its influence on the

[143] See Georg Jellinek, *Allgemeine Staatslehre* (Athenaeum Verlag, Bodenheim 1982).

former, it is of course the former that is the object of this analysis. The distinguishing factors pertaining to *global* constitutionalism are defined here as the three common assumptions of global constitutionalism. They are not key themes in a substantive sense since they are necessary prerequisites for the idea of global constitutionalism to exist. The three common assumptions are (1) that constitutions can exist beyond the nation State, (2) that there is minimum unity/homogeneity evident in the international sphere and (3) that the idea of global constitutionalism itself is universal. These assumptions will be discussed in more detail in Chapter 3.

The preoccupations of scholars of constitutionalism on a global scale underwent certain trends, going from the philosophical in Antiquity to the theological-philosophical in the Middle Ages to procedural and institutional in modern history. Today's key themes seem to be a combination of all of these influences. It has emerged that contemporary global constitutionalism is undoubtedly strongly influenced by Western political and philosophical thought. The following chapter will seek to establish whether this influence causes specific blindspots and biases, which may prompt the question of whether global constitutionalism as it is today really is *global*.

CHAPTER THREE

QUESTIONING THE CONTRIBUTIONS OF PUBLIC INTERNATIONAL LAW TO THE DEBATE ON GLOBAL CONSTITUTIONALISM

Every portrait that is painted with feeling is a portrait of the artist, not of the sitter.[1]

Introduction

We have already learnt that the contemporary debate is largely confined to the trajectories of liberal democratic political tradition, so why not already dismiss it as not 'global'? In his collection of essays, *The Thing*, G. K. Chesterton contemplates, *inter alia* reform and how to go about it. He imagines the existence of a certain institution or law, which he exemplifies as the installation of a fence or gate across a road. Chesterton considers that the modern type of reformer says he does not see the point of the fence and demands for it to be taken down. The more intelligent type of reformer will respond: 'if you don't see the use of it, I certainly won't let you clear it away.' He urges the modern reformer to go away and think about what the use may be; 'Then, when you come back and tell me that you *do* see the use of it, I may allow you to destroy it.'[2]

The following will critically examine the dimensions of global constitutionalism, will raise questions about their tenability, and (as the intelligent type of reformer would do) will consider the use of the contemporary visions. At the heart of the analysis lies the question of whether the liberal democratic idea of global constitutionalism can appropriately be treated as the *only available* reference-point for global constitutionalism.

To begin with, it must briefly be explained which traditions are meant when the term 'liberal democratic' is employed. Distinctive of liberalism are the two themes of formal autonomy and abstract equality. Ideas of limiting State power and accountability emanate from these traditions – ideas that are today often believed to be realised through democracy. According to David Held, one can distinguish between three different types of democracy.[3] Firstly, there is the direct or participatory democracy that is often associated

[1] Oscar Wilde, *The Picture of Dorian Gray* (Wordsworth Classics, London 1992).

[2] G. K. Chesterton, *The Thing: Why I am a Catholic (originally printed in* 1929) (Dodo Press, Gloucester 2009).

[3] See David Held, *Democracy and the Global Order* (Stanford University Press, Stanford 1995) 5–16.

with ancient Athens. In such a democracy, citizens are directly involved in the decision-making processes. Secondly, there is liberal democracy, in which representatives bound by the rule of law are elected to act on behalf of the body of citizens as a whole in decision-making processes. Thirdly, there is the (socialist) one-party model of democracy. The first type of democracy is often regarded as unworkable at a national level of government (and certainly at an international level), particularly as a pure model, and the third type of democracy is regularly viewed as not democratic at all – at least in terms of how it has historically played out. When speaking of democracy, most writers (of international law) therefore refer to the second type of democracy.[4] This chapter is dedicated to questioning precisely such premises: What does it mean to assume that the politically dominant form of liberal-democracy is associated with the democratic functions of constitutionalism? It seems most sensible to begin with an examination of the five key themes that inform the current debate. However, it has emerged that there are in fact certain common presumptions that underlie the five key themes. While the key themes are the building blocks of the dimensions, there is something that makes the blocks what they are in the first place.

Section I begins with an examination of these basic common assumptions of global constitutionalism. The sections are all arranged similarly in that they follow the same structure: A description of the respective assumption or key theme including, where appropriate, a brief outline of the historical background; the concerns that grow out of the assumption or key theme; and the relevant dimension of global constitutionalism influenced by the assumption or key theme. The first common assumption discussed here is the belief that constitutions can exist beyond the domestic legal system and the nation State. The second common assumption maintained in prevailing international law visions of global constitutionalism is that a certain unity or homogeneity of the international sphere exists. The universality of the idea of global constitutionalism itself is the third common assumption depicted here. Section II scrutinises the key themes of global constitutionalism found to inform the prevailing dimensions of global constitutionalism. Rather than this being a criticism of liberal democratic government, the study attempts to unveil some of the ways in which liberal democratic traditions limit global constitutionalism. It is contended that the seeming divergences of the visions of global constitutionalism of public international law simply reflect the different visions and trajectories of liberalism. The critique that will be undertaken in the following is a synthesis of writings by critical scholars, rather than exclusively a composition of new ideas. The novelty lies in the association of the critique

[4] As it happens, most democratic politics involve a mixture of the first and second types of democracy at the national level.

with visions of global constitutionalism within public international law. The literature relied on is that which aims to bring marginalisations into the spotlight. I have drawn on feminist theory, Marxist theories, thoughts on anti-imperial impulses and other theories that centre diversity and inclusion and have applied them to the contemporary debate on global constitutionalism.

Section I: Examining the Basic Common Assumptions

Each of the international law contributions to the debate on global constitutionalism bases its arguments either expressly or implicitly on three common assumptions: firstly, the assumption that constitutions can exist beyond the nation State; secondly, the assumption that there is a certain unity on the international plane; and finally the assumption that the idea of global constitutionalism itself is global.

A. *Constitutions can exist beyond the Nation State, in the International Sphere*

The first assumption that is made by proponents of global constitutionalism is that constitutionalism is not necessarily a notion tied to the nation State. Some scholars are explicit in this assumption, but most are not. Writers rather refer to changes on the international sphere that remind them of familiar (domestic) constitutional systems. The discussions that are explicit about the applicability of a constitution to the international sphere commonly begin by distinguishing a constitutionalism that is apt for applying to the world as distinct from national constitutions. The former is sometimes referred to as constitutionalism in a wide sense and the latter to constitutionalism in a narrow sense. Descriptions of constitutionalism in a wider sense include observations along the lines that 'any reasonably developed legal order'[5] can be conceived of as having a constitution, and that 'the fundamental legal order of any autonomous community or body politic'[6] can be regarded as such a constitution. It is proposed that international law is 'multifarious' and does not exclude the possibility of 'transferring the concept of constitution from states to the international sphere …'[7] It is moreover observed that constitutionalism 'is and ought to be applicable to any institution that exercises

[5] Stefan Kadelbach and Thomas Kleinlein, 'International Law – a Constitution for Mankind? An Attempt at a Re-appraisal with an Analysis of Constitutional Principles' (2007) 50 German Yearbook of International Law (GYIL) 308.

[6] Bardo Fassbender, 'The United Nations Charter as Constitution of the International Community' (1998) 36 Columbia Journal of Transnational Law 532–538, 555–561.

[7] *Kadelbach, Kleinlein, 2007* (n 5) 309.

power'.[8] After the determination that any particular legal order can be framed by a constitution, it is then commonly discussed in what way the *international* sphere constitutes a (separate) legal order. The question of the existence of a separate legal order is mostly of the same tenor as the question of the existence of an international (legal) community. Those tacitly assuming the applicability of the concept of a constitution beyond the nation State mostly begin their analysis here.

A variety of methods are engaged to address the question of an international community. Either it is simply asserted that a global constitutional order exists since an international community exists (see e.g. Tomuschat[9]) or it is considered necessary to demonstrate the existence of an international community for the purpose of determining the existence of a global constitutional order (see e.g. MacDonald[10]). In any event, the existence of some form of international legal order is believed to be a requirement of a global constitution. Constitutions are thought to provide the framework for a legal order of a society. Constitutions themselves are regarded as being part of this legal order. No matter whether the constitution is viewed as *framing* the regular powers of a society and its political system or whether it is viewed as *mirroring* them, the idea of an overarching regulating framework is emphasised. Proponents of global constitutionalism commonly submit that certain changes in the national and the international sphere have facilitated the existence or emergence of an international legal order embraced by a constitution. Some reservations need to be voiced as regards this seemingly simple transition from international law to an international legal order to a global constitutional order. Describing this as a move to coherence of the international order could oversimplify what is in fact a complex body of law and politics, theory and actions. The description of a constitutionalist vision (particularly Normative Constitutionalism, with its abstract rules and principles) of the international legal order could in particular ignore the influence of politics on the international sphere. A concern that flows from this possible oversimplification is that certain patterns from already existing legal orders are observed on the international sphere and are thus provided with the stamp of the familiar legal systems. This is particularly so for Analogical Constitutionalism. The danger, in short, could amount to a downplaying of the particularities of the international system. Yet, it is not only the coherence that the international sphere is lacking in comparison to

---

[8] Miguel Poiares Maduro 'From Constitutions to Constitutionalism: A Constitutional Approach for Global Governance' in Douglas Lewis (ed) *Global Governance and the Quest for Justice* vol. I (Hart Publishing, Oxford and Portland, Oregan 2006) 251.

[9] Christian Tomuschat, 'Obligations Arising for States Without or Against Their Will' (1993) 241 Receuils des Cours 216.

[10] Ronald St. John Macdonald, 'The International Community as a Legal Community' in Ronald St. John Macdonald and Douglas M. Johnston (eds), *Towards World Constitutionalism – Issues in the Legal Ordering of the World Community* (2005) 863.

the nation State. Ulrich Haltern, a critic of global constitutionalism, rejects analogies on the basis that he believes that international law lacks the 'symbolic-esthetical dimension' inherent in national constitutional law.[11] The world is host to a great diversity of different environments, ethnicities, customs, and value systems. Let it suffice to say at this stage that, given the diversity prevalent in the world, the *assumption* cannot be made that the international sphere is a legal order that can be home to a common set of norms. Not only can such an order not be assumed, the rationalising of such an order could provide grounds for imposing certain political and philosophical concepts that have their roots in Western Europe and can thus not necessarily be universalised.

So what has happened to international law that causes some to talk of constitutionalisation and some to talk of fragmentation? Scholars believing in a 'paradigm shift' in international law commonly begin their observations with a portrayal of changes in domestic legal systems.[12] The nation State is not (and indeed never was) absolutely sovereign in regard to many issues that are traditionally thought to be within the sole jurisdiction of the nation State. Trade with other nation States has necessitated cooperation and thus the regulation of relations on a sphere distinct from the respective domestic jurisdictions. The member States of the European Union have altogether given up their freedom of action over numerous issues previously reserved for the sphere of national sovereignty. States have furthermore surrendered some additional aspects of their sovereignty through membership in international/regional organisations such as the UN, the WTO, or NATO. Even such areas as security, traditionally in the exclusive domain of the nation State, have been limited through international agreements. These changes to the domestic sphere are often sweepingly referred to as the effects of 'globalisation'. Mary Kaldor identifies three accounts of the effects of globalisation on the State. The most extreme position would be to argue that the State has become an anachronism and that we are moving towards a single world community. The opposite view is that globalisation is an invention of the State and can therefore easily be reversed. Yet others insist that globalisation does not mean the end of the State but rather its transformation.[13] Regardless of the position one takes, domestic legal systems have certainly undergone a change through a higher level of interconnectedness in so far as jurisdiction has been transferred from the domestic legal system to the international sphere.

---

[11] Ulrich Haltern 'Internationales Verfassungsrecht?' (2003) 128 Archiv des Öffentlichen Rechts 511–556.

[12] See eg Anne-Marie Slaughter, *A New World Order* (Princeton University Press, Princeton 2004) Chapter 1, 36–61.

[13] Mary Kaldor, 'Beyond Militarism, Arms Races and Arms Control' Social Science Research Council/After Sepr.11, 2 <http://www.ssrc.org/sept11/essays/kaldor_text_only.htm>

The changes to domestic legal systems have (simultaneously) had a large impact on international law. Institutions have been established and a host of inter-State agreements have been reached that deal with inter-State matters. The international sphere has become a forum of animated legal activity. If one views the international sphere as having a dynamic of its own (distinct from the realist vision that international law lies exclusively within the competence of national power), one can claim that the international sphere has in turn influenced changes to the nation State. The transfer of jurisdiction from the national to the international sphere has led to claims concerning the changing face of international law. In the 1980s a debate was sparked concerning the question of 'relative normativity' in international law, i.e. the emergence of a hierarchy of norms. Prosper Weil, anxious about graduated and diluted normativity, questioned whether international law can be viewed as a legal order that contains the supremacy of certain norms.[14] In his view, distinguishing between different types of legal norms poses a threat to the unity, coherence, and legal certainty of international law. The recently (re)triggered debate on global constitutionalism in public international law could indeed be seen as the extension of the debate on relative normativity.[15] Global constitutionalism could be viewed as a concept which provides relative Normativity, a procedural phenomenon, with material content.

The issue of whether an international legal order exists goes to the core of the existence of international law itself. The question – familiar to all those that have studied public international law – is 'is international law really law?' For the most part, it refers to the alleged tug-of-war between international law and politics. According to one view, international law is not a distinct body of law that has an obligating force of its own but rather that it is solely the product of the (military and economic) self-interest of States, which ceases to exist as soon as the self-interest of the State ceases to exist.[16] According to realists, if cooperation and coordination are visible, it is purely due to the expediency of States. Taken to the extreme, the exclusion of an *international* interest means that international affairs are but an assemblage of self-interests (an anarchy), barring the possibility of a separate international legal order. Advocates of a global constitutional order promote the other extreme by asserting that a loose international order has given way to a comprehensive international order. They therefore not only submit that an international legal order exists, but go a step further by claiming that the international legal order is a constitutional order. The purpose of the above description of the different camps of

[14] Prosper Weil, 'Towards Relative Normativity in International Law? (1983) 77 AJIL 413.

[15] See Normative Constitutionalism, particularly contributions about a hierarchy of norms.

[16] See eg Jack L. Goldsmith and Eric A. Posner, *The Limits of International Law* (OUP, Oxford 2005).

international law was to briefly highlight that there is a large discrepancy between the belief that international law is 'merely power politics' and the belief that the international legal order is so comprehensive as to accommodate a common set of constitutional norms. Thus, the simple assumption that the international sphere is a legal order and thus a constitutional order simplifies an ongoing debate that can by no means be considered as solved (if at all there is a 'solution'). Certainly, any descriptions of an international legal order (and with that a constitutional order) cannot turn a blind eye to the complex levels of interaction between hard law and soft law, international law and municipal law, consensus and compulsion, that make up the body of what we refer to as international law.

Abstraction of reality is a tradition of constitutionalism which has been prevalent since theorists such as Locke and Kant. Thinkers of the age of Enlightenment attempted to reduce the structures of the State to a small set of concepts. Kant's vision was that such abstraction and reduction could lead to a type of blueprint for the universal creation of the rationalised or good society.[17] Constitutionalist debates are often couched in abstractions. David T. ButleRitchie criticises this, maintaining that abstract form is often valued over the content of social and historical circumstances.[18] Visionaries of global constitutionalism employ the same methodology: they observe certain occurrences in the international sphere – such as increased communication through digitalisation or the establishment of international institutions – and bring these occurrences into a language of abstract concepts or patterns suitable for universalisation. The language used for the global constitutional project is a language made up of terms such as 'global values', 'international legal community', 'international order' etc. Martti Koskenniemi suggests that such a systemic approach to international law and the (project of the) portrayal of an international order is itself to no avail since such ideas only exist in the academic world.[19] In his assessment, such rationalising is removed from reality in the sense that occurrences are rationalised and categorised that cannot in reality be rationalised or categorised.

It seems that there are three possibilities regarding the motivation for such rationalisation. Firstly, it could indeed be entirely innocent in the sense of what the writer believes to be a neutral observation. Secondly, the purpose of rationalisation could be for developing international law itself. Or, thirdly,

[17] See Immanuel Kant, Lewis White Beck (tr), (*Zum Ewigen Frieden*) *Perpetual Peace* (Bobbs-Merrill, Indianapolis 1957).

[18] David T. ButleRitchie, 'Organic Constitutionalism: Rousseau, Hegel and the Constitution of Society' (2006) 6 JLSociety 67.

[19] Martti Koskenniemi, *The Gentle Civilizer of Nations: The Rise and Fall of International Law 1870–1960* (CUP, Cambridge 2004) 3.

the purpose could be more reprehensible in that it could be a means to further hegemonic ambitions. Let us take a closer look at these possible motivations: To begin with, the first scenario; one may observe that scholars make analogies with their own constitutional orders simply because it is the natural benchmark against which other legal phenomena are measured. Antonio Cassese argues: 'We all live within the framework of national legal orders. We therefore tend to assume that each legal system should be modelled on State law, or at least strongly resemble it.'[20] This approach could even be regarded as something habitual: the rationalising of familiar features to familiar structures. Indeed, David Kennedy writes that it should not surprise us that international lawyers from different national cultures should build their visions of 'international law' on the basis of whatever in their own experience is most associated with the term 'law'.[21]

Bardo Fassbender argues in favour of the second possible scenario, that international lawyers are eager to develop international law into an international legal system of greater cohesion and effectiveness.[22] Fassbender considers the debate on global constitutionalism to be central to this undertaking:

> International constitutionalism is a progressive movement which aims at fostering international cooperation by consolidating the substantive legal ties between states as well as the organizational structures built in the past.[23]

Of course, such rhetoric of 'progression' could be a means of veiling a more hegemonic vision – the third scenario, certain standards, generally associated with stronger Western States, are imposed on weaker States in the international sphere. Reasons may vary, but, if concerned with hegemony will usually revolve around a form of control. Abstraction could be a very handy tool in this endeavour. Since the tradition of abstraction was central to the work of scholars that helped define liberalism, their approach is often accepted as the only viable method.[24] For who dares question thinkers such as Locke and Kant? Abstraction is a method of universalisation. Modern theorists of abstraction could therefore be accused of attempting to universalise their traditions rooted in liberal democracy, which are not suited to a diverse world. After all, the international arena does not resemble a liberal democratic system. Although arguably the most influential States in the international sphere have a liberal democratic tradition, the majority of States are not liberal

---

[20] Antonio Cassese, *International Law in a Divided World* (Clarendon Press, Oxford 1986) 9.

[21] David Kennedy, 'The Disciplines of International Law and Policy' (1999) 12 LJIL 18.

[22] *Fassbender, 1998* (n 6) 551.

[23] *Ibid* 552.

[24] David T. ButleRitchie states that the work of these scholars has been 'fetishized' in our century: David T. ButleRitchie 'Critiquing Modern Constitutionalism' (2004) 3 AppalachianJL 38–40.

democracies.[25] Besides, it can be argued that the influence of China in the world economy and therefore in global political processes is mitigating the influence of liberal democracy in the international arena. Philip Allott even writes of the 'decline and fall' and 'withering away' of liberal democracy that has allegedly taken place.[26] Could, therefore, the idea of global constitutionalism be employed as a means of regaining liberal democratic ground on a global scale?[27]

It is certainly true that the international sphere does not have the same level of coherence as a domestic legal system. Yet, it is not only the coherence that the international sphere is lacking in comparison to the nation State. As noted above, Ulrich Haltern believes that international law lacks the 'symbolic-esthetical dimension' inherent in national constitutional law.[28] Certainly, the international sphere cannot simply be viewed as analogous to a domestic legal system. As was discussed above, this view is open to the critique that it could facilitate the imposition of certain traditions generally associated with Western liberal democratic principles. The dimension of Analogical Constitutionalism could thus be criticised for glossing over the unique features of the world community on the one hand and enabling ideologically motivated measures on the other hand. Normative Constitutionalism similarly draws on abstraction in a form that needs to be tested against a diversity much larger than that of any single domestic legal system.

If one applies the concept of constitutionalism to the international order, it must therefore be in accordance with the particularities of the international sphere. The definition of 'constitutionalism' that is employed in the discourse on 'global constitutionalism' must therefore be sufficiently wide for it to leave space for features specific to the international sphere.

B. *Unity/Homogeneity in the International Sphere*

Strongly intertwined with the assumption of an international legal order is the assumption of unity of the international sphere. Unity of a legal society is often understood as homogeneity. Such homogeneity is thought to enable the

---

[25] Freedom House, which rates the status of States according to categories of 'free', 'partly free' and 'not free', rated 89 States of 193 as 'free' in its 2010 *Freedom of the World Survey*. Freedom House states: 'The survey operates from the assumption that freedom for all peoples is best achieved in liberal democratic societies'. The report and the methodology employed can be found at <http://www.freedomhouse.org/template.cfm?page=15>.

[26] Philip Allott, 'The Emerging International Aristocracy' (2003) 35 New York University Journal of International Law and Politics 310, 311.

[27] For a deepter analysis into the appeal of global constitutionalism, see Chapter 4.

[28] Ulrich Haltern 'Internationales Verfassungsrecht?' (2003) 128 Archiv des Öffentlichen Rechts 511–556.

existence of a common framework that unites that which may be initially diverse to something that can be viewed as one. Advocates of global constitutionalism assume the necessity of some form of unity of the order, for which a global constitution would constitute a framework. The idea of unity can be expressed in a two-fold manner: Either, unity of the international sphere already *exists*, so that the constitution is a *description*, or the constitution would fulfil the purpose of *creating* unity, in the form of a *prescription*.

1. Unity Exists

Some visions of global constitutionalism, particularly those based on the idea of an international legal community (Social Constitutionalism and Normative Constitutionalism) assume the existence of unity. However, this may be counterposed to concerns of fragmentation and hegemony.

In light of a fragmentation of international law a holistic approach such as that implied through a global constitution could seem unfeasible and idealistic. General international law has developed into specialist fields or systems, which each possess their own principles and rules.[29] Additionally, the lines between the municipal and the international level are increasingly blurred. International regulation is affecting domestic regulation and domestic interpretation of international rules provides for an array of different rules.[30] In 2002, the International Law Commission, on the initiative of Martti Koskenniemi, formed a study group on the fragmentation of international law. The group found that fragmentation has resulted in conflicts between rules or rule-systems, deviating institutional practices and, possibly, the loss of an overall perspective on the law.[31] In times of fragmentation, can a global constitution, an over-arching mechanism binding everyone in the international community, really be recognised and accepted? Christian Walter believes that the flourishing of sectoral regimes in international law specifically precludes the existence of a single overarching international constitution.[32] Walter points to the disaggregation of the State as public authority and the decentralisation of international law as aspects of fragmentation, and declares that these features 'require abandoning the idea of *a* constitution'.[33] Jan Klabbers has observed that the constitutionalisation of international organisations (such as the WTO and the ILO) may indeed lead to a deeper fragmentation, as

[29] *Slaughter* (n 11).

[30] David Kennedy refers to a 'porous boundary' in 'The Forgotten Politics of International Governance' (2001) 6 European Human Rights Law Review 120.

[31] Report of the Study Group of the ILC, 58th session (2006) A/CN.4/L.682 [8].

[32] Christian Walter, 'Constitutionalizing (inter)national Governance – Possibilities for and Limits to the Development of an International Constitutional Law' (2001) 44 GYIL 191–196.

[33] *Ibid* 173.

the various competing regimes and organisations are 'locked in constitutional place'.[34] Elsewhere, Klabbers describes the observations on fragmentation as 'somewhat panicky'.[35]

According to Antonio Cassese, the world community lost its homogeneity after 1917.[36] Before this period, international law was a strictly Western law, applicable to States that shared a similar history, religion, and culture. Cassese observes that '[t]he emergence in the 1960s of numerous developing countries delivered the fatal blow to its former cultural and ideological unity'.[37] Certainly during the period of the Cold War, with two ideologies competing for world domination, the question of unity was not at the forefront of international law discourses. From 1989 onwards, when the end of the polarised bloc politics was perceived and a new world order was proclaimed,[38] the hopes for a united world grew. With the domination of liberal States and the word-of-the-century 'globalisation' in everyone's mouths, it was believed that a coherent system of international law was now possible, maybe even inevitable. And yet, liberalism and globalisation did not bring about the expected coherence of the international system; on the contrary.[39] Today, international law is constituted by a panoply of hard law and soft law, with overlapping areas of competence and colliding norms. Some areas that were formally accepted as belonging to international law have now detached themselves to become 'self-contained' regimes.[40]

Rather than providing a response to the question of whether the introduction of a global constitution is possible in light of fragmentation, the purpose of this investigation is to highlight that certain issues must be addressed if one aims to promote global constitutionalism. This is especially so as the idea of constitutionalising international law, though maybe less convincing, seems even more *appealing* in a situation of fragmentation.[41] As was observed earlier, international lawyers often rationalise the international sphere according to a pattern that they find attractive (idealism). In this sense, international lawyers could be accused of clouding the difference between the 'is'

---

[34] Jan Klabbers, 'Constitutionalism Lite' (2004) 1 International Organizations Law Review 32.

[35] Jan Klabbers, Anne Peters, Geir Ulfstein, *The Constitutionalization of International Law* (OUP, Oxford 2009) 11.

[36] *Cassese* (n 19) 32.

[37] *Ibid.*

[38] President Bush referred to a 'new world order' in a speech in 1991, just hours after the US and Allied troops commenced air raids against Iraq. <http://bushlibrary.tamu.edu/research/public_papers.php?id=2217&year=1990&month=9>.

[39] Martti Koskenniemi & Päivi Leino, 'Fragmentation of International Law? Postmodern Anxieties' (2002) 15 LJIL 559.

[40] See eg Math Noortmann, *Enforcing International Law: From Self-Help to Self-Contained Regimes* (Aldershot, Ashate 2005).

[41] *Walter* (n 31) 191.

of the international sphere and their idea of the 'ought'.[42] The appeal of a global constitution amidst fears of fragmentation of international law is central to the concern of self-legitimising which will be addressed in connection to the creation of unity. Particularly those advocates who describe an already existing set of norms as constituting a constitution for the world (Institutional Constitutionalism and Normative Constitutionalism) could be accused of neglecting the reality of fragmentation.[43]

Unity of international law could also be disputed on the grounds that it ignores the hegemonic dimension of international law. The imperialist history of international law, defined by the hegemony of European States and later of the United States, could be a continuing force that stands in strong contradiction to an alleged unity in the international sphere. International law was historically not an *international* law at all. If one pinpoints the beginnings of international law with the Treaty of Westphalia of 1648 and the birth of the notion of sovereignty, then one finds that international law was at its beginnings a European law.[44] As mentioned in the previous chapter, the terms imperialism and colonialism are often employed synonymously, colonialism is often referred to as a consequence of imperialism and is described as the territorial manifestation of power. Colonialism therefore implies the extension of sovereignty beyond the borders of the coloniser to the colonised. When speaking of colonialism, writers typically refer to European expansionism abroad beginning around the 15th century. These new challenges prompted questions as to whether the colonised territories should be recognised as sovereign and should hence be subject to the law of nations. The answer to this question was particularly pertinent since it would have implications for whether the colonised people could justifiably defend their territories and wage war. During this time, sovereignty was increasingly believed to be a secular rather than a religious notion.[45] Scholars such as Francisco de Vitoria and Hugo Grotius were extremely influential in their submissions that it was the State itself that was sovereign, rather than the ruler who had formerly claimed his right by the decree of God. Hence, justification to rule was increasingly detached from divine law. A problem was attached to this. If sovereignty was a secular rather than a religious notion, all territories could make a claim to sovereignty regardless of whether they were home to Christians or heathens. If all

---

[42] Wouter Werner, 'The never-ending closure: constitutionalism and international law' in Nicholas Tsagourias (ed), *Transnational Constitutionalism* (CUP, Cambridge 2007) 348.

[43] To be sure, eminent authors of global constitutionalism address fragmentation in regards to constitutionalism in some depth, see for example numerous references in *Klabbers, Peters, Ulfstein* (n 34).

[44] See eg Peter Malanczuk, Michael Barton Akehurst, *Akehurst's Modern Introduction to International Law* (7th edn Routledge, London 1997) 11, 12.

[45] Antony Anghie, *Imperialism, Sovereignty and the Making of International Law* (CUP, Cambridge 2008) Chapter 1.

territories could be recognised as sovereign, then they would also have to be recognised as equal. This outcome was naturally undesirable for the hegemony of European States, since it would have caused a diminution of power and influence over the colonised territories. The scholars that called themselves international lawyers devised a number of legal arguments to prevent the colonised territories from being acknowledged as sovereign. Antony Anghie has written extensively about the Spanish international lawyer Vitoria who developed and interpreted the idea of sovereignty to exclude the colonised people from the benefits of sovereignty.[46] With the use of this argument, set notably in the language of international law, the Spanish colonies were thus able to maintain their hegemony. With further secularisation it was increasingly the legal language that provided the arguments for the hegemony of European States (it had before been the religious terminology). It is significant that the secular scholars nevertheless kept up the strong moral undertone in their legal justifications of the imperialistic operations. Europeans projected Western needs onto non-Europeans, prompting a self-congratulatory mood in respect of their justness, foresight and magnanimity. John Locke, writing about the aboriginal peoples in America, stated that the indigenous peoples were rich in land but poor in all the comforts of life. Consequently, it is for their own good and comfort to become part of the commercial system and assimilate to European ways, for they too can then share the commodities and jobs and general conveniences of the Europeans.[47] It was this combination of legal blended with moral language that made the justifications of imperialistic advances so compelling. By the end of the 19th century, the United States had emerged a strong colonial power; meanwhile, the power of the European States was waning with the beginning of decolonisation. At the end of the Second World War, decolonisation first occurred through anti-colonial struggle, and was eventually enabled (and controlled) by the recognition of a right to self-determination of the imperial powers.

Critical writers submit that Empire is not a European phenomenon of the past, but is prevalent in a contemporary hegemony of Western powers in the non-Western world. There are a variety of ways in which hegemony has been described. A common argument is that today's domination by standards that are rooted in the West is a 'conceptual imperialism'. Although formal imperialism has been abandoned, some States are believed to have adopted this new means of imperialism. Conceptual imperialism in constitutionalism is the conceptual domination of constitutional ideas rooted in a distinctly European tradition. This type of imperialism does not entail violence or oppression in the obvious way practiced in the 15th to 20th centuries; it is

[46] *Anghie* (n 44).

[47] John Locke, Peter Laslett, (ed), *Two Treatise of Government* (CUP, Cambridge 1991) 41.

more subtle, taking place partly in the form of the above-mentioned abstraction and rationalisation. Indeed, as David T. ButleRitchie pointedly states, conceptual imperialism is

> cloaked in terms of liberty and freedom. Yet the rigidity and abstract formalism of modern constitutionalism constrains contemporary founders to a conceptual landscape which is ideologically very narrow...[48]

One of the main limitations of constitutionalism is, according to James Tully, that constitutions largely 'recognise one culture at the expense of excluding or assimilating all others'.[49] Submissions such as these make it necessary to consider whether imperial history still pervades both international law and constitutionalism and has therefore promoted a culture of exclusion. Justifications for colonisation came from what have since been regarded as the great thinkers in European history beginning with Hugo Grotius.[50] When Locke and Kant referred to what they saw as European and therefore 'good' ways, there is often an imperialistic undertone. Modern writers on constitutionalism tend to see the conclusions of Locke and Kant as authoritative premises and traditions of interpretation and therefore either overlook the imperialistic origins or take them for granted.[51] Of course, it is not only international law, but also – if not more so – the initial ideas of modern constitutionalism that are predicated on the thoughts of men such as Locke and Kant.

According to Edward Said, Western States, particularly the United States, carry out their form of imperialism through the façade of democracy and freedom.[52] Said claims that modern imperialism is carried out through abstract notions such as democracy and freedom, themselves expressed in representations and images that dominate the imaginations of the hegemon and the oppressed.[53] Anne Orford writes of how international law operates in the realm of imagination and manifests imperialistic patterns, or reaffirms the existing order. According to Orford meanings are created in a way which enables certain narratives of identification.[54] E. Ann Kaplan has described this perspective in cinematic terms as the 'imperial gaze'.[55] Kaplan asserts that the imperial gaze invites the viewer of a narrative to identify with the powerful,

---

[48] *ButleRitchie, 2004* (n 23) 45.

[49] James Tully *Strange Multiplicity – Constituionalism in an Age of Diversity* (CUP Cambridge 1995) 7.

[50] See eg Amos Shartle Hershey, *The Essentials of International Public Law* (The Macmillan Company, New York 1912) 56f.

[51] *Tully* (n 48) 7.

[52] Edward W. Said, *Culture and Imperialism* (Alfred A. Knopf, New York 1993).

[53] *Ibid.*

[54] Anne Orford, 'Muscular Humanitarianism: Reading the Narratives of the New Interventionism' (1999) 10 EJIL 678–689.

[55] E. Ann Kaplan, *Looking for the Other: Feminism, Film, and the Imperial Gaze* (Routledge, New York 1997).

white character. The imperialist character is associated with attributes such as freedom, creativity, authority, civilisation, power, democracy, sovereignty and wealth. These positive features are contrasted with a second character in the narrative: the black, native or colonised subject.[56] The second character is employed as a tool that allows the white man to imagine himself as civilised and free in contrast to savagery and slavery.[57] Actors on the international sphere, whether the Security Council, the UN, NATO or the US can accordingly be identified with this hero image.[58] Constitutionalism too inescapably evokes 'seductive' associations of freedom, democracy and legitimacy.[59] Some visions of global constitutionalism could thus facilitate the manifestation of hegemonic structures, while cloaking these ideas in a heroic project shaped through terms such as 'values', 'democracy' and 'the common good'. Visions that involve the United Nations could particularly be charged with the manifestation of the 'imperial gaze'. As is well known, the power allocation in the UN Security Council was established as reflecting the distribution of political power at the end of the Second World War. Philip Allott submits that an 'international aristocracy' has emerged through the arrangements that were put in place at that time. He criticises the UN Charter as creating the groundwork for an international 'oligarchy of oligarchies'.[60] Such indications of hegemony certainly call the unity of the international sphere into question.

The international sphere may also be said to be home to gender hegemony. Hilary Charlesworth, Christine Chinkin and Shelley Wright have famously developed thoughts on the inherently gendered nature of international law. International law is not neutral towards women, but rather strengthens their social subordination.[61] It is asserted that the absence of women in the development and drafting of international law and its norms has produced a body of law that is biased in favour of men. The monopoly of a male elite in the development of international law has produced a jurisprudence that legitimates

---

[56] *Orford* (n 53) 687, 688.

[57] Toni Morrison, *Playing in the Dark: Whiteness and the Literary Imagination* (HUP, Cambridge MA 1992) 44.

[58] *Orford* (n 53) 686.

[59] *Klabbers, Peters, Ulfstein* (n 34) 344, referencing Ronald MacDonald and Douglas M. Johnston, 'Introduction' in *idem* (eds), *Towards World Constitutionalism: Issues in the Legal Ordering of the World Community* (Martinus Nijhoff, Leiden 2005) xiii–xviii, at xvii.

[60] *Allott, 2003* (n 25) 336.

[61] Hilary Charlesworth, Christine Chinkin, Shelley Wright, 'Feminist Approaches to International Law' (1991) 85 AJIL 613–645; Hilary Charlesworth 'Feminist Methods in International Law' (1999) 93 AJIL 379–394; Hilary Charlesworth, Christine Chinkin, *The Boundaries of International Law* (Melland Shill Studies in International Law, Manchester University Press 2000); Christine Chinkin, Shelley Wright, Hilary Charlesworth, 'Feminist Approaches to International Law: Reflections from Another Century' in Doris Buss, Ambreena Manje (eds), *International Law: Modern Feminist Approaches* (Hart Publishing, Oxford 2005) 17–45.

the unequal position of women around the world.[62] Male interests are therefore perceived as objective and neutral, which reinforces gendered and sexed assumptions.[63] The alleged hegemony of men is a particular theme of the work of Catherine MacKinnon. Gender discourses, according to MacKinnon, are not about equality and difference, but rather about domination and subjugation, about hierarchy: 'Difference is the velvet glove on the iron fist of domination. The problem is not that differences are not valued, the problem is that they are defined by power.'[64] Irrespective of whether one adheres to this view, it must be taken into account that women are still underrepresented in the institutions in which international law is created and applied.[65] Constitutionalism is of course open to much the same critique, being originally written by men for men. The hegemonic and therewith exclusionary history of both international law and constitutional law could have the potential to cause a principle such as global constitutionalism to be a toxic mix of hegemony. Visions of Institutional Constitutionalism in particular could manifest the gendered nature of international law or would at least be open to criticism from this perspective.

In summary, it is necessary to consider the history of international law – and constitutionalism – when referring to a supposed unity of the international sphere. It has become evident that the ongoing history of imperialism and international law are intertwined. Indeed, imperialism relies on the use of vocabulary of law, democracy and freedom to fuel its mission. It has also been observed that the decision-making processes in international law were and still are dominated by men, meaning that male interests are more likely to be represented. The supposed unity of the international sphere could obscure these hegemonic struggles taking place. Indeed, they could *institutionalise* hegemonic domination.

2. Unity can be Created

Some scholars believe that a global constitution would in fact *create* unity on the international sphere (i.e. an international legal order) that is necessary for the legitimacy of international law. It has been stated that a global constitution is necessary for the creation of unity in order to prevent all decisions on the international level from being viewed as arbitrarily made in a situation of international anarchy.[66] Two concerns must be addressed in regard to the

---

[62] *Charlesworth, Chinkin, 2000* (n 60) 1.

[63] *Ibid* 18.

[64] Catherine MacKinnon, *Towards a Feminist Theory of the State* (HUP, Cambridge MA 1989) 219.

[65] Anne Peters, 'Völkerrecht im Gender-Fokus' in Andreas Zimmermann/Thomas Giegerich, *Gender und Internationales Recht* (Duncker&Humboldt, Berlin 2005) 213.

[66] *Kadelbach, Kleinlein, 2007* (n 5) 308.

creation of unity: First, the concern that global constitutionalism could be an effective tool for awarding self-legitimacy. Second, there is the concern that the establishment of unity could be seen as a creation of uniformity.

a. Self-Legitimation

The rhetoric of global constitutionalism could be (mis)used to award legitimacy to global constitutional ideas themselves. The descriptions of cooperation, the force of the law that is believed to exist despite violations, and other constitutionalist parlance can be viewed as the attempt of advocates of global constitutionalism to bring about what they describe as already existing.[67] The concept of global constitutionalism could be a welcome tool for legitimacy in view of such features as fragmentation of international law, the democratic deficit of international institutions, and demands for accountability. To be sure, the lack of an international legislator and the growing influence of NGOs have created a legitimacy problem for international law. Certain visions of global constitutionalism, particularly those associated with a normative project, could be open to criticism of confusing the *is* with the *ought*. The process of self-awarded legitimacy is, of course, a phenomenon of constitutionalism in general. Most constitutional States and organisations are viewed as 'constituted' by the document that is then termed the constitution. The drafters of the constitution grant themselves with an *ex post* legitimacy for the act of drafting and therewith of constituting. Particularly adherents of Normative Constitutionalism, who advocate for the recognition or the drafting of a higher set of norms are privy to issues of self-legitimacy. The lack of a global legislator gives particular weight to visions of international law that declare the hierarchical superiority of certain norms. Visions of international law as a 'system' could indeed incorporate the purpose of being utilised as a tool for the development of international law.[68] Since it is contrasted with the anarchy of realism, a systemic vision provides coherence to the entire subject. Without the rationalisation for coherence of the international system, all international law would merely be a jumble of bilateral and multilateral treaties drafted and agreed for the purpose of State interest. The systemic view deeply depends on placing international law in the ambit of law rather than politics.

Normative Constitutionalism, and in particular the key theme of the standard-setting capacity of constitutions, makes particular use of the systemic method. Visions that incorporate such concepts as *jus cogens* norms and

[67] Wouter Werner (n 41) 348.

[68] Andreas L. Paulus, 'The International Legal System as a Constitution' in Jeffrey L. Dunoff and Joel P. Trachtman (eds), *Ruling the World: Constitutionalism, International Law, and Global Governance* (CUP, Cambridge 2009) 69–109; Eyal Benvenisti, 'The Conception of International Law as a Legal System' (2008) 50 GYIL 393.

norms *erga omnes* could not only be viewed as purveying specific norms of international law with a compelling nature; they could also be viewed as attempting to lift international law out of the realm of a normative anarchy and into the realm of a normative order. The interpretation of such norms as global constitutional norms in turn provides legitimacy to the new realm of order. This would legitimise one particular type of interpretation, while rendering any other interpretation illegitimate. For example, the interpretation of the norm of the freedom of expression as a global constitutional norm would (somewhat ironically) reduce the scope for discussion of this particular norm. Furthermore, any norm that may collide with it (such as the right to non-discrimination, for example) would be required to take a back seat if it were not also marked with the same stamp. This is, of course, a process that must be regarded critically in view of any possible bias and marginalisation. Certain norms could be elevated to the status of higher norms, which would clearly favour some rights over others. Hilary Charlesworth has commented on the male bias pertaining to interpretations of the content of *jus cogens* norms. She has shown that, for example, the right to be free from racial discrimination has been labelled a *jus cogens* norm, but the right to be free from sexual discrimination has not been acknowledged as such: '*jus cogens* norms reflect a male perspective of what is fundamental to international society that may not be shared by women or backed up by women's experience of life.'[69] Of course not all systemic visions of international law are upheld for the *purpose* of legitimacy. But systemic visions of global constitutionalism, such as seen in Normative and Institutional Constitutionalism, would inescapably presuppose such legitimacy – a presupposition that could be considered highly undemocratic.

b. Creation of Uniformity

The project of the creation of unity may be inspired by the aim of seeking to eliminate difference in favour of uniformity. Visions of global constitutionalism that hope to bring forth unity in international law could be accused of trying to impose a certain 'constitutional culture'. In the theories of Hobbes and Pufendorf uniformity causes unity and which itself causes strength and power needed to hold out in the competition with other European powers over the wealth and labour of the non-European world.[70] James Tully contrasts this with visions emphasising diversity. Diversity is often viewed as prompting

---

[69] Hilary Charlesworth, 'Remarks' in *Contemporary International Law Issues: Opportunities at a Time of Momentous Change: Proceedings of the Second Joint Conference held in The Hague, The Netherlands July 22–23, 1993* (Martinus Nijhoff Publishers 1994) 423; Hilary Charlesworth, Christine Chinkin, 'The Gender of *Jus Cogens*' (1993) 15 Human Rights Quarterly 63–76.

[70] Howard Schweber, *The Language of Liberal Constitutionalism* (CUP, Cambridge 2007) 31; Christopher B. Gray, *The Philosophy of Law: An Encyclopedia* (Taylor & Francis, 1999) 706.

disunity, weakness, dissolution and lastly death.[71] In the tradition of Hobbes and Pufendorf, unity is believed to perform the function of advancing peace. Unity is particularly central to those ideas of global constitutionalism that emphasise universal values and the key theme of social idealism in the language of rights (human rights and *jus cogens*, for example). Angelika Emmerich-Fritsche's idea for world law distinctly incorporates these themes. She submits that it is necessary to consider law in connection with its ethical/philosophical foundations in a time of fear of a clash of civilisations.[72] According to her, substantive consensus is a requisite for the achievement of peace.[73]

Suggestions implying the creation of unity through a global constitution stress the importance of universalism to an extent that cultural diversity could be threatened. Since there is no natural uniformity on the international plane, the call for unity could be understood as a call for the *imposition* of uniformity. It can be convincingly argued that the imposition of uniformity does not lead to unity but rather to resistance, further repression and disunity.[74] Judith Squires, in considering the role of liberalism for modern constitutions claims that the transcendence of particularity and difference in the name of equality and universality is often associated with the liberal ethos.[75] The rhetoric of unity could therefore be deemed an attempt at the reaffirmation or expansion of the existing order of States that are already embedded in liberal tradition. While the recognition of differences is important in liberalism, it is a difference of interests, rather than a difference of identities that is stressed.[76] Diversity of interests is thought to be accommodated in a homogeneity of identities. Scholars that demand unity and universality by means of the promotion of common identity (constituted through common values) could therefore be accused of imperial intentions through culture rather than strictly though law. Unity and uniformity are therefore not only promoted through black-letter law; there is a metaphysical dimension to constitutionalism, which seeks to foster a particular constitutional culture. Imperial powers typically seek to import their culture to the dominated powers. National and regional constitutions have a history of being adopted to enforce a certain 'constitutional culture' on citizens and therefore to unify them according to this culture. The phrase 'constitutional culture' was used by Howard Caygill

---

71 *Tully* (n 48) 196.

72 Angelika Emmerich-Fritsche, *Vom Völkerrecht zum Weltrecht* (Duncker & Humboldt Berlin 2007) 197.

73 *Ibid.*

74 *Tully* (n 48) 197.

75 Judith Squires, 'Liberal Constitutionalism, Identity and Difference' in Richard Bellamy and Dario Castiglione (eds), *Constitutionalism in Transformation: European and Theoretical Perspectives* (Blackwell Publishers, Oxford 1996) 209.

76 *Ibid* 210.

and Alan Scott to describe Rousseau's 'social spirit'.[77] Writing about successful constitutions, Rousseau stated: 'the social spirit, which should be created by these institutions, would have to preside over their foundation; and men should be before law what they should become by means of the law.'[78] According to Rousseau, therefore, it is not only necessary to have the constitutional document; a 'social spirit' or a 'constitutional culture' is also necessary in order for the constitution to flourish. A non-liberal democratic example is the preamble to the 1977 Soviet Constitution, which also aimed to introduce a constitutional culture by openly seeking to 'mould the citizen of communist society'.[79] Some of the dimensions of global constitutionalism that were identified in Chapter 2 could be accused of attempting to impose a certain constitutional culture on international law. Such dominating constitutional culture necessarily marginalises any opposing cultures. As Caygill and Scott pointedly state: 'An important aspect of constitutional politics is, as we all know but perhaps do not say, the deconstitution of existing social relations and their reconstitution under the new constitutional order.'[80] Such a description of the functionality of constitutions implies that constitutions are a means for achieving political ends. In light of the diversity – of cultures, identities, etc – on the international sphere, instituting a common constitutional culture seems entirely unrealistic. Minorities are particularly vulnerable in the international sphere. It is in the international sphere that even more voices need to be considered than in the relatively more homogenous national legal systems. It seems that it is not unity or commonality that define us in the international sphere; rather it is particularity and diversity. With regard to the debate on the universality of human rights, Susan Marks and Andrew Clapham refer to the dominating 'dissensus rather than consensus'. While those promoting universalism search (in vain) for commonalities and agreement, they should rather direct their attention to the 'experiences of uncertainty, disagreement and renegotiation'.[81]

Unity is considered as a paramount necessity for constitutions by many authors. Robert Uerpmann, for example, who in fact supports the project of global constitutionalism, criticises the United Nations Charter as inapt for being dubbed the global constitution because it is too fragmented to be a

---

[77] Howard Caygill and Alan Scott, 'The Basic Law versus the Basic Norm? The Case of the Bavarian Crucifix Order' in Richard Bellamy and Dario Castiglione (eds) *Constitutionalism in Transformation: European and Theoretical Perspectives* (Blackwell Publishers Oxford 1996) 99.

[78] Jean-Jacques Rousseau, G.D.H. Cole, (tr), *Social Contract and Discourses* (Dent, London 1973) II vii: 'The Legislator'.

[79] See <http://www.servat.unibe.ch/icl/r100000_.html>

[80] Howard Caygill and Alan Scott, 'The Basic Law versus the Basic Norm? The Case of the Bavarian Crucifix Order' in Richard Bellamy and Dario Castiglione (eds), *Constitutionalism in Transformation: European and Theoretical Perspectives* (Blackwell Publishers, Oxford 1996) 99.

[81] Susan Marks and Andrew Clapham, *Human Rights Lexicon* (OUP, Oxford 2005) 397.

comprehensive global constitution.[82] Submissions such as this signify to what extent unity is assumed as a necessity for a constitution. The international social sphere manifests no natural unity. Scholars advocating a vision of global constitutionalism by way of a systemic approach could be attempting to unite a pre-constitutional chaos in a constitutional order. The above has shown that the attempt at uniting could be viewed as an imperialistic endeavour to secure the majority culture at the expense of minority cultures. Such possible attempts at establishing a 'constitutional culture' which manifests the marginalisation of those who are already being marginalised must be rejected and prevented. This applies particularly to aspects of Normative and Institutional Constitutionalism.

C. *The Idea of Global Constitutionalism is Global*

The third common assumption on which advocates of global constitutionalism base their theses is the assumption that the idea of global constitutionalism itself is universal. However, it appears that the idea may in fact be specific to a particular region. As was exemplified in Chapter 2, the majority of scholars concerned with constitutionalism are Germans or other continental Europeans. If the *idea* of global constitutionalism is itself limited to a certain region, it would be unsuitable to argue in favour of a unified global legal order subscribing to this idea. Europeans are generally more accustomed than people elsewhere to the idea of a constitution that transcends State borders. In regard to debates on the (failed) Treaty for the Constitution of the European Union, European scholars are of course not only familiar with the *idea* of a supra-national constitution; many are also familiar with *defending* such an idea.

Jed Rubenfeld, engaging in a comparison between constitutional Europe and the United States, argues that 'international constitutionalism' is a distinctly European conception.[83] In his view, international constitutionalism emerged in Europe as the result of the failure and defeat of nationalism after the end of World War II. The Allies viewed the end of the war as a victory *over* nationalism.[84] To the United States, the end of the war marked a victory *of* nationalism. Thus, the United States practice unilateralism and what Rubenfeld signifies as a nationalistic 'democratic constitutionalism' that stands in contrast to 'international constitutionalism'.[85]

It has also been argued that a reconfiguration of international law in the form of constitutionalism is a means for the European States to respond to

---

[82] Robert Uerpmann, 'Internationales Verfassungsrecht' (2001) 56 Juristen Zeitung 565.

[83] Jed Rubenfeld, 'The Two World Orders' (2003) 27 The Wilson Quarterly 28ff.

[84] *Ibid.*

[85] Jed Rubenfeld, 'Commentary: Unilateralism and Constitutionalism' (2004) 79 New York University Law Review 1971.

their loss of international power post World War II. Armin von Bogdandy suggests three visions of world order that European States may choose from:[86] First, European nations could follow the superpower most closely aligned with their own interests and convictions. This vision of world order, as the most realist of all the visions, might be associated with the United Kingdom. Second, European countries that adhere to the vision of a powerful Europe could strive to build a unified Europe equal to other global powers. He suggests that this might be the favoured approach of France. And the third vision, one associated with constitutionalism, is of a global community. Adherents to this vision strive for a global legal community that frames and directs political power in light of common values and a common good. According to von Bogdandy, this could be regarded as the German approach to public international law. While he explains that it would be erroneous to believe that this is the exclusive approach of German public international lawyers, he goes on to say that '[n]ontheless, understanding current international law as a building block of a global legal community has been a constant thread of thought among many German international law scholars.'[87]

As Stefan Kadelbach and Thomas Kleinlein explain, with only a lawyer's tools it is difficult to ascertain whether the debate on the constitutionalisation of public international law is indeed European, or indeed German. And yet, 'the idea that international law is the constitution of mankind has found many adherents in German legal writings.'[88] Kadelbach and Kleinlein point out certain favourable conditions in German legal history and theory that have encouraged this phenomenon to flourish. They argue that the coherence of a legal system is a central theme of German legal theory.[89] Eyal Benvenisti, asked to write about the most distinctive aspect of the German approach to public international law, declared the systemic vision (identified above as an approach adopted, among others, by Kant) as the main characteristic. It is asserted that the systemic vision entails 'the effort to envision the various legal norms as arranged within a hierarchy, composing together a coherent, logical order.'[90] Juliane Kokott raised a further point about German scholars' work regarding the systemic approach. According to her,

> Post-War Germany still has identity problems. For example, it is much more difficult for German politicians to articulate national interests than for French

[86] Armin von Bogdandy, 'Constitutionalism in International Law: Comment on a Proposal from Germany' (2006) 47 HarvardIntlLJ 223.

[87] *Ibid* 224.

[88] *Kadelbach, Kleinlein, 2007* (n 5) 304.

[89] *Ibid*; Stefan Kadelbach, Völkerrecht als Verfassungsordnung? Zur Völkerrechtswissenschaft in Deutschland' (2007) 67 ZaöRV 599.

[90] Eyal Benvenisti, 'The Conception of International Law as a Legal System'(2008) 50 German Yearbook of International Law 393.

> politicians. In comparison, it is easier for Germany to make its voice heard as the advocate or guarantor of legal principles.[91]

The recent history of Germany is certainly an influential factor for the legal and political preferences of German international law scholars. Moreover, public international law has always had a strong connection with constitutional law in Germany so that, even today, German academics of international law are required also to qualify to teach constitutional law and often publish in both areas. Notably, Anne Peters, who has of course written extensively about global constitutionalism, is appointed Professor of International and Constitutional Law.

The above shows that it cannot be assumed that global constitutionalism is a global idea. It indeed suggests the necessity for some empirical work, animated by the aim of discovering global constitutionalist impulses from outside the Western world. Indeed, the entire Section I has attempted to demonstrate that a number of alleged features of global constitutionalism cannot be assumed. It cannot be assumed that the concept of a constitution can exist in the international sphere; it cannot be assumed that unity exists or should exist on the international sphere; and it can also not be assumed that the idea of global constitutionalism has resonance throughout the world.

Section II: Questioning the Key Themes of Global Constitutionalism

A. *The Limitation of Power*

As was discovered in the previous chapter, the limitation of power is possibly the oldest key theme of global constitutionalism. The limitation of power, as a core liberal theme, is believed to be achieved through participation and accountability. Modern visions of global constitutionalism that stress the importance of participation on a global scale presuppose that the limitation of power can best be attained through democratic structures. In particular, visions of Social Constitutionalism stress the importance of participation and therefore make frequent reference to the necessity for democratic structures. Institutional Constitutionalism focuses on governance and is pre-eminently concerned with accountability. It is believed that participation and accountability can be attained through a system that constantly seeks to justify the sovereign power of the State while at the same time setting limits to that power.[92]

---

[91] Juliane Kokott, 'Report on Germany' in Anne-Marie Slaughter, Alec Stone Sweet, J.H.H. Weiler (eds), *The European Court and National Courts – Doctrine and Jurisprudence: Legal Change in its Social Context* (Hart Publishing, Oxford 1998) 77, 126.

[92] *Held* (n 3) 9.

These correlations and associations require some further analysis. The idea of representative democracy finds its roots in Montesquieu's notion of checks and balances which is facilitated through the separation of powers.[93] The idea is that the danger of despotism can only be addressed if measures are put in place to prevent the three branches of power (judicial, legislative and executive) from uniting. Montesquieu adopted the republican thesis that the best means of ensuring that legislation reflects the common interest is to have it made by the people. Montesquieu criticised direct participation for confusing the power of the people with its liberty. He claimed that this form of participation subverts the distinction between legislative and executive powers. Besides being unworkable in nation States, as opposed to the ancient *polis* where it was practiced, the people collectively are 'extremely unfit' to discuss affairs.[94] His suggestion was to introduce representative democracy, which remedies the defects of direct participation and introduces a system of checks into the democratic process. Montesquieu's suggestion was to select only the more capable citizens and reduce those involved in debating public issues to more manageable sizes in a proportionary manner.[95] The bestowal of political power on the people – and therefore the legitimacy of political power – was believed to have its basis in the equality of all people. This has its European intellectual roots in Christian notions of individuality. Democratic constitutions were viewed as the best means to promote equality. Equality in this context is assumed to be equality in terms of rights and duties, also known as legal equality. Thus, it is believed that constitutions are preconditions of democracy and create equality. Hence, a correlation between constitutions, democracy, and equality was established, and it persists in many prevailing visions of global constitutionalism to this day.

Liberal democratic constitutionalism does not only limit power however, it also grants power. While the visions of global constitutionalism concentrate on the limiting of power, they do not address the fact that this also implies bestowal of power. In these visions, power is allocated to an international decision-making organ, a force that could then itself deprive people of political and social freedom.[96] This inevitability is most obvious, yet rarely discussed, in the characterisation of the United Nations Charter as the constitution of the world (Institutional Constitutionalism). While the Charter grants rights (and therefore limits power), its recognition as a global constitution would at the same time enlarge the power of the United Nations as an institution.[97] While the United Nations possesses regulatory and coercive capabilities, this

[93] Charles de Secondat, Baron de Montesquieu, *The Spirit of Law* (Francis Douglass and William Murray, Aberdeen 1756) (vol I book XI ch III) 163.

[94] *Ibid* (vol I book XI ch VI) 168.

[95] *Ibid.*

[96] *Held* (n 3) 9.

[97] See the cosmopolitan visions of David Held, (n 3) 269.

is currently restricted through fragmentation, through colliding competences of other institutions, and through State interests – in short through the lack of a comprehensive order in the international sphere. The designation of the UN Charter as the global constitution (and the consequent establishment of a hierarchy in international law) would elevate the United Nations likewise into a position of superiority. Problems emanating from elevation – the oligarchy of oligarchies, the gendered nature of the UN, etc – have already been highlighted.

The inclusion of the notion of legal equality in a constitution grants power to the individual which in itself is of course to be embraced. Yet, this formal type of equality gives rise to concerns about cultural diversity and about gender inequalities. The liberal concern with reason, lawful government and freedom of choice is believed to be dependent on the recognition of political equality of all mature individuals.[98] A strong focus on the equality of individuals could come at the expense of cultural diversity in that equality could be viewed as only applying to the individuals that conform to what can be coined the 'dominat*ing* culture' in a community, thus excluding the 'dominat*ed* cultures'. More and more instances of intervention occur in which equality is 'imposed' in conflict or post-conflict States by means of democracy promotion. The central value of equality is commonly parcelled in the form of a constitution. Equality of the people is viewed as a means of promoting peace and preventing despotism. It must, of course, be taken into account, that such intervention is today a complex interplay between the 'imposition' of certain ideas by strong States (determined by such factors as respect in the international community, economic strength, and military strength) and their acceptance and even demand by weaker cultures. But, there is a real danger that equating equality with individualism and peace could marginalise minorities that identify themselves in groups. Those who are different are pushed into the role of dissenters and destabilisers; a threat to peace. The belief that legal equality is a tool for preventing the concentration of power anywhere else than in the individual encourages, according to James Tully, an imperial culture and has in fact led to an embodiment of imperial culture in most constitutions.[99] In order to maintain the *status quo*, cultural diversity is repressed.

> The constitution, which should be the expression of popular sovereignty, is an imperial yoke, galling the necks of the culturally diverse citizenry, causing them to dissent and resist...[100]

Notions of legal equality in constitutional traditions are furthermore associated with gender inequality. When legal equality was first introduced into written constitutions, these constitutions only referred to the equality of men,

[98] *Ibid* 9.
[99] *Tully* (n 48) 7.
[100] *Ibid* 5.

not of men and women. When modelling global constitutionalism on established constitutional frameworks, it is mostly left unremarked that the old constitutions were framed by men for men with disregard of the women that would one day fall within its ambit.[101] Ideas of legal equality must therefore confront the shortcomings of a possible exclusion of minorities and the interests of women.

In sum of the above, visions of global constitutionalism that refer to the limitation of power in a liberal democratic tradition are mostly silent on the fact that such a constitution would in fact concentrate the power on the international sphere. In order to see that the concentration of power is not a necessity for a constitution, legal equality must be uncoupled from the political notion of democracy, and liberal democracy must be uncoupled from constitutionalism. Those visions of global constitutionalism that stress the coupling of liberal democracy with constitutionalism, particularly some visions of Social Constitutionalism, must therefore be viewed critically, as possible visions of dominating cultures. Also problematic are visions of global constitutionalism that depend on the concentration of power in one locus, such as certain forms of Institutional Constitutionalism.

B. *The Institutionalisation of Power*

The institutionalisation of power is thought to provide the organs that exercise influence on a global scale with accountability. This theme is particularly prevalent in what was termed 'Institutional Constitutionalism'. The origins of recorded thoughts on the institutionalisation of power can be found in the work of Aristotle. Aristotle reasoned that some people were born to rule while others were born to serve. The structures of politics should enable the former to rule for the common good and in the public interest.[102] The institutionalisation of power rests on the notion of the separation between the public and the private spheres. The separation of the public and the private spheres and the location of the political within the public is an assumption that is enshrined in most views of constitutionalism of a liberal democratic tradition. A constitution either makes this distinction itself (constitutes it) or renders this distinction obligatory (requires it). The institutionalisation of power is always aimed at directing the locus of power. In some cases the direction of the locus of power can be aimed at one particular body. In the national sphere, the direction of the locus of power in a liberal democratic system is aimed at the executive. Commonly a system of checks and balances is included in such a system. In some public international law visions of global constitutionalism,

---

[101] *Ibid* 3.

[102] Aristotle, Ernest Barker (tr), *The Politics of Aristotle* (Clarendon Press, Oxford 1948) (1254a v 2) 12.

power is also directed to one body. It should be recalled here that not all of the ideas of global constitutionalism pertain to a single global locus of power. On the contrary, some visions – such as the idea of a civil world law or ideas of global governance – encompass ideas of dispersing power. The following is therefore a critique of visions which provide for a *single locus* of power. For example, in the accounts that hold the UN Charter to be the global constitution, it is believed that the locus of political power (at least for political decisions regarding international law) should rest with the UN Security Council.[103] While one might be tempted to think that Institutional Constitutionalism would be specifically susceptible to criticisms relating to the orientation of a single locus of power, this only holds true for those visions that regard a single institution as the centre of global constitutionalism. However, *all* visions grouped under the dimension of Institutional Constitutionalism imagine an environment in which the public is clearly distinct from the private.

Feminist voices were the first to use the slogan 'the personal is political' to express problems inextricably linked with the public/private dichotomy.[104] Some feminists argued that the 'masculine' ethical orientation is for justice and rights and the 'feminine' ethical orientation is for care and responsibility.[105] While justice is allocated to the public sphere, care is allocated to the private sphere, leading to the exclusion of female assertions in the public sphere. The division public/private is in this way mapped onto the division male/female.[106] This dichotomy between the public and the private and the male and the female is often described in more abstract ways as the 'normal' and the 'other'. The first feminist thinkers had groundbreaking ideas concerning the philosophy of the 'other'. Deliberations about the 'other' are generally seen as a means of defining 'the self'. Simone De Beauvoir first brought this philosophical notion into connection with male-dominated culture, signifying that women are seen as the 'other' or 'second' sex in society, in contrast to the 'normal' male sex.[107] Hilary Charlesworth and Christine Chinkin applied this idea to international law:

> Men and maleness are assumed to be the norm from which women and femaleness are to be differentiated. Women are construed as the 'other', the deviant from the norm.[108]

[103] See eg Macdonald (n 10) 863.

[104] See Carol Hanisch, 'The Personal is Political' in Shulamith Firestone, Anne Koedt (eds), *Notes from the Second Year: Women's Liberation in 1970* (Radical Feminism, New York 1970). In a new Introduction from 2006, Carol Hanisch clarifies that she was not the one to give the original paper its title, but rather that it was the editors, Firestone and Koedt.

[105] Carol Gilligan, *In a Different Voice* (HUP, Cambridge MA 1982).

[106] Seyla Benhabib, *Situating the Self* (Polity, Cambridge 1992) 158.

[107] Simone De Beauvoir, H. M. Parshley (tr), *The Second Sex* (Vintage Books New York 1989).

[108] *Charlesworth, Chinkin, 2000* (n 60) 2.

Such polarities led to the subordination of women. Women were traditionally not expected to take part in the public sphere and were thus trapped in the private sphere.[109] Accordingly, women's interests could not be adequately represented. This meant that any abuses, of a physical or psychological nature, taking place in the home were not regarded of concern to the society at large and could be masked on the basis that it took place in the distinctly private sphere. Such subjugation of women often also supports the pre-eminence of civil and political rights (associated with male interests), as opposed to economic, social and cultural rights (associated with female interests).[110] The theme of the 'other' has been taken up by scholars writing about the exclusion of groups and minorities that are similarly underrepresented or have limited access to the public sphere. Questions of the interests of homosexuals,[111] minority cultures,[112] and colonised peoples[113] have been situated in discussions of the 'other'.

Concerns about the single locus of political power on a global scale prompt the question of the 'right to have rights', as articulated by Hannah Arendt. The idea of the single locus of political power was formed along with the concept of absolute sovereignty, which itself had its origins in absolute monarchy. From resistance to absolute sovereignty of the monarch grew the idea of absolute sovereignty of the nation State through the people. At the end of the 18th century, constitutions came progressively to be identified with written statutes and charters of rights through which monarchical power recognised the liberties of the citizens and their participation in public affairs.[114] This model perceives constitutionalism as a political doctrine. A constitution is a means by which political power and, particularly the power of the government over individuals, is limited. Dario Castiglione argues that constitutions have been presented as 'the centre piece in the strategy for the limitation of power.'[115] Such a close link between the constitution and politics allows for the concept of citizenship – an important aspect of the institutionalisation of power. If citizenship is embedded in a constitution, a circle is created: 'on the one hand, the constitution is meant to reflect the balance of equality between the citizens, while, on the other, the extent of citizenship depends on the constitution itself.'[116] So long as there is only one *locus* of political power, the circle can

---

[109] *Peters, 2005* (n 64) 217, 218.
[110] *Ibid* 218.
[111] Eduardo De Jesus Douglas, 'The Colonial Self: Homosexuality and Mestizaje in the Art of Nahum B. Zenil' (1998) 57 Art Journal 15–21.
[112] Iris Marion Young, *Justice and the Politics of Difference* (Princeton University Press, Princeton 1990) particularly 161–170.
[113] Eg *Said* (n 51).
[114] Dario Castiglione, 'The Political Theory of the Constitution' in *Constitutionalism in Transformation: European and Theoretical Perspectives* (Blackwell Publishers Oxford 1996) 7.
[115] *Ibid* 5.
[116] *Ibid* 12.

only be broken by this power. Visions of Social Constitutionalism that combine constitutionalism with a civil world law could be susceptible to such concentration of power.

A single locus of political power implies that the political power determines who can enjoy citizens' rights and who cannot. Such a form of constitutionalism carries a risk of unchecked political rule. It also underlines how rights in the abstract (such as human rights) could be empty shells without a political structure that defines citizenship. This thought goes back to the work of Arendt. Reflecting on the status of the Jews in the Third Reich in Germany and the rest of Europe, Arendt argued that one needs to be part of a political community in order to make claims, even those claims that are usually associated with the 'abstract nakedness of being human', such as the claim to physical protection or life.[117] If then, as Arendt suggested, our perception of humans is connected to ourselves as *social* beings, every human would need to be part of a global political or democratic community in order for global constitutionalism to be effective. A global community, however, seems to be exactly what is being contrasted with Arendt's point. Since there is no global community of *abstract* humans, people are only recognised as having rights within national communities as *specific* humans in specific places. Normative visions of global constitutionalism (Normative Constitutionalism) focus on certain fundamental rights that are often believed to transcend State borders. Human rights are commonly viewed as such fundamental rights and seen as having constitutional significance.[118] Arendt views the idea of universal human rights critically. Since human rights are advocated as distinct from a political community, Arendt would claim that they have no significance. As a global constitution would (by definition?) be a framework for abstract humans, Arendt would not be in favour of such a structure. If their interests are not respected, who can individuals appeal to in such an order? What if these interests are minority interests or regarded as down-right undesirable for the community at large?

Seyla Benhabib considers the significance of belonging to a political community for her theory of cosmopolitan justice. She advocates a cosmopolitan theory of justice which incorporates a vision of just membership.[119] Benhabib attempts to overcome the conflict that Arendt identified between human rights and citizens' rights by incorporating citizenship claims into a universal human rights regime.[120] This solution would make human rights subject to political decisions and possibly a particular ideology. While no solution to this

---

[117] Hannah Arendt, *The Origins of Totalitarianism* (Allen and Unwin London 1951) 299.

[118] Eg Erika de Wet, 'The Emergence of International and Regional Value Systems as a Manifestation of the Emerging International Constitutional Order' (2006) 19 LJIL 613–614.

[119] *Benhabib* (n 105) particularly 3.

[120] *Ibid* 22.

problem is suggested here, the above seeks to highlight limitations inherent in the designation of a particular locus of political power.

A further concern connected to a single locus of political power has again to do with minority cultures. A hierarchical form of government encourages a majority culture and the demand for assimilation of minorities. The perceived link between constitutionalism and liberal (representative) democracy brings home the seeming impossibility of representing the world in all its diversity. Martti Koskenniemi gets to the crux of the matter when he says 'there is no representative of the whole that would not be simultaneously a representative of some particular'.[121] If one particular demands assimilation of another particular, not only could cultural diversity be at stake, but it raises the question of why this particular and not the other? Historically, the expectation of assimilation to a dominating culture took place during colonisation. For example, the liberal democratic constitutions that promoted equality for all European citizens in the days of colonisation did not extend this privilege to the aboriginal peoples of the territories that they settled in. The demand for assimilation of the aboriginal peoples to the majority culture took place in Canada, the USA, Australia and many parts of South America. The settlers saw themselves as being in a position to judge over the rights of the aboriginal peoples, leaving the impression of some being more equal than others. These uneven structures of 'equality' have persisted up until today, where minority cultures struggle for the acknowledgment of their need to accommodate their cultural requirements. 'Cultural requirements' refers not only to the recognition of cultural particularities (language, practices, etc), but also to the need for political participation.

Today, the demand for assimilation to the majority culture is arguably an issue within the trend towards increased transnational migration.[122] Labour migration is growing through ease of travelling and increasing rights to work internationally, refugee flows and displacements are on the rise due to the prevalence of civil conflict and other circumstances that prompt flight, and finally internal migration through urbanisation is a trend that has continued from the 19th century to the 21st century.[123] In times of intensified migration, where ethnic backgrounds of the citizens are multiplying rapidly, there have been political debates about enforcing and recognising a majority culture within the nation States. Discussions have been taking place in Germany, one of the most popular countries for immigrants in Europe, on the implementation of the so-called *Leitkultur* – a dominant German

---

[121] Martti Koskenniemi, 'International Law and Hegemony: A Reconfiguration' (2004) 17 Cambridge Review of International Affairs 199.

[122] For an analysis of questions of migration and 'the other' see *Benhabib* (n 105).

[123] For the distinction between these three types of migration, see Patrick Manning, *Migration in World History* (Routledge New York 2005).

culture.[124] In the UK, there have been calls to introduce 'Britishness' to immigrants, and Britishness tests have been launched for anyone wanting to become a citizen. One dares not imagine what such a dominant culture would demand in terms of assimilation on a global scale.

There are, then, limitations to the key theme of the institutionalisation of power. To summarise briefly: the institutionalisation of the dichotomy between the public and the private on the international sphere could lead to concerns for those whose lives are lived primarily in the private sphere. Furthermore, the link between the political and the legal through the institutionalisation of power raises questions regarding the right to have rights for those not belonging to any political community. Another possible limitation of the institutionalisation of power is that it risks marginalising minority cultures and even eliminating them. Thus, the visions of global constitutionalism that provide for a single locus of political power, particularly visions of Institutional Constitutionalism, should be viewed critically vis-à-vis visions that provide for a dispersion of power.

C. *Social Idealism*

Social idealism is a key theme of global constitutionalism that is mostly translated into the human rights language in visions of global constitutionalism. As explained in Chapter 1, idealism in this context is the designation of an ideal for the future in terms of the idea of 'the good life' for all members of a given society. Legal equality of people, the preservation of each individual's human dignity, or the opportunity of participation in political life, may be ideals familiar from some domestic constitutions. In visions of global constitutionalism, particularly in Normative Constitutionalism, ideals are frequently based on what are termed 'common values' of the international community. The incorporation of ideals in visions of global constitutionalism can be traced back to natural law and its roots in Classical Antiquity. Values in modern visions of global constitutionalism are exhibited in law as normative interests (in contrast to Antiquity where ideals were viewed as abstract principles). Constitutional values are considered as defining people and their ways of life. Values are therefore not only thought to pre-exist in all individuals; they are also held to shape the collective identity of the people living under the constitution.[125]

It is customarily believed that constitutions incorporate the most important (objective) values of a society, and that a global constitution would incorporate the common values of a global society. Normative Constitutionalism

---

[124] See eg Norbert Lammert, *Verfassung, Patriotismus, Leitkultur: Was unsere Gesellschaft zusammenhält* (Hoffmann und Campe 2006).

[125] See the analysis on the encouragement of a 'constitutional culture' above.

focuses on the interpretation of certain fundamental norms – deemed reflective of common values – as global constitutional norms. In global constitutional visions, common values of mankind are mostly thought to find their authoritative expression in human rights. Many visions of global constitutionalism view human rights as the 'ideal' normative language. There are two concerns that follow from the association of constitutional ideas exclusively with human rights. On the one hand, human rights themselves are an abstract notion that has to be filled with content. The interpretation of (the content of) human rights is often undertaken in a way which is particular to a certain philosophical, historical, and ethical viewpoint that is not necessarily universal. On the other hand, human rights are commonly equated with civil rights. Such equation makes the concept susceptible to political determination, which can be a token of their progressive potential but also raises concerns about the possible influence of political ideology. The assumption of the universality of a particular interpretation as a matter of course obstructs the possibility of critical appraisal. This in turn opens up the field for the possibility of favouring certain rights over others (commonly the preference for civil and political rights). The declared universality of human rights and their designation as a bill of rights in a global constitution could also obscure the significance of the diversity of values and forms of life.

There are various ways in which writers assert the objective supremacy of human rights as common/universal values of mankind. Those writing about global constitutionalism often make reference to the near universal recognition of the Universal Declaration of Human Rights (UDHR), the wide-spread entrenchment of its norms in domestic constitutions, and the inclusion of those norms in numerous other international agreements.[126] It is generally accepted that there was a shared conviction on the part of the victorious powers after the Second World War that such disregard for human dignity as was demonstrated during the Nazi regime should not be repeated, and that human dignity must be protected through law. While the UN Charter of 1945 did not include specific references to human rights (although some provisions have been interpreted as such), the United Nations General Assembly soon remedied this omission through the UDHR.

It is maintained that the prevalent interpretation of the content of human rights is in fact an interpretation common to traditions historically associated with the ideology of political liberalism of the West. 'The West' is, needless to say, not a coherent term in this context. References to 'the West' do not only refer to a common territory, but also to a common political, religious, and philosophical set of traditions, sometimes referred to as a common ideology.

[126] Louis Henkin makes reference to these indicators, which famously caused him to use the term 'age of rights': Louis Henkin, *The Age of Rights* (Columbia University Press New York 1990), see particularly ix.

Within 'the West' there are, of course, paradoxes, contradictions, and other internal discrepancies. However, as was seen in Chapter 2, 'the West' experienced certain milestones of thought that affected international law and political theory. Thus, it can be asserted that certain notions of global constitutionalism are biased towards 'the Western' historical development of ideas. There are two main arguments in favour of this assertion in regard to human rights. Firstly, that the *abstract* notion of human rights and its philosophical foundations have a 'Western' bias. Secondly, it can be submitted that the *content* of human rights norms favours 'Western' values.

The *abstract* idea of human rights is criticised for its bias towards individualism and its focus on civil and political rights. The concept of human rights – as we understand it today – is believed to be a product of the Enlightenment, which took place in Western Europe of the 17th and 18th century. In the Enlightenment, the individual was placed at the centre of all philosophical ideas and developments. The idea of certain inviolable rights of the individual vis-à-vis the State power was shaped in this time. Influenced by liberal ideas of autonomy and equality, the ideas took effect in democratic notions of participation and accountability, itself prompting the importance of civil and political rights. Many scholars, including a number mentioned above, base their normative vision of global constitutionalism on Kant's ethical ideas and proposals for perpetual peace, often invoking and giving priority to human rights.[127] Patrick Capps has highlighted that Kant's vision of constitutionalism – the idea that all States should be 'republican' – does not necessarily imply human rights protection at all.[128] Kant was 'minimally' referring to the restriction of political power, not necessarily linking it to individuals' democratic rights.[129] This amplifies the above argument that Kantian ideas are often regarded as authoritative premises and also that an interpretation of authoritative premises is too readily assumed to demand the protection of human rights.

The *content* awarded to (the abstract idea of) human rights by way of their interpretation could also be parochial. Modern human rights were arguably first conceptualised in the UDHR. Although aspiring to universality and the inclusion of every human being, the adoption of the UN Charter and the UDHR following it were clearly dominated by Western political philosophy.[130]

---

[127] See eg *Emmerich-Fritsche* (n 71).

[128] Patrick Capps, 'The Kantian Project in Modern International Legal Theory' (2001) 12 EJIL 1006, referring to Fernando R. Tesón's interpretation of 'republican' as 'what we would call today a liberal democracy, that is, a form of political organization that provides for full respect for human rights', Fernando R. Tesón, *A Philosophy of International Law* (2nd ed Westview Press, Boulder, CO 1998) 3.

[129] *Capps, ibid* 1006.

[130] Virginia Leary, 'The Effect of Western Perspectives on International Human Rights' in Abdullahi Ahmed An-Na'im and Francis M. Deng (eds) *Human Rights in Africa: Cross-Cultural Perspectives* (The Brookings Institution Washington DC 1990) 15.

The participants in the drafting process of the UN Charter and the UDHR were undoubtedly predominantly either Western countries or Western-dominated countries; this was prior to decolonisation, so colonial powers also represented the interests of their colonised regions. The UDHR places greater emphasis on civil and political rights rather than social, economic and cultural rights and that the rights of peoples (self-determination, for example) are entirely omitted.[131] It is asserted that the focus on the individual and particularly on civil and political rights gave Western countries an opportunity of 'universalising' their ideology in the time of the Cold War.[132] This Western bias is said to have continued through the Cold War, where it was also instrumentalised. Not only was the Western ideology of individual rights to be spread; it was also to be set against the Eastern European socialist ideology. Establishing the importance of civil and political rights in the international arena was a way of disadvantaging socialist countries.[133] The content of human rights is not only shaped through their intellectual roots; the content is also determined on the basis of what is politically expedient at that time.[134] Universalists refer to human rights as an objective given which can be determined through rationality; the implication of such 'rationality rhetoric' is of course that all people in the international community *would* consent to the common set of values if they were rational.[135] To spell it out: this suggests that individuals that do not subscribe to liberal values are not as rational as others. Such reasoning inevitably prompts the recollection of the early international apologists for colonialism who argued in terms of the rationality of concepts that could not be grasped by the non-Western States.[136]

Human rights may not only be employed as a means for conceptual imperialism; they may also be employed to rationalise and legitimise interventionist policies ('conceptual *colonialism*'). Interventionist policies may be aimed at ensuring that change occurring in developing States is on par with the economic interests of industrialised States.[137] References to certain rational concepts originally alien to non-Western States could then be understood as a means of veiling the 'civilising mission' of the West.[138] Makau wa Mutua states that if one considers the history and development of human rights norms it is indeed 'implausible to openly deny that the human rights corpus is

---

[131] *Cassese* (n 19) 299.

[132] Makau wa Mutua, 'The Ideology of Human Rights' (1995–1996) 36 Virginia Journal of International Law 588–657.

[133] *Cassese* (n 19) 298.

[134] *Mutua* (n 131) 591.

[135] *Tully* (n 48) 69.

[136] See e.g. Anthony Pagden and Jeremy Lawrence (eds), *Francisco de Vitoria: Political Writings* (CUP, Cambridge 1991) 233.

[137] *Marks, Clapham* (n 80) 387.

[138] *Ibid.*

the construction of a political ideology'[139]. Mutua argues that despite attempts at presenting human rights discourse as non-ideological, human rights and Western liberal democracy are virtually synonymous; human rights are in his estimation in fact the universalised version of Western liberal democracy.[140] Whether this is overstated or not, the deep interconnectedness between liberal democracy and human rights cannot be denied.

Advocates of universal human rights argue that the history of the norms is no longer relevant. It is claimed that the universal applicability of human rights norms today cancels out any historical unevenness. Mutua retorts that there are other ideas, such as the view that free markets are the best engine for economic development, that are equally or more universally accepted today. One need only think about universal ideas of the past to discover that colonialism, for example, was also universally accepted.[141] The quantitative approach shows that universally accepted values are not necessarily 'good' values. Such an approach could simply be indicative of the widespread application of a certain dominating ideology. Insofar as advocates of universal human rights deny these points, human rights become cloaked in an aura of almost mystical superiority that remains unchallenged and unquestioned. *Faith* in human rights, in the sense of complete trust, leaves no space for a critical appraisal of the underlying values.[142] Yet, subjective valuations may lie hidden behind apparently objective value-based reasoning.[143] The objectification of value-orientation has been taken to its greatest extent in the concept of *jus cogens* norms. Bardo Fassbender describes *jus cogens* as the 'Decalogue of a secularised world … in accordance with contemporary "Western" values.'[144]

The debate of universal values is often expressed as the dichotomy between universalism on the one hand and relativism or particularism on the other. In simplified terms, universalists declare the universality of certain values, while relativists claim that moral systems differ around the world and therefore no single set of values can have universal validity.[145] Although some challenge the dichotomy,[146] advocates of human rights are commonly universalists.[147]

---

139 *Mutua* (n 131)

140 *Ibid* 592, 607.

141 *Ibid* 628.

142 Peter Fitzpatrick, 'What are the Gods to us now?: Secular Theology and the Modernity of Law' (2007) 8 Theoretical Inquiries in Law 161–190.

143 *Kadelbach, Kleinlein, 2007* (n 5) 334.

144 Bardo Fassbender, 'The Meaning of International Constitutional Law' in Ronald St. John Macdonald and Douglas M. Johnston (eds), *Towards World Constitutionalism – Issue in the Legal Ordering of the World Community* (Martinus Nijhoff, Leiden 2005) 845.

145 For a concise description of the discourse see 'Universality' in *Marks, Clapham* (n 78) 385–388.

146 See eg Chih-yu Shih, 'Opening the Dichotomy of Universalism and Relativism' (2002) 2 Human Rights and Human Welfare 13–24.

147 See eg Michael J. Perry, 'Are Human Rights Universal? The Relativist Challenge and Related Matters' (1997) 19 Human Rights Quarterly 461–509.

Universalists often accuse relativists of providing legitimacy for political suppression. Relativists and moderate universalists submit that universalism glosses over differences; to their mind, belief in the universality of human rights and the denial of its ideological roots risks obscuring awareness of the diversity of ways of life. Universalists respond that they are committed to diversity, and that it is for that reason that they recognise human rights. Thus, paradoxically, the commitment that the human rights corpus shows towards diversity is only fostered within the ideology of Western political democracy.[148] The recognition of diversity within that ideology narrows the scope for the acknowledgment of differences other than those within the Western discourse. For instance, it has been claimed that there is not only one ethical orientation in the form of justice and rights. In *In a Different Voice*, Carol Gilligan argues that one can distinguish between two ethical orientations: that of justice and rights on the one hand and that of care and responsibility on the other. It is asserted that the latter requires a contextuality, narrativity and specificity not valued in the former. Gilligan states that women are more likely to manifest the latter than men, providing them with a different (not inferior) moral sense.[149] If such other orientations are not highlighted, the dominant orientation is provided with an absoluteness that is not reflected in the complexity of reality.

In sum, it is problematic that human rights are viewed as a universal concept and yet their interpretation is linked to a certain philosophical, historical, and ethical viewpoint. This in effect means the universalisation of a particular. Central to the critique here is that, firstly, human rights are viewed as the only available means of expressing a constitutional ideal, and secondly, the interpretation afforded to human rights (both as an abstract concept as well as its specific content) is a particular interpretation that may militate against the possibility of its universalisation. Normative Constitutionalism is particularly exposed to such concerns.

D. *The Standard-Setting Capacity*

Standard-setting refers to prescriptive-practical norms that make up a fixed system of law, which have the purpose of acting as guidance for societal development. The key theme of standard-setting implies constant development in terms of a progression of the international legal order within a given organised plan. Discussions of global constitutionalism are premised on the belief that a global constitutional order is *progressive*. Bardo Fassbender, referring to Article 13 of the UN Charter, which speaks of the progressive development of international law, explains that international constitutionalism is a

---

148 *Mutua* (n 131) 654.
149 *Gilligan* (n 104).

'progressive' movement. Indeed, Fassbender speculates that those who are satisfied with the current state of affairs (and are thus not interested in 'development') would not even bother with the notion of global constitutionalism.[150] In a similar vein, Brun-Otto Bryde claims that a regressive adjustment is no longer possible and that 'development' is therefore inevitable.[151] Development towards unity and cooperation are seen as features of the age of globalisation. A global constitution could therefore be perceived as a *symbol*, as well as a *system*, for this development. It is claimed that there has been a development (whereby striving for development is in our nature and therefore inevitable), in which our day and age is the most developed yet.[152] According to this view, development is in our nature, and development is judged as 'good'; we are therefore getting increasingly better at becoming what we are meant to be. Kristin Ross has described this phenomenon (with reference to French decolonisation) as 'modernisation ideology'. Modernisation ideology enables people to believe in the 'fantasy of timeless, even, and limitless development'. This is connected to a self-congratulatory attitude, in that '[a]ll societies will come to look like us, all will arrive eventually at the same stage or level, all the possibilities for the future are being lived now.'[153] In adoption of this view, progression towards global constitutionalism can therefore be understood as a historical inevitability.

Difficulties arise when the idea of standard-setting in the sense of a systematisation of law is linked to the idea of progression, and when the idea of progression is itself believed to be tied to a liberal democratic tradition. Notions of progress could be employed as justifications for the spread of certain ideas rooted in a liberal democratic tradition. The problem is one of progression on the one hand (standard-setting of a constitution) and the static features of constitutions on the other hand. In some ways, all visions of constitutionalism include an element of belief in the importance of standard-setting. All scholars of constitutionalism presume to some extent that their designation of a global constitution can set a standard or be used as a *plan* for progression. Normative and Social Constitutionalism in particular include the idea of setting a standard for the future.

In the past, the idea of progress was of course used to justify expansionist policies. In the 19th century, for example, European expansion was justified

[150] *Fassbender, 2005* (n 143) 846.

[151] Brun-Otto Bryde, 'International Democratic Constitutionalism' in Ronald St. John Macdonald and Douglas M. Johnston (eds) *Towards World Constitutionalism: Issues in the Legal Ordering of the World Community* (Martinus Nijhoff Publishers, Leiden 2005) 110.

[152] Some writers therefore even claim that development has gone so far that history and political evolution have come to an end. See particularly Francis Fukuyama who claims in *The End of History and the Last Man* (Free Press, New York 1992) that the universalisation of Western liberal democracy signals the end of mankind's ideological evolution.

[153] Kristin Ross, *Fast Cars, Clean Bodies: Decolonization and the Reordering of French Culture* (The MIT Press, Cambridge MA 1996) 10.

by making it appear as a step towards the fulfilment of the universalist promise.[154] Today, such expansionism could be on a purely conceptual level. The declared universality of human rights norms, which have (as we have just seen) a history that is intertwined with changes of perception in the West, could be viewed as modern expansionism under the justification of progress. Human rights are often cloaked in a blanket of sanctity that creates the image that it is the most progressive form of protecting individuals from State power. For Wouter Werner, however, the ongoing violations of fundamental norms taking place despite the emergence of peremptory norms and the creation of standard-setting treaties are the 'most obvious challenge to a constitutional reading of international law'.[155] More than anything, this is seen as drawing attention to the contradictions of liberalism.[156] Such imperfections and contradictions can be detected in the visions of Social Constitutionalism. On the one hand, liberal democracy is viewed as the most progressive form of a political system and one that must be reflected in a global constitution; on the other hand, experience of liberalisation and democratisation is distinctly mixed. The political transformation that that took place (and is still taking place) in the post-1989 former Communist states is the second attempt at establishing liberal democracy through constitutionalism.[157] The first attempt, which was part of the general political settlement following the First World War, was almost wholly unsuccessful.[158] As Istvan Pogany points out:

> Despite international guarantees respecting the treatment of national minorities and the drafting of impeccably democratic constitutions, frequently modelled on that of the Third French Republic, the region rapidly succumbed to nationalism, dictatorship and political extremism.[159]

Istvan Pogany is therefore cautious with respect to late 20th century history. In his assessment: 'People, unlike laws, have memories and established patterns of behaviour. These can be changed only gradually, if at all.'[160] Importantly, Pogany points out that the power of words and the evocation of supposed common values in the texts of the new constitutions is therefore limited. It must also be mentioned that the process of constitutionalisation in Eastern Europe in the early 1990s has led to the creation of more, not fewer nation States. No regional constitutional solutions emerged from the reshuffle. This is

[154] *Koskenniemi, Gentle Civiliser, 2004* (n 18) 3.

[155] *Werner* (n 41) 341.

[156] *Mutua* (n 131) 593.

[157] Istvan Pogany 'Constitution Making or Constitutional Transformation in Post-Communist Societies?' in Richard Bellamy and Dario Castiglione (eds) *Constitutionalism in Transformation: European and Theoretical Perspectives* (Blackwell Publishers Oxford 1996) 157.

[158] Antony Polansky, *The Little Dictators: The History of Eastern Europe since 1918* (Routledge and Kegan Paul London, 1975).

[159] *Pogany* (n 156) 157 (footnote omitted).

[160] *Ibid* 159.

not only an argument against the 'progress narrative' of constitutionalism but also an indication that constitutionalisation is believed to be a feature of nation States and not of regional, let alone global, formations. Time will tell.

A global constitutional vision based on liberal democratic principles risks manifesting such contradictions on a global scale – this would particularly apply to Normative Constitutionalism. Written constitutions have a fairly static nature. They are drafted as documents that encompass the needs of the present and of the future. There are commonly mechanisms built into the constitution which enable their amendment only on the basis of a strict procedure with high hurdles. This raises particular issues where a *global* constitution is concerned.

It is noteworthy that those advocates of global constitutionalism who consider possible weaknesses of liberal-democratic standards do not consider the possible necessity of a reorientation of the debate. Instead, they argue for *more* liberal democracy.[161] The above discussion suggests that the standard-setting element as a key theme of global constitutionalism should be uncoupled from the belief that a liberal democratic model is the most progressive model. It must be added that, even then, the standard-setting element by itself is problematic. Constituting a model, system, or fixed plan for society is inevitably always a step behind reality. The static nature of a plan for society is not only unrealistic but also limited and frequently one-dimensional. As a final note, it should be mentioned that ambitions for progression are of course not in and of themselves bad.

E. *Individual Rights Protection*

A recurring key theme of global constitutionalism is the centrality of the protection of individual rights. Individual rights are regarded as the best means to protect the existence and interests of the individual in and from society. Especially those visions of global constitutionalism that were categorised in Chapter 1 as 'Normative Constitutionalism' focus on certain individual rights as global constitutional norms. As has already been elaborated, the ideas of global constitutionalism that centre the protection of rights mostly stress internationally recognised human rights.

Critique of individual rights includes concerns that have been touched on already, but are worth reconsidering in this context. To begin with, visions of global constitutionalism refer to the *recognition* of certain individual rights. The recognition of rights is contrasted with their creation through a legislative (political) process. One approach to Normative Constitutionalism is to declare the global constitutionalist qualities of so-called fundamental norms.

---

[161] See eg Jürgen Habermas, Ciaran Cronin (tr), 'Does the Constitutionalization of International Law Still Have a Chance?' in *The Divided West* (Polity, Cambridge 2006) 116ff.

Fundamental norms are understood as either pre-existing the relevant political order or at least as existing independently of that political order.[162] This pre-political and independent justification of rights is – again – associated with liberalism. It has its origins in Christianity and European philosophy in as much as it is often portrayed as emanating directly from the Christian concern for the individual and his or her personal salvation, and from the influence that this had on theories of natural and divine law. Theories of constitutionalism of the age of the Enlightenment were not discovered from a void, but rather found their basis in natural law thought of Antiquity. Natural law norms were believed to be independent of a political process. In contrast to positivism, which requires the identification of a specific source for a norm to be valid, natural law norms find their source in the nature of being. Thus, Carl J. Friedrich writes,

> The constitution is meant to protect the *self* in its dignity and worth; for the self is believed to be primary and of penultimate value. This preoccupation with the self, rooted in Christian beliefs ... eventually gave rise to the notion of rights which were thought to be natural.[163]

Friedrich highlights here the deep link between the Western philosophical and religious tradition and individual rights. According to B. Obinna Okere, approaches in Africa (for example) are quite different: the African conception of man is not founded on the liberal vision of autonomy and individuality, but rather man is viewed as 'an integral member of a group animated by a spirit of solidarity'.[164] On the basis of statements like these it has been argued that some societies rather place much emphasis on the community itself while individual rights take a back seat. Cognisant of the danger of sounding trite, such statements call attention to the possibility of alternative conceptions to our incessant focus on individual rights.

A constitutionalism that is based on the notion of the individual legal person as the bearer of rights is also viewed critically by some feminist voices.[165] Some feminists believe that the notion of individual rights could alienate and exclude women from the public sphere. Rights, since formulated to apply to every individual, have universalist assumptions; particularities are set aside, as the bearer of individual rights is conceived as an abstract agent. This understanding of rights reinforces the public/private divide. While men have

---

162 See eg Erika de Wet regarding *jus cogens* norms (n 117) 613.

163 Carl J. Friedrich, *Transcendent Justice: The Religious Dimension of Constitutionalism* (Duke University Press, Durham N.C. 1964) 17.

164 B. Obinna Okere, 'The Protection of Human Rights in Africa and the African Charter on Human and Peoples' Rights: A Comparative Analysis with the European and American Systems' (1984) 6 Human Rights Quarterly 148.

165 *Gilligan* (n 104) 17 with reference to Jean Baker Miller, *Toward a New Psychology of Women* (Beacon Press, Boston 1976).

traditionally been regarded as asserting their interests in the public sphere, women remain captives of the private sphere, unable to adequately assert their interests.[166] The State (the public) is constructed on the basis of abstract equality and serial individuals, whilst the private becomes the site for individuality. One could therefore claim that individual rights help to produce, maintain and reinforce gender divisions, even as they promote norms of non-discrimination. The suspicion of this is even greater if non-revisable; *jus cogens* norms could be implicated here. *Jus cogens* norms, as compelling norms of international law, have a nature that allows for no interpretation and no discussion. Once their content is identified, there is no going back, and limited room is left for development or change. Undoubtedly, feminists laid the groundwork for addressing questions of exclusion. On the basis of their work, there have since been calls for the recognition of collective rights,[167] or group rights[168], in order to give collective identities the possibility of assertion. Within a constitutionalist debate, attention must therefore be drawn to the rights that are *not* included in the constitutions. Needless to say, if particular rights are not included, then the interests that these norms could protect are also not protected. In the case of the international sphere, it would seem particularly unnatural to exclude the interests of groups and collectives since they play such an important role in the international arena, more so sometimes than in the national.

The indeterminacy of individual rights is a further point of discussion with regard to specific visions of global constitutionalism. Indeterminacy regards the conception that what laws 'mean' and the aims they may appear to have will depend on the judgment of application.[169] Although rights are considered the most objective form of securing values, it is plain that disputes still arise regarding their interpretation, *inter alia* as to which interests and values deserve special protection, who the rights apply to, the weight to be accorded to the protected interests and values vis-à-vis other moral principles and social considerations, and how the rights are to be implemented in particular contexts.[170] Such indeterminacy is particularly prevalent in the supposedly pre-political domain of human rights. Significantly, despite their alleged universality, there is no agreement on the scope, content, or philosophical bases

---

[166] *Squires* (n 74) 212, citing *Carol Gilligan* (n 104).

[167] Jürgen Habermas, 'Struggles for recognition' in Amy Gutmann (ed) *Multiculturalism: Examining the Politics of Recognition* (Princeton University Press Princeton 1994) 107.

[168] *Young* (n 111).

[169] Martti Koskenniemi 'Constitutionalism as Mindset: Reflections on Kantian Themes about International Law and Globalization' (2007) 8 Theoretical Inquiries into Law 11. Reference to Hans Kelsen, Bonnie L. Paulson & Stanley L. Paulson (tr), *Introduction to Problems of Legal Theory* (Clarendon Press, Oxford 1992) 81.

[170] Richard Bellamy 'The Political Form of the Constitution: the Separation of Powers, Rights and Representative Democracy' in R Bellamy and D Castiglione *Constitutionalism in Transformation: European and Theoretical Perspectives* (Blackwell Publishers Oxford 1996) 27.

of the human rights corpus.[171] The constitutionalisation of rights does not and cannot rid rights of their contentiousness, but rather shifts discussions. This indeterminacy could in the extreme lead to a superfluousness of the law itself. Hans Kelsen contended that indeterminacy of words in legal texts denotes that where different interpretations are possible, the appliers of law are free to choose between the meanings; in his view, all of the meanings would be equally valid.[172] If the content of norms is indeterminate, the definition of a norm may then lie solely with the policy-maker, which is particularly pertinent in the international sphere.

The absence of general and compulsory jurisdiction for the international arena is significant here. Although there are international courts (such as the International Court of Justice) and committees (such as the Human Rights Committee) that have a wide-reaching jurisdiction, the fact that there is no court, which has the single highest authority of norm-interpretation, means that each State may resort to 'auto-interpretation' of legal rules.[173] Such 'auto-interpretation' can be viewed in the varied interpretations of what constitutes torture despite the definition of the term in the United Nations Convention against Torture of 1984 and its interpretation through different international institutions.[174] Due to the lack of coherency of norm-interpretation in the international sphere, human rights are consequently even more indeterminate in the international arena than civil liberties are in domestic jurisdictions. Auto-interpretation could be a problem in regard to interests of the weaker participants in the international sphere if a particular model of global constitutionalism were to be recognised to the exclusion of another. Since constitutional rights are indeterminate, they could be open to interpretation by dominant actors alone. One of the main concerns of Prosper Weil, when he criticised ideas of relative normativity in international law was precisely the power of a few powerful States seemingly to speak on behalf of the international community. He argued that

> ... as the international community still remains an imprecise entity, the normative power nominally vested in it is in fact entrusted to a directorate of this community, a *de facto* oligarchy.[175]

For James Tully it is essential to recognise that the language employed in modern constitutionalism (by contrast to ancient constitutionalism that was ever-changing and determined by customs), only expresses the dominant side in

---

[171] *Mutua* (n 131) 590.

[172] Hans Kelsen, *Reine Rechtslehre* (Verlag Österreich, Wien 2000) 346–348.

[173] *Cassese* (n 19) 14.

[174] See eg the discussion on the Bybee Memorandum for the U.S. Bush administration. Jeremy Waldron, 'Torture and Positive Law: Jurisprudence for the White House' (2005) 105 Columbia Law Review 1681ff.

[175] *Weil* (n 13) 441.

social relations. Terms such as 'constitutions, nations, societies, cultures, recognition, citizens, rights, sovereignty, justice, institutions, and the common good' have been coined and defined from one perspective only.[176] Tully invites his readers to see a parallel between the searches for authoritative definitions of these terms and Wittgenstein's 'craving for generality'.[177] This craving has its source in the preoccupation with positivist thought, with its striving for comprehensive theory: As discussed above, a particularly compelling discourse for German scholars.

It must also be mentioned that the use of language as a constitutive tool of constitutionalism is also criticised by some scholars of international law, who have, in the tradition of French post-structural theory, highlighted that, since law is made up of language, language *generates* rather than simply *describes* legal rules.[178] This is particularly the case with international law since a primary source is treaty 'law'. While such treaties may be purely contractual or codificatory, they often have a law-generating function. Similarly, concepts and principles of international law may reconfigure the realities they purport simply to respond to. This observation principally emphasises the strength of the law rather than reduces it to pure semantics. Anghie exemplified how the language of 'State sovereignty' had the ability to exclude the colonised peoples from claiming their own sovereignty.[179]

Indeterminacy of constitutional terms, linked with the belief in the neutrality of constitutional values, offers an ideal instrument for the realisation of an agenda. Constitutions are often considered the epitome of impartiality. The rights enshrined in them are seen as the most fundamental rights of modern societies, and the institutional organisation is seen as the best possible means of balancing power and checking abuses. It is this appearance of impartiality that offers fertile ground to various self-interests. If an agenda is not viewed as an agenda but an objective necessity, it is particularly powerful. What makes matters more pertinent is the fact that constitutions are generally fairly static. A clash of interests in global constitutionalism could be set in stone through the drafting of a constitution or through the recognition of certain existing norms as global constitutional norms. Such setting in stone could substantiate and institutionalise the limitations in an unprecedented way. Indeterminacy is however not just an enemy; it could also be a friend. The dynamic nature of politics as opposed to law enables a much-needed contextuality. Possibly, our view should shift away from the inevitable indeterminacy of norms to the

---

[176] *Tully* (n 48) 111.

[177] Peter Docherty, Ludwig Wittgenstein, *The Blue and Brown Books: Preliminary Studies for the 'Philosophical Investigations'* (2nd edn Wiley-Blackwell, Oxford 1969) 17.

[178] Deborah Z. Cass, 'Navigating the Newstream: Recent Critical Scholarship in International Law' (1996) 65 NordicJInterlLaw 359–362.

[179] *Anghie* (n 44) Chapter 1.

model of politics that underlies it. If wider participation is ensured, so would the representation of more diverse interests.

The above has highlighted the limitations to individual rights. Not only do they have a history entrenched in Western philosophy (which in turn influenced political and legal thought), this history has manifested itself in the language and interests that are protected in individual rights. The indeterminacy of individual rights adds to the potential for partiality or the entrenching of hierarchies.

Conclusion

Under critical scrutiny, it has been revealed that prevailing visions of global constitutionalism in international legal perspective are subject to significant limitations. Visions of global constitutionalism, despite their complexity and multi-dimensionality, are largely rooted in the same legal-political traditions, historically engrained in Western Europe. The divergences of the dimensions of global constitutionalism largely reflect the different visions and trajectories of liberalism. Such limited views have been found to burden prevailing approaches to global constitutionalism with important blindspots and biases. Arguments of global constitutionalism could be regarded as a manifestation of the liberal democratic ethos in international law. It was firstly revealed that the visions of global constitutionalism as portrayed in Chapter 1 have common assumptions:

1) Constitutions can exist beyond the nation State: The danger in this view is that patterns of the international sphere are interpreted analogically to features of the nation State. Thus, the complexity and uniqueness of the international sphere could be oversimplified and rationalised.
2) Unity/Homogeneity of the International Sphere: The assumption that a unity in the international sphere exists can be met with objections concerning fragmentation and hegemony of international law. The assumption that unity can be created by means of a global constitution gives rise to concerns about self-awarded legitimacy and the danger of uniformity.
3) The idea of global constitutionalism is global: This assumption can be questioned on the basis that most of the literature on global constitutionalism written by public international lawyers comes from Europe, particularly from Germany.

Subsequent to an examination of the common assumptions, a spotlight was directed towards the key themes of global constitutionalism. In Chapter 1 it was found that the prevailing visions of global constitutionalism are all shaped by the key themes of global constitutionalism, with different key themes being centralised for different visions. Under critical scrutiny, certain biases and omissions were revealed:

1) The limitation of power: Attention was drawn to the fact that the limitation of power also includes a granting of power. Furthermore, it was revealed that the notion of legal equality (that gives rise to the need for the limitation of power) could lead to the marginalisation of minorities.
2) The institutionalisation of power: The analysis of this key theme showed that the consequent division of the public from the private sphere is prone to reproduce gender hierarchies. The domination of one locus of power could moreover endanger the right to have rights and the representation of interests of subordinated groups.
3) Social idealism: Idealism in visions of global constitutionalism is predominantly reflected in the pre-eminence of human rights. The limitations of human rights were identified as their susceptibility to imperialistic interpretations and therefore the danger of repressing diversity.
4) Standard-setting: This key theme is often associated with the belief in progress according to a fixed plan. The danger in this concerns the way 'progress' may be coupled with a belief in the model of liberal democracy as the sole or most advanced model.
5) Protection of individual rights: An issue that must be raised in terms of the centralisation of individual rights is their indeterminacy. Indeterminacy betokens receptiveness to political decision-making processes.

The critique of the key themes therefore engenders a critique of the dimensions of global constitutionalism identified in Chapter 1:

1) 'Social Constitutionalism' strongly relies on a model of 'constitutional democracy'. Such a model is susceptible to a concentration of power in a single locus, thus potentially contributing to the marginalisation of vulnerable groups and the domination by a majority culture.
2) 'Institutional Constitutionalism' is in the spotlight for not taking fragmentation and hegemonic tendencies of international law into account, instead rather idealistically advocating for a certain set of umbrella norms to frame the international sphere. Institutional Constitutionalism could also cause an institutionalising of the marginalisations intrinsic to liberal democratic political models.
3) 'Normative Constitutionalism' was examined in regards to the self-legitimating nature of its approach to international law. This dimension was also criticised for making use of means such as individual rights that are inherently indeterminate and could thus occasion exclusions.
4) 'Analogical Constitutionalism' is criticised for being open to the possibility of glossing over the particularities of the international sphere.

> Furthermore, it is alleged to foster the imposition of certain traditions generally associated with liberal democratic ideas of constitutionalism.

It is notable that many advocates of global constitutionalism are indeed aware of these limitations.[180] Interestingly, this awareness does not provoke conclusions of abandonment or a reorientation of the project. On the contrary, it is in fact advocated that the limitations show the need for *more* constitutionalisation.[181] Chapter 4 ventures to ask these questions: Should the project of global constitutionalism be abandoned? Why does the global constitutional project carry such great appeal to public international lawyers? And should the debate be reoriented to reach beyond its current confines, and how might that be achieved?

---

[180] Anne Peters, 'Compensatory Constitutionalism: The Function and Potential of Fundamental International Norms and Structures' (2006) 19 LJIL 602ff.
[181] *Werner* (n 41) 342.

CHAPTER FOUR

A SUGGESTION FOR A REORIENTATION OF THE DEBATE TOWARDS ORGANIC GLOBAL CONSTITUTIONALISM

The constitution is a becoming not a being.[1]

Introduction

The past chapters have taught us that contemporary global constitutionalism is shaped by the history of constitutional and international legal thought. The history is one of a distinctly liberal democratic tradition and could cause the emergence or the manifestation of significant marginalisations. So can the term be recast in a way that prevents marginalisations? James Madison warned not to separate text from historical background: 'If you do, you will have perverted and subverted the Constitution, which can only end in distorted, bastardized form of illegitimate government.' Should we follow Madison's warning? If so, does this mean that the 'project' of global constitutionalism should be entirely abandoned? Indeed, *can* the idea be abandoned? If the debate on global constitutionalism is here to stay, why is this? And, if the project should not or cannot be rejected, what should be the focus of global constitutionalism for it not to suffer from such limitations – is there a possibility for redeeming the idea of global constitutionalism? This chapter strives to find answers to these questions.

Section 1 briefly examines whether the limitations of the prevailing vision of global constitutionalism require an abandonment of the idea. It is concluded that the debate is so prevalent in international law that the demand for its abandonment is impractical. Section 2 analyses the appeal of the idea of global constitutionalism for public international lawyers. Three aspects of global constitutionalism are highlighted as supplying the idea with its tenacity. It is found that the idea of global constitutionalism embodies important concerns of public international lawyers about the current status of their field. In other words, these concerns can be *expressed* by means of the idea of global constitutionalism. First, visions of global constitutionalism are all concerned with the exercise of power on the international sphere, whether this be political power, economic power, or some other form of regulatory power.

---

[1] Philip Allott, *Eunomia: New Order for a New World* (2nd edn OUP, Oxford 2001) (9.19) 139.

Since constitutions are often viewed as frameworks for allocating power, the labelling of phenomena as 'constitutional' expresses the relevance of power allocations. Second, visions of global constitutionalism are entrenched in the belief that law has the potency to impact on social reality. Events that are of international concern are often met with demands for more law, whether this be the affairs at the Guantanamo Bay detention camps or the recent financial crisis. Third, the global constitutional debate speaks to the appeal for providing international law with legitimacy. Section 3 introduces an alternative to prevailing international legal approaches to global constitutionalism, the form of what is referred to as 'organic global constitutionalism'.[2] Organic global constitutionalism endeavours to overcome the shortcomings and limitations that the other visions of global constitutionalism have been shown to entail.[3] Organic global constitutionalism tries to take a step back from the dream of a global constitution of certain common legal techniques and pre-political values, and suggests a more fluid and flexible approach to constitutionalism. Importantly, it is not presented as a coherent 'new concept' of global constitutionalism; rather, a compilation of relevant themes. These themes, although initial and tentative, do not point to a process that will one day accumulate or amalgamate to 'a global constitution'; rather, what is involved remains constitutional*ism* and can be implemented as a 'corrective' to the contemporary debate.[4] The section introduces the thoughts of certain scholars and applies these thoughts to the discourse on global constitutionalism. For the largest part, this chapter does not rely on the work of international lawyers, but rather on the work of political scientists and philosophers. The work of James Tully on domestic and comparative constitutionalism will be referred to extensively. Jürgen Habermas' discourse theory will be placed into the context of organic global constitutionalism. Furthermore, it is suggested that Ernesto Laclau's idea of the negative universal can be adopted in the context of global constitutionalism. Finally, Jacques Derrida's idea of the future as a promise without content will be suggested as a theme of organic global constitutionalism.

[2] The term 'organic constitutionalism' was first introduced by G.W.F. Hegel (see T.M. Knox (tr), G.W.F Hegel, *Philosophy of Right* (OUP, Oxford 1952) § 271, 272). His meaning of the term is different to the way I use the term in that Hegel spoke of constitutionalism for the national rather than the international sphere: 'organic' for him meant that constitutions should be in tune with the historical situatedness and culture of a given society. This type of 'organic' is only truly 'organic' at the time the constitution is drafted. After the constitution has been written, it is again fixed. David T. ButleRitchie argues for a similar type of domestic constitutionalism (explaining his use of the word 'organic' as referring to the social and political context within a State: 'constitutional formation should be homegrown') in 'Organic Constitutionalism: Rousseau, Hegel and the Constitution of Society' (2006) 6 JLSociety 36–81 (particularly at 41). 'Organic' for global constitutionalism is also sensitive to historical backgrounds, present circumstances and cultures, but is significantly never-ending in this sensitivity and fluidity.

[3] Christine E. J. Schwöbel, 'Organic Global Constitutionalism' (2010) 23 LJIL 529–553.

[4] See Chapter 5 for a further probing of the idea of organic global constitutionalism as a corrective.

David Kennedy will be the only international lawyer whose work will be referred to in depth. Kennedy's suggestion regarding the politicisation of international law will be highlighted as a theme that could have relevance to global constitutionalism. The themes of organic global constitutionalism emerging from these ideas are: firstly, constitutionalism as an ongoing process; secondly, the politicising of the discourse of global constitutionalism; thirdly, global constitutionalism as a negative universal; and fourthly, global constitutionalism as a promise for the future.

The possible shortcomings of the idea of organic global constitutionalism are addressed subsequently. It is observed that there are two limitations to the idea of organic global constitutionalism that are noteworthy from the outset. The need to work within structures and procedures of participation 'freezes' some aspects of the fluid and contextual plurality of identities. A further shortcoming of organic global constitutionalism is that not everyone comes to the discourse as equals. While no specific procedure of participation is suggested here, the limitations of international law in terms of participation (in broad terms, that it is biased towards Western, white, male subjects) could apply to global constitutionalism too. However, it is concluded that these limitations to organic global constitutionalism can be mitigated, and are therefore not necessarily inherent in the concept. The chapter concludes by returning to the key themes of global constitutionalism and identifying which aspects of these are incorporated in the suggestion for organic global constitutionalism.

Section I: Should and Can the Idea of Global Constitutionalism be Abandoned?

Seeing that the project of global constitutionalism is currently impaired by limitations, this short section asks whether it should be entirely abandoned. It seems reasonable to begin with an examination of why the abandonment of the idea of global constitutionalism might be a worthwhile cause. One could, after all, claim that the idea of global constitutionalism is merely an academic exercise, with no practical significance. The rationalisation of certain occurrences in the international sphere by international lawyers may have some academic merit, but such musings of academics in their ivory towers could be removed from reality. However, the idea of global constitutionalism also always includes a *project* of global constitutionalism. Contributors to the debate on global constitutionalism never believe that the idea by itself is sufficient. For them, the idea is inherently linked to a practicable project.[5] Ideas on global constitutionalism therefore always also consider the implementation of

[5] Anne Peters states global constitutionalism is 'an agenda' in 'The Merits of Global Constitutionalism' (2009) 16 Indiana Journal of Global Legal Studies 397.

the idea of global constitutionalism. If the current *ideas* of global constitutionalism include limitations, the *project* will also include such limitations.[6]

Before it is ascertained whether the debate on global constitutionalism *should* be abandoned, it is elementary to determine whether the debate *can* be abandoned. There is no need for a detailed analysis of this here. As scrutinised in Chapter 2, the idea of global constitutionalism, or elements of what we would today regard as a vision for global constitutionalism, have been on the minds of thinkers for thousands of years. The emergence and consolidation of public international law provided a forum in which to express this idea. In the past years, there has been a great influx of literature within this forum. The idea of global constitutionalism evidently carries a strong appeal to public international lawyers. It seems that the debate is here to stay and cannot be ignored. It is not practical to consider abandonment of the idea; rather it appears necessary to explore the reason for its tenacity.

Section II: The Appeal of the Project of Global Constitutionalism

In the past chapters, there has been frequent reference to facets of global constitutionalism that draw international lawyers to the idea. The following recalls these facets and attempts to group them together. Needless to say, there is a large diversity of motivations for partaking in the discourse on global constitutionalism. It has already been mentioned that there are clusters or centres of the discourse on global constitutionalism. For example, one centre for the discourse is in Germany. It was found in Chapter 3 that the concentration of writers on global constitutionalism in or from Germany is linked to both deep-rooted historical and philosophical considerations, as well as the modus in which international law is taught at the universities. Beyond this, there are certain aspects of the idea of global constitutionalism that make the discourse appealing to international lawyers. The following tries to depict those aspects that determine the appeal of the idea. In the following, three motivations have been selected as representing what it is about global constitutionalism that carries such a strong appeal. The three motivations are closely related and interdependent: The first motivation – the restriction and allocation of political power – carries within it a central attribute of regulation (the second motivation), which itself can only be enforceable if the legitimacy of international law (the third motivation) is ensured. The distinction between the three motivations may appear a somewhat artificial nitpicking; however,

[6] Global constitutionalism as a 'project' is correspondent with David Kennedy's understanding of public international law as a whole. He regards international law as 'a set of particular human projects situated in time and space'. See David Kennedy, 'The Disciplines of International Law and Policy' (1999) 12 LJIL18.

the distinctions highlight different facets of constitutionalism, which deserve to be mentioned separately.

1. The Motivation of the Allocation of Power in the International Sphere

The first issue that may elucidate the appeal of global constitutionalism concerns the allocation of political power in the international sphere. The allocation of power, which includes the aspect of 'constituting' as well as the aspect of 'restricting', through law is an ongoing concern of international lawyers. In a sense, it is a lawyer's 'bread and butter' to restrict political power: We require lawyers to ensure that there is an objective standard by which decision-makers can be restricted in their discretion and can be held accountable for any actions that would be an abuse of that discretion. The restriction of political power on the international sphere has become more urgent since the exercise of power (to be understood here as the political process of decision-making) has become more difficult to trace and therewith more difficult to grasp. This has of course occurred through the ubiquitous processes of globalisation. Globalisation processes are described as, *inter alia*, the increasing number of networks that transcend State borders, whether economic, political, social, or legal;[7] the increasing number of norms, institutions, and procedures in the international sphere;[8] the changing relations in the world post World War II which have gone from systems of coexistence to systems of cooperation;[9] and the shift of public decision-making away from the nation State towards international actors.[10] International lawyers translate this factual dimension into legal terminology: A shift has occurred from a sovereignty-centred system towards a value-oriented or individual-oriented system.[11] A shift has occurred from international law as a contractual system, in which sovereignty (in its external dimension) was the paradigm, to 'a true legal order of a supra-State kind.'[12]

While some international lawyers claim the comprehensiveness of the international legal order, allegedly occurring through globalisation processes,

[7] See eg David Held, *Democracy and the Global Order: From the Modern State to Cosmopolitan Governance* (Stanford University Press, Stanford 1995) 267f; Anne-Marie Slaughter, *A New World Order* (Princeton University Press, Princeton 2004).

[8] Bernhard Zangl, Michael Zürn 'Make Law Not War: Internationale und Transnationale Verrechtlichung als Baustein für Global Governance' in Bernhard Zangl, Michael Zürn (ed), *Verrechtlichung – Baustein für Global Governance?* (Dietz, Bonn 2004) 12ff.

[9] Anne Peters, 'Global Constitutionalism in a Nutshell' in Liber amicorum Jost Delbrück, *Weltinnenrecht* (2005) 536.

[10] Erika de Wet, 'The Emergence of International and Regional Value Systems as a Manifestation of the Emerging International Constitutional Order' (2006) 19 LJIL 612.

[11] Christian Tomuschat, 'International Law: Ensuring the Survival of Mankind on the Eve of a New Century' General Course on Public International Law (1999) 281 Recueil des Cours 237.

[12] Luigi Ferrajoli, 'Beyond Sovereignty and Citizenship: a Global Constitutionalism' in Richard Bellamy (ed) *Constitutionalism, Democracy and Sovereignty: American and European Perspectives* (Avebury, Aldershot 1997) 154.

there is at the same time an ongoing discussion within the profession regarding the fragmentation of this very order. It is widely argued that the field of international law has become fragmented into a collection of specialised and independent areas of law.[13] Due to the diverging principles of law, definitions of norms, and institutional procedures, it is maintained that there is no longer a comprehensive and overarching international law.[14] Global constitutional parlance therefore appeals to those international lawyers who wish to emphasise that a common framework in the form of overarching, universal concepts is required and that they have ownership over this framework. It is asserted here that it is not fragmentation itself that causes concern to international lawyers; it is rather the fear that fragmentation will make it difficult or even impossible to limit and control political power.

Take for example international environmental law; tracing the exercise of power back to a particular source is a huge challenge. There is a plethora of bilateral and multilateral treaties with no evident hierarchy among them; some of these specialised treaties have established institutions, which are authorised to adopt regulations; then, there are the (openly) political decision-making activities such as the Copenhagen Climate Conference in 2009; how these treaties and political bodies relate to public international law principles, indeed how they relate to one another, is highly complex.[15] This raises questions of who the actors are that make international environmental law – Heads of State, international institutions, individual lawyers, or diplomats – and who should be held accountable for any breaches of this law – States as such, specific governments, individuals, or businesses.[16] These multiple sources of power, some national, some international, some transnational, have inspired discussions, predominantly by scholars of international relations, on global governance and the 'disaggregated State'.[17] International lawyers are somewhat sceptical of global governance and decentralised power; they prefer to see power centralised. If they consider global governance, then it is usually within the framework of squeezing it into well-known centralised structures of accountability and more generally public law.[18]

---

[13] *Slaughter* (n 7).

[14] David Kennedy refers to a 'porous boundary' in 'The Forgotten Politics of International Governance' (2001) 6 European Human Rights Law Review 120.

[15] Daniel Bodansky, Jutta Brunée, Ellen Hey, 'International Environmental Law: Mapping the Field' in Daniel Bodansky et al. (eds), *Oxford Handbook of International Environmental Law* (OUP, Oxford 2007)1ff.

[16] For an analysis of the constitutional properties of these sources of international environmental law, see Daniel Bodansky, 'Is there an International Environmental Constitution?', (2009) 16 Indiana Journal of Global Legal Studies 574–584.

[17] Anne-Marie Slaughter first introduced the term of the 'disaggregated State' (n 7).

[18] For an analysis of the public nature of global governance, see Armin von Bogdandy, 'Developing the Publicness of Public International Law: Towards a Legal Framework for Global Governance Activities' (2009) 9 German Law Journal 1375.

With variations as to the extent of their efforts, international institutions have been attempting to centralise their areas of expertise within their respective institution in order to counter the pull of decentralisation. Constitutionalism does not only serve the function of constraining power, it also 'constitutes' power according to the will of those that craft the constitution in the first place.[19] This is of course no big revelation, but it is a point that is sometimes swept under the carpet: when establishing an international organisation, for example, power of the member States is not only restricted, it is also constituted within the organisation. Examples of localisation as a reaction to globalisation can be found in the various institutions: the United Nations has, in its Charter, attempted to centralise legal matters regarding the use of force; the World Trade Organisation has attempted to centralise issues regarding international trade; the International Criminal Court's project is to centralise international criminal law matters; and the International Labour Organisation is attempting to centralise labour standards. These international-norm-hubs are also power hubs. The restriction of political power through law is not merely a responsive tool; international institution will also be granted with law-*making* powers that extend to its member States and sometimes beyond. Once the power has been allocated through law, the exercise of that power is largely within the discretion of that specific institution A prime example is the UN Security Council; this UN organ has declared itself as having legislative powers (see the resolutions regarding the funding of terrorism), executive powers (take for example the power to impose and oversee the implementation of sanctions), institution-building powers (see the criminal tribunals of Rwanda and the former Yugoslavia). It is in fact unclear where the powers of the Security Council end and this is where concerns of parochialism arise. Jan Klabbers observes, with the caveat that it is a heuristic device, that this is part of a chain of action and reaction, move and counter-move: 'globalisation calls forth localisation, which then at the same time, by looking like parochialism, may inspire yet other manifestations of the global through de-localisation.' Again, the UN Security Council is an excellent example; it has centralised so much power that it is unclear what would happen if it were to act *ultra vires*, indeed, whether there is a space for an *ultra vires* at all.[20] This has prompted demands for Security Council reform in order to globalise what has been localised. The limitation of power that constitutionalism promises does of course not end with international organisations. Constitutionalism promises a framework that would encircle all actors of international law.

---

[19] *Bodanksy* (n 16) 572.

[20] Jan Klabbers, *An Introduction to International Institutional Law* (CUP, Cambridge 2009) 168.

The discourse on global constitutionalism thus provides international lawyers with a tool for allocating power and tracing accountability hierarchies within a framework that may otherwise seem chaotic at best or the fruits of hegemonic power struggles at worst. The use of globalisation terminology – notably within their specialised language of 'accountability' and 'legitimacy' – therewith looks like an attempt by international lawyers to reclaim some of the debate that they may have lost hold of in the globalising and yet localising world. Discussions of global constitutionalism by public international lawyers could therefore be understood as attempts at denial or 'management' of fragmentation and as a part of a bid to regain relevance. Global constitutionalism, no matter how loose, would necessarily acknowledge a certain set of universal concepts, whether rights, principles, or the legal language in general. The recognition or rather introduction of such universal concepts would indeed settle the debate on the fragmentation of international law – at the very least in regard to a loss of an overall perspective on the law. This in turn would then allow international lawyers to exercise control over political processes.

It appears appropriate to note here that this concern for the allocation of political power through law, in particular through a constitution, is one-sided in that it assumes a division of politics and law that is prevalent in the liberal-democratic model of constitutionalism. Constitutional law is in some way believed to pre-date politics and is therefore largely left unquestioned. What is omitted in this view is the complex power-structures that enable law-making in international law in the first place. This can very easily be highlighted through a reminder of the 'sources' of international environmental law: In a simplified sense, one can always trace the source back to political decision-making: Who is it that generates law from treaties? State parties. Who represents the State parties in such treaty-making procedures? Politicians and diplomats. The idea of law as the objective tool that can keep the subjective political tool in check will be explored further in the following motivation for taking part in the debate on global constitutionalism.

2. The Motivation of the Regulation of International Society through Law

Closely related to the lawyers' desire for the limitation of political power is the desire for the regulation of society through law. Lawyers like to think of law's objective standard-setting properties that stand in contrast to the mere principle of might is right. Participants in the debate on global constitutionalism consider that a global constitution would provide a framework that regulates social life in the international (as well as sometimes the national) sphere. This perception of constitutionalism reflects a perception of a wide-ranging potency of the law. International lawyers tend to respond to international events with a demand for the greater or better application of law. Any changes in global social reality are believed to call for new or enhanced regulation. International lawyers tend to have an anxiety about the lack of law.[21] One often encounters the argument that there is a dichotomy between law on the one hand and politics on the other, with politics obstructing the way to a true legal system. Issues making the headlines such as the plight of the detainees in the detention camps at Guantanamo Bay have given rise to demands that are predicated on the strong belief that more law would be transformative of current (political) standards. Indeed, Lord Steyn of the UK House of Lords famously referred to Guantanamo Bay as a 'legal black hole'.[22] Lord Steyn argued that injustices in the name of politics and security have been perpetrated towards individuals who have no effective recourse to law. In a way, this is of course true, but what is left out of the picture is the enabling power of law in the first place. Human rights law, or rather the lack of it, is at the centre of much of the debate on the potency of law to regulate social reality. Human rights law in its traditional sense – as a negative obligation on the State power to refrain from doing something to the detriment of individuals' rights – is believed to be the chief tool with which arbitrary power can be made accountable. Ralph Wilde has argued that law, particularly human rights law, is associated with a general redemptionist idea.[23] The need for redemption of supposed exercise of arbitrary power causes a demand for more law.[24] But not only is law seen as the appropriate medium with which to harness arbitrary power and to therewith promote democracy, it is also seen as the appropriate medium for promoting peace throughout the world.[25] The use of global constitutional language provides international lawyers with a legal tool that they regard as a tool for regulating *a better* global social reality.

In my mind, the worldwide financial crisis reignited the 'law as redemption' perspective, if with a less explosive terminology than that used for human rights. The most commonly used description of what happened in the global meltdown is that market forces spiralled out of control due to a lack of regulation. Howard Davies, Director of the London School of Economics and Political Science, writes:

---

[21] Susan Marks, 'State-Centrism, International Law, and the Anxieties of Influence' (2006) 19 LJIL 339–347.

[22] Johan Steyn, 'Guantanamo Bay: The legal black hole' 27th F. A. Mann Lecture (25 November 2003).

[23] Ralph Wilde, 'Casting Light on the "legal black hole": Some Political Issues at Stake' (2006) 5 European Human Rights Law Review 554.

[24] In his book titled *Law and Irresponsibility*, Scott Veitch explores the possibility that legal norms are not only complicit in the production of suffering, but that they also *organise* irresponsibility. Scott Veitch, *Law and Irresponsibility* (Routledge Cavendish, 2007).

[25] Jürgen Habermas, Ciaran Cronin (tr), 'Does the Constitutionalization of International Law Still Have a Chance?' in *The Divided West* (Polity, Cambridge 2006) 116ff.

> One widely accepted conclusion emerging from analyses of the financial crisis that began in 2007 is that international networks of regulators have not kept pace with the increasing globalisation of financial markets ...[26]

Davies' response to this in the 'Practitioners Special Section' of Global Policy is that 'the problem' is the absence of a hierarchy between the various regulatory bodies and the absence of a 'central body with the authority to require any of the other organisms to act, on any particular time frame'.[27] Lawyers join the economists in the rhetoric of disapproval that – in Davies' words – 'no one is in charge of anyone else' by explaining (self-importantly?) that increased regulation would restrict this powerful yet elusive 'market force' from causing more havoc in the future. Law can fix any blips in society's usually ordered progress towards perfection. One could of course observe that lawyers possess the necessary expertise for using law as a tool for social change and that therefore there is nothing wrong with lawyers (as experts) in using this tool. Reflecting on the politics of expertise that may be implicated if international lawyers invoke authority, the authors of the article '*We are Teachers of International Law*' consider two aspects: On the one hand, the expertise lies in the legal training, experience and label of 'lawyer'; on the other hand, law can be such a powerful tool of impacting on social reality that it cannot be down to certain individuals (even if they bear the label 'lawyer') to claim knowledge of what 'justice' or other similarly influential terms is and means.[28] Lawyers have an undeniably strong interest in maintaining the associations of expertise that the label 'lawyer' invokes. David Kennedy observes that international lawyers are aware of the danger of losing control over impacting on social reality when he states:

> A great deal of the urgency in the progressive case for building international institutions has always come from the fear that the international regulatory project would fall behind the natural advances of the international market.[29]

When referring to law as a regulating force, one would customarily speak in terms of public law structures. Public law supplies the hallmarks of order and control that characterise a hierarchical system affixed with a single locus of power at its apex. In many legal systems around the world – particularly those legal systems that are home to scholars of global constitutionalism – a constitution is the mechanism that encapsulates the entire legal system. However, as seen above, other forces also appear to have the capacity to regulate society on

---

[26] Howard Davies, 'Global Financial Regulation after the Credit Crisis' (2010) 1 Global Policy 195.

[27] Ibid.

[28] Matthew Craven, Susan Marks, Gerry Simpson, Ralph Wilde, 'We are Teachers of International Law' (2004) 17 LJIL 370.

[29] David Kennedy, 'The Disciplines of International Law and Policy' (1999) 12 LJIL 53.

the international sphere; for example, market forces.[30] Along with market forces, there is an increase in private law issues on the field that we know as public international law. Take for example private military companies that derive their obligations from their contracts, or the provisions for the reparations of victims in the Rome Statute. For international lawyers the dividing line between the public and the private is extremely significant: public law enables lawyers to predict outcomes, it means the universalisation of certain standards, it means *control*. Private law on the other hand provides legal subjects (note nevertheless the terminology of *subject*) a largely impenetrable legal bubble in which they are accorded with contractual freedom. Certainly, this freedom is restricted by public law, for example as regards the legal age of the legal subjects. But, the plethora of contracts means that there is a huge body of law which is more intangible and obscured or even invisible. A constitutionalised international law would reintroduce the 'publicness' of public international law in a way that it would act as a framework for this currently obscured or invisible sphere of legal relationships. The framework would provide a mechanism of making these legal relationships more controllable. It is after all control and order that provide the comforting duvet (or is it a security blanket?) for lawyers. Constitutionalism, the quintessence of the 'public', would thus undoubtedly confirm the power of law to regulate international society.

3. The Motivation of the Legitimation of International Law

Wouter Werner states that the discussion on a global constitutional order implicates a normative project in that advocates of a global constitutional order are at the same time trying to bring such an order about.[31] What is thus happening is a self-allocation of power to international lawyers which at the same time rather usefully settles the debate about the legitimacy of international law itself: The very term 'constitution' carries with it a promise of legitimacy.[32] The legitimacy of international law is often questioned in the context of a debate – familiar to all those that have studied public international law – on whether 'international law is really law?' For the most part, this discussion is couched within the context of the lack of enforcement mechanisms on the international sphere. A lack of enforcement means a lack of legitimacy in that there may be no need to obey international law.[33] Some authors state that an

---

[30] This should of course not tempt us into viewing market forces as entirely distinct from law. The enabling power of law applies here too.

[31] *Ibid* 348.

[32] Jan Klabbers, 'Constitutionalism Lite' (2004) 1 International Organizations Law Review 47.

[33] In terms of the moral duty of citizens to obey international law, see Mattias Kumm, 'The Legitimacy of International Law: A Constitutionalist Framework of Analysis' (2004) 15 EJIL 908.

effective enforcement mechanism is thus central to any legal system and that the absence of such an enforcement mechanism on the international sphere at the same time means the absence of law. Other authors believe that all actions by States are determined by (military and economic) self-interest of States. Thus, there is no effective international law where the self-interest of States does not accord with it.[34] Taken to the extreme, the exclusion of an *international* interest means that international affairs are but an assemblage of self-interests (an international anarchy), barring the possibility of a separate international legal order. To recap considerations from Chapter 3, advocates of a global constitutional order promote the other extreme by asserting that a loose international order of coordination has given way to a comprehensive international order of cooperation. They therefore not only submit that an international legal order exists, but go a step further by claiming that the international legal order is a *constitutional* order. The question of whether international law is really law is one which has been underlying the field since the first treaties were signed, so why the recent interest in constitutionalism? It appears that the new legitimacy crisis of international law is, again, connected to globalisation processes: Globalisation has to a certain extent displaced State consent as the source of legitimacy since it has brought with it a large number of non-consensual norms thus leaving a vacancy for legitimacy.[35]

It is an assumption underlying all ideas of constitutionalism that, just as there is no society without law (*ubi societas, ibi jus*), so too there is no law without society. Constitutionalism is the legal framework that pertains to the coexistence of humans on a given territory; in other words, it is the legal framework of a society, a legal community. Correspondingly, *global* constitutionalism is the legal framework of *international* society. With this in mind, the first point to be made is that global constitutionalism puts a stop to questions about whether an international legal order exists. For it is impossible to contemplate the topic of global constitutionalism without recognising its basis in an international *legal* society. This seems all the more apparent when one calls attention to the root of the word constitutionalism as being the verb 'to constitute'. A constitution 'constitutes' a legal society. The constitutionalist language automatically evokes ideas of a normative framework that is ordered and *good*: it is a framework that has the potential to largely remain unquestioned, not simply by international lawyers, but by entire societies.

Werner states that the rise of global constitutional debates (he calls this 'international' constitutionalism) can 'partly be understood as an attempt to make sense of some (recent) developments in international law'.[36] I believe the

---

[34] See eg Jack L. Goldsmith and Eric A. Posner, *The Limits of International Law* (OUP, Oxford 2005).

[35] *Bodansky*, (n 16) 583.

[36] Wouter Werner, 'The never-ending closure: constitutionalism and international law' in Nicholas Tsagourias (ed), *Transnational Constitutionalism* (CUP, Cambridge 2007) 331.

project of these international lawyers is directed towards something more than a desire to rationalise and order. Their goal is to regain some of the influence that they may have lost in the thickets of globalisation processes – or indeed may never have had due to the supposedly unresolved question of the legitimacy of the field itself. The above three motivations all share the common theme that international lawyers are seeking a means of expressing their concerns of their own (possibly dwindling or alternatively never existing) influence. International lawyers hope to express and rationalise and perhaps *manage* globalisation processes on their field. The proliferation of international forces (globalisation processes) has partly displaced and at any rate decentred international law discourses. International lawyers are observing the factual changes on the international sphere such as the increase in interconnectedness and the international market and wish to address these with legal structures that uphold their own relevance. Global constitutionalism offers the perfect solution: It is flexible enough to take politics and economics into account and at the same time provides ground for a strong normative framework. The appeal of a strong regulating framework that at the same time is realistic enough to take other (non-normative) forces into account is overwhelming.

Section III: Appeal, Survival, or Addiction?

Let us then examine this 'appeal'. I am interested in particular in the question of how strong the appeal of global constitutionalism is for international lawyers. What appears to be at the centre of the debate on the tenacity of global constitutionalism is its possible regulating and legitimising properties which at the same time secure the relevance of international lawyers as such. It is no secret that international lawyers – indeed lawyers at large – like to think of legal systems as unified and coherent systems. Mimicking the sovereign power that international lawyers are familiar with from their respective domestic legal settings (see Analogical Constitutionalism), the UN as an organisation is rationalised to encompass a hierarchical structure with a centralised power system. As David Kennedy observes, this is a paradoxical enterprise, since what is happening is a struggle to somehow 'reinvent at an international level the sovereign authority it was determined to transcend' in the first place.[37] Interestingly, Kennedy describes this enterprise as an 'obsession'.[38] Maybe, what we are in fact dealing with is not only an 'appeal' but something more irresistible. Conditioned by their legal training, lawyers attempt to find a 'principle' in the chaos, a 'structure' in the confusion and a 'definition' in the varied

---

[37] David Kennedy, 'The International Style in Postwar Law and Policy', (1994) 7 Utah Law Review 14.
[38] *Ibid.*

interpretations. Legal training, albeit to a larger extent in the civil law system, is about learning a structure and definitions in abstract and then applying cases to these abstract legal rules. No wonder then, that lawyers have a desire for structure. In the domestic legal setting, these structures and definitions are extremely useful for reasons of legal certainty and social stability. It is seen as a necessary evil that there will be exceptional individual cases (so-called 'hard cases') in which the application of the structure and definition will lead to injustices;[39] and indeed the system normally provides enough flexibility for adapting the structure if the individual cases become the norm. In international law, a greater extent of caution is required when it comes to such abstractions. It is certainly true that the international sphere does not have the same level of coherence as a domestic legal system.

International lawyers are uncomfortable with embracing legal pluralism; their legal training tells them there must be a structure and a definition that can be universalised. For them, international law with its plurality and diversity is a challenge; possibly even in the form of an uncut diamond that requires some legal attention until it will shine in all its clarity. But, taking the above considerations about non-regulatory forces on the international sphere into account, one could however consider whether the debate on global constitutionalism is much more than a desire, whether it is in fact a survival mechanism. In the face of the fragmentation of international law into specialised legal areas and weakening of sovereignty, could international lawyers be fighting for the survival of their profession? If this is the case, and if international law is indeed in the midst of a legitimacy crisis, should one regard the model of a global constitution, which provides a normative framework for all of international society, as the saving grace for the profession? In that event, international lawyers could hardly be blamed for the urgency with which global constitutionalism is presented. This survival argument is however only persuasive if one assumes that every legal system requires a determinate set of rules – or perhaps values – in order to be respected. This view presupposes that individuals can voice preferences in terms of who can make legal decisions and that once this preference has been ascertained, the political body can act upon them and other issues arising from them. But, as Martti Koskenniemi explained in *From Apology to Utopia*, this view is a premise of liberalism.[40] Thus, international law would only have a legitimacy crisis if it were exclusively predicated on the political model or tradition of liberal-democracy. This outcome is impossible as it would naturally stand in contradiction to its 'international' nature. It would go beyond the scope of this book to state what

[39] Martti Koskenniemi, *From Apology to Utopia* (CUP, Cambridge 2005) 595.
[40] *Ibid* 75.

the premises of international law are and whether they lie in a particular political tradition, suffice it to say that international law could also derive its legitimacy (assuming it requires this) from other sources, other democratic models for example. The discourse on global constitutionalism is therefore not one of survival.

It seems that Jason Beckett is accurate in his assessment when he writes of international lawyers 'craving' constitutionalisation.[41] A craving is stronger than a mere appeal since it carries with it a sense of compulsion, but it also acknowledges that whatever one is craving is dispensable. Lawyers are accustomed to structures and definitions from their domestic legal systems and therefore long for them when dealing with international law (withdrawal). It is difficult to defy the pull of order, which offers itself as a relief to the chaos. The compulsive side of a craving is often due to an addiction. An international lawyer's addiction for order, as any other addiction, comes with a health warning: The more the craving is fed with order, the stronger the desire and the greater the dependency. The stronger the desire, the more arduous it becomes to question ones behaviour and any possible significant problems inherent in that which gives relief. In a sense, global constitutionalism is an overdose of order in the international legal sphere: it generates hierarchies where they are not self-evident and by doing this excludes some of the richness that is part and parcel of diversity and to a certain extent chaos. What is the antidote then to this overdose? I suggest it lies in the embracing of indeterminacy. Applied to the issue at hand, embracing indeterminacy means embracing global constitutionalism as an ongoing process. Although this may seem less comforting than a set of rules enshrined in a given hierarchy, there may nevertheless be the possibility of taking comfort in ones own discomfort. Importantly, the discomfort does not point towards a structural deficiency of international law, it is merely an indicator of the appeal for order. In the Epilogue to the reissue of *From Apology to Utopia*, Martti Koskenniemi aims to save indeterminacy from disrepute by stating that indeterminacy is neither a scandal nor about deficiency, it is indeed 'an absolutely central aspect of international law's acceptability.'[42] He explains that it is necessary to recognise indeterminacy as a mechanism for accommodating not only for the different, and often conflicting, purposes of legal rules but also to accommodate for change. Rules must stand the test of time and for this, they must be indeterminate – at least to a certain extent. So, although it may be possible to order the international legal sphere in hierarchies and to design a global constitution, this would at the same time only be one possible interpretation. As soon as one attempts to

[41] See Jason Beckett, 'The Politics of International Law – Twenty Years Later: A Reply', EJIL: Debate: http://www.ejiltalk.org/author/jason-beckett/.

[42] *Koskenniemi* (n 39) 591.

define the indeterminate, one inevitably excludes all the other potential interpretations. These thoughts serve as an apt introduction to the following suggestions for a reorientation towards organic global constitutionalism.

Section IV: A Reorientation towards Organic Global Constitutionalism

While the previous section addressed the appeal of global constitutionalism, Chapter 3 demonstrated that despite this appeal, the discourse remains limited in important ways. The following proposes a new perspective on global constitutionalism which aims to avoid such limitations. The introduction of *organic* global constitutionalism as a new dimension to global constitutionalism seeks to reorient the debate away from its current trajectories towards a more flexible, participation-centred model.[43] This suggestion is an attempt at re-engagement with the topic of global constitutionalism.

Chapter 1 revealed that the prevailing visions of global constitutionalism all incorporate the five key themes of constitutionalism. All key themes of global constitutionalism were subjected to criticism in Chapter 3. Significantly, some aspects of some key themes of global constitutionalism were criticised more than others. It seems that those dimensions which rely heavily on the centralisation of power and a common set of values are subject to the more serious limitations. Institutional Constitutionalism (e.g. the idea that the United Nations Charter is the global constitution) and Normative Constitutionalism (e.g. the idea that *jus cogens* norms are the global constitution), along with Analogical Constitutionalism (e.g. the idea that global constitutionalism should mirror national or regional constitutional models), were specifically criticised in regard to these two features. Both the centralisation of power and the designation of certain values as *common* values include a sense of fixation or stasis. The fixation of these two elements must be avoided in the international sphere. If liberal democratic ideas such as unity and legal equality are admitted to the international sphere, then they should be so only in a form which allows for corrections and changes and treats liberal democracy as a work-in-progress rather than as an end-product. Organic global constitutionalism tries to maintain the idea of global constitutionalism, but to dispense with those aspects of global constitutionalism that cause stasis.

The reconfiguration of global constitutionalism is based on four themes: first, that constitutionalism should be regarded as an ongoing process; second, that the debate on global constitutionalism should be political and discursive; third, that a vision of global constitutionalism should be predicated on the idea of the universal as a negative, or in other words, constitutionalism as an

[43] *Schwöbel* (n 3) 538–553.

'empty space'; finally, that global constitutionalism should be viewed as a promise for the future – a future devoid of predetermined content. These four themes will be introduced by reference to their respective intellectual origins.

A. *Constitutionalism as an Ongoing Process*

The first theme of organic global constitutionalism that is introduced is the theme of constitutionalism as process. Rather than a given set of norms, the word 'constitutionalism' itself refers to an idea or practice. In most visions of global constitutionalism, that idea or practice is directed towards the amalgamation or composition of 'a global constitution'. The reference to constitutionalism as process refers to an *ongoing* process that is not aimed at hardening to form a specific constitution. Recourse will be made to the work of James Tully, who has been mentioned numerous times in the previous chapters, and will now be relied upon more extensively. In his book *Strange Multiplicity: Constitutionalism in an Age of Diversity*, Tully challenges the predominant ideas of constitutions in nation States.[44] The focus of the book is to demonstrate that cultural recognition is possible through constitutionalism without imperialism if the present-day language of constitutionalism is reoriented. Tully's ideas on constitutionalism, which he developed for the national sphere, are applied to the international sphere for organic global constitutionalism. This allows the reconfiguration to take place within an agenda of organic global constitutionalism acting as an anti-imperial concept; it emphasises the need for the accommodation of cultural diversity; and it aims to avoid assimilation of minority cultures in favour of a dominant majority culture.

Tully begins by asking: 'Can a modern constitution recognise and accommodate cultural diversity?'[45] He approaches the debate from the perspective of the struggles of aboriginal peoples for constitutional recognition. The strange multiplicity of cultural identities, which he suggests, is illustrated through an account of a sculpture by Bill Reid named 'The Spirit of *Haida Gwaii*'. The sculpture depicts a canoe containing thirteen passengers, each a different character from the aboriginal Haida mythology. During the time of European imperialism, the Haida, like many other aboriginal governments, were deprived of their land and were forced to assimilate to the imperial European culture.[46] Tully encourages his readers to imagine the canoe and its passengers and to approach it with a willingness to listen to its culturally diverse spirits. Such willingness could enable one to imagine the sculpture as a constitutional dialogue of mutual recognition.[47] The constitutional dialogue is facilitated

---

[44] James Tully, *Strange Multiplicity: Constitutionalism in an Age of Diversity* (CUP, Cambridge 1995).
[45] *Ibid* 1.
[46] *Ibid* 17–24.
[47] *Ibid* 23, 24.

through the language of constitutionalism. Tully stresses that the appeal of the constitutional language lies in the fact that it is open to change; that it accommodates anti-imperial undertakings through its flexibility.[48] The problem is that the predominant language of constitutionalism today only puts the spotlight on the dominant, inflexible and imperial aspects.[49] For Tully, the politics of cultural recognition constitutes a third movement of anti-imperialism and constitutionalism; with the difference that cultural recognition means recognition in a constitutional order without the claim to becoming a nation State.[50] The first wave of constitutional nation-State-building took place when European nation States arose in opposition to the papacy and the Holy Roman Empire. The second wave of constitutionalism can be attributed to the struggles for independence of former colonies vis-à-vis the European imperial powers. Not only have the anti-imperial struggles inside and outside of Europe taken place within the constitutional language, the struggles of women and other suppressed groups have also been waged and justified in these terms.[51]

Judith Squires explains that even the most radical feminists who had completely detached themselves from constitutionalism, condemning the constitutional language as masculine, European and imperial, returned to it. Throughout the 1960s and 1970s many feminists within the Women's Movement advocated direct participation in women's autonomous organisations, arguing that women's energies should not be devoted to existing political institutions and electoral policies.[52] The theory of abstract individualism, the rights-based ethic of justice, the practice of institutionalised politics and the clear demarcation of public and private spheres were all rejected, thus displaying a critique of the foundations and operation of liberal constitutionalism.[53] Formal structures were abandoned in favour of mechanisms of rotating responsibilities and validating personal experience as a mode of political expression.[54] However, these mechanisms ran up against two problems: The first problem was the insularity that it ensued. The radical cohesiveness that was propagated among feminists led to denying and suppressing differences within political groups or movements.[55] The second problem was that of accountability, which arose through the process of rotation and could not be resolved. This suggests that the language of constitutionalism is a language

[48] *Ibid* 38.
[49] *Ibid* 31.
[50] *Ibid* 16.
[51] *Ibid* 37.
[52] Judith Squires, 'Liberal Constitutionalism, Identity and Difference' in R Bellamy and D Castiglione *Constitutionalism in Transformation: European and Theoretical Perspectives* (Blackwell Publishers Oxford) 212.
[53] See Chapter 3.
[54] *Squires* (n 52) 212.
[55] Iris Marion Young, *Justice and the Politics of Difference* (Princeton University Press, Princeton 1990) 312.

that all may be comfortable with as a language of struggles for recognition in the public sphere. It also suggests that some form of (democratic) structure, possibly in the form of representation, is necessary. The latter point will be addressed in the following section on politicisation. The former point is that constitutional language has proved *adjustable*. When minorities make a claim to constitutional recognition, they are arguing that the prevailing terms and conditions of constitutionalism are exclusionary to their interests and that those terms and conditions should be adjusted to include them.[56] Significantly therefore, not only imperialists use the language of constitutionalism, but also anti-imperial movements and minorities. Tully therefore contends that the

> composite, contemporary language of constitutional thought and practice need not be either blindly defended against any claim to cultural recognition or blindly rejected for its male, imperial and Eurocentric bias. Rather, it can be amended and reconceived to do justice to demands for cultural recognition.[57]

Tully's ideas that the constitutional language is one of flexibility and adaptability, but also one of stability is very compelling. While the features of flexibility and adaptability allow for participation, and change, the feature of stability can facilitate imperialism and exclusion. On the basis of his findings, he encourages a reconfiguration of domestic constitutionalism.

The above thoughts can be applied to the discourse on *global* constitutionalism. First and foremost, and possibly banally, global constitutionalism must be a language available to all that would be both subject to it and possible participants in it. Constitutional language despite its limitations is an apt language for participation since it is a language that is available to majorities as well as minorities; not only to imperial but also to anti-imperial struggles. Current visions of global constitutionalism make use of the imperial aspects while giving insufficient weight to the anti-imperial aspects. Just as Tully criticises contemporary constitutionalism from a comparative law perspective, so too is it possible to criticise current approaches to global constitutionalism from an international law perspective. As was found in Chapter 3, one of the primary limitations of the prevailing visions of global constitutionalism is that the models involved do not deserve the title 'global'. They have a tendency to marginalise minority cultures. What is more, the inflexible nature of the visions of global constitutionalism *manifests* such marginalisation in the international sphere. Thus, current participants in the debate on global constitutionalism make use of the flexibility of the language of constitutionalism to fill it with their respective liberal democratic interpretations. Their specific interpretation of global constitutionalism is subsequently stabilised. Organic global constitutionalism, however, embraces the fluidity of the constitutional language.

[56] *Tully* (n 44) 40.
[57] *Ibid* 31.

Stabilisation leads to exclusions; in contrast, flexibility leaves room for the recognition of diversity and plurality. The need for constitutionalism to be viewed as a process and open to change is additionally stressed in the model of global constitutionalism presented here through the prefix 'organic'. While the first point highlighted that constitutional language is open to change, the word 'organic' suggests that it must (paradoxically!) *remain* open to change. The flexibility of the language of constitutionalism should therefore be promoted rather than obstructed.

It should be stressed at this point that the discourse on global constitutionalism is of course complex and that some contributors to the discourse have indeed given thought to the need for flexibility. As was highlighted in Chapter 1, Stefan Kadelbach and Thomas Kleinlein argue in their vision of global constitutionalism that principles should replace rules, which they consider as too rigid. They regard principles as having the advantage of being dynamic rather than final.[58] Similarly, Anne-Marie Slaughter suggests an informal set of principles as an alternative to formal codification of a global constitution. In her view, formal global constitutionalism would inevitably lead to a global government and thus flexible principles should be favoured.[59] Philip Allott's vision of the three constitutions should also be mentioned here. Allott envisions the integrating of the three constitutions as a 'process of generation'. He makes it clear that 'the constitution is a process not a state of affairs'.[60] The flexibility and fluidity of organic global constitutionalism should not be regarded in a negative sense, as exclusively an anti-imperial tool, it should also be seen as something positive with emancipatory properties. Viewing constitutionalism as an ongoing process ensures that a vaster amount of the richness in diversity, communication and texture can be taken into account.[61]

B. *Politicising the Discourse of Global Constitutionalism*

Another theme of organic global constitutionalism is that it is regarded as inescapably political. It was illustrated in Chapter 3 that, no matter to what extent one tries to rationalise constitutionalism, it is not a neutral or non-political ground. Rather, the political should be included in constitutionalism, indeed should be provided with a priority status. This entails the recognition that constitutionalism is not predicated on pre-political convictions, but rather that normativity is determined discursively or politically. It is suggested that

---

[58] Stefan Kadelbach and Thomas Kleinlein, 'International Law – a Constitution for Mankind? An Attempt at a Re-appraisal with an Analysis of Constitutional Principles' (2007) 50 GYIL 345.

[59] *Slaughter* (n 7) 245.

[60] *Allott, 1990* (n 1).

[61] David T. ButleRitchie argues in favour of 'organic constitutionalism' on a domestic scale on this basis. David T. ButleRitchie (n 2) 69.

such 'politicising' of the debate involves democratisation of the debate. By this is meant a participatory and discursive methodology of specifying which issues are viewed as 'constitutional'. Notably, political determination is used synonymously with participatory determination and does not refer to any particular political model. This proposed theme of organic global constitutionalism will be introduced in two steps. First, David Kennedy's work will drawn on as a significant contribution to the idea of politicising legal debates that have become too technical. It is then put forward that Jürgen Habermas' discourse theory should be employed, albeit in a modified way, for substantiating the abstract constitutional language and to satisfy the necessity for a normative element.

In contrast to the other themes of organic global constitutionalism, this theme begins with an observation of an international lawyer – David Kennedy. The following will primarily rely on his seminal essays in *The Disciplines of International Law and Policy* to represent his thoughts.[62] Kennedy emphasises the pluralism of the international law profession. Not only are international lawyers diverse, but so are their views on what international law is. As he puts it, international lawyers have certain projects (personal, professional, or political) that they pursue using the argumentative, doctrinal and institutional materials which the discipline offers.[63] In the areas of both foreign policy and the international economy, international law has, according to Kennedy, become too legalistic. Public international law institutions are too focussed on the State and too formal in their approach to law to be able to be at the centre of the debate on the construction of a modern market regulatory regime.[64] International institutions are too dependent on outdated concepts such as 'sovereignty' to be effective or taken seriously in this field. Thus, *political* engagement in the international sphere, in international law, is crucial. This implies a necessary focus on participation, rather than on ascertaining a unity as a common basis.[65] Kennedy goes on to introduce the international legal theory that positions itself outside of this liberal mainstream (referred to *inter alia* as New Approaches to International Law and Critical Legal Studies). Many ideas of this legal theory were introduced in the preceding chapters when criticising the one-dimensional application of liberal democratic precepts that have been extrapolated to the international sphere. Kennedy explains that methodologically this shares with the U.S. mainstream an image of law both as rules and policies.[66] It observes the stability of rules on the one hand and the flexibility of policies on the other hand. In contrast to the mainstream,

[62] *Kennedy, 1999* (n 6).
[63] *Kennedy, 1999* (n 6) 14, 83.
[64] *Ibid* 53.
[65] See Susan Marks, *The Riddle of all Constitutions* (Oxford University Press, Oxford 2003).
[66] *Kennedy, 1999* (n 6) 34.

its critique is directed against the liberal policy conclusions and legalist sympathies of the mainstream discipline itself.[67] Kennedy's thoughts on the need to politicise international law from the perspective of United States international lawyers can be applied to the debate on global constitutionalism. Politicisation responds to a concern that any form of global constitutionalism which distances itself from liberalism may be taken as undemocratic.[68] The idea of politicising the legal debate is in fact an attempt to make the discourse *more* democratic. Constitutionalism is an inherently political matter and cannot be regarded as neutral. Rather, constitutionalism includes both legal and political matters. As Wouter Werner asserts, global constitutionalism 'should take the political seriously'.[69] The proposal for an organic form of constitutionalism pays heed to the fact that the identities of participants and therewith the respective interests represented on the international level are fluid. Crucially therefore, politicisation means participation. Those wanting to be heard in the international sphere – and making use of a space of global constitutionalism – may come there in a variety of ways. Cultural identity, determined through cultural affiliations, is itself fluid and open to change. Identities cannot be defined through looking at national borders, or sexes, or even languages. Individuals adopt an ever more disparate set of personal identities, meaning that they have affiliations with a number of groupings. Personal identities can be evidenced by ethnic affiliation, religious allegiances, views of personal morality, ideas about what is valuable in life, tastes in music, art etc.[70] Participants may identify themselves as citizens of a particular country; as belonging to a certain sex; as belonging to a cultural group; or as part of a profession. Identities are as fluid as the plurality in the world. If constitutionalism is to be global, then this fluidity of identities must be accommodated.

A further central reason for politicising the debate is the necessary rejection of specific entrenched pre-political values in the international sphere. Rather than declaring particular values as given and unalterable, an open debate would determine which questions are constitutionally pertinent. The problems inherent in a debate centred on common values were discussed in Chapter 3. It was demonstrated that prevailing visions of global constitutionalism manifest exclusions in the international sphere by designating certain norms as global constitutional norms. For example, it was shown that the designation of the United Nations Charter as the global constitution could manifest certain hegemonic structures already existing in the international sphere (those structures that are in place through the internal constitution of the United Nations such as the designation of the permanent members in the

[67] *Ibid* 35.
[68] *Squires* (n 52) 209.
[69] *Werner* (n 36) 348.
[70] David Miller 'Citizenship and Pluralism' (1995) 43 Political Studies 432.

Security Council). Furthermore, it was discussed that the designation of certain norms as *jus cogens* norms could not only exclude other norms, but would indeed exclude any form of discourse on the excluded norms. It was shown that the nomination of certain universal values (such as human rights norms) begs the question of the convictions behind such norms. For example, are these supposed fundamental and universal norms based on a religious conviction, such as the Christian belief in the personal salvation of individuals or on a philosophical conviction, such as the Kantian notion that every person has certain rights merely by virtue of being human? Furthermore, are these supposed fundamental and universal norms based on a Western tradition? And, are such norms not limited by their indeterminacy in any case? The above examples clarify that the idea of entrenched pre-political norms offers much room for dispute. If the focus is shifted to a discursive determination of norms, participation is moved to the forefront.

It must be noted here that, while rejecting entrenched pre-political norms, we cannot envision discourse as proceeding from a 'clean slate'. It must be accepted that participants come with pre-political values firmly entrenched in their identities. Participants are likely to have specific cultural, religious, ethical or other beliefs that they will wish to see represented. The challenge is to allow a hearing of these beliefs. The discourse must thus be lodged in the respective cultural, societal, or religious context. It cannot be free-floating discourse; all discourses are in some way predetermined through the participants to it. The rejection of entrenched pre-political norms simply means that no *specific* pre-political value is prioritised over another. The rejection of a common pre-existing ethical basis for constitutional matters raises questions of legitimacy. Yet, legitimacy should in fact be easier to achieve through a political process. Richard Bellamy summarises this phenomenon aptly:

> Once societies are no longer viewed as naturally constituted according to some moral order, then the norms that animate and regulate human affairs have to be politically constructed and legitimated by those who are to submit to them.[71]

The inherent difficulty facing any suggestion of a political constitutionalism is to overcome the tension between the need for flexibility and fluidity on the one hand and the need for formal procedures and the stability of norms on the other hand. It is possible that organic global constitutionalism could thus run into self-contradiction. It was demonstrated in Chapter 3 that a central limitation of the prevailing visions of global constitutionalism is that they not only suffer from weaknesses in terms of exclusions, but also manifest these weaknesses in the international sphere. Such manifestations occur through the

---

[71] Richard Bellamy 'The Political Form of the Constitution: the Separation of Powers, Rights and Representative Democracy' in Richard Bellamy and Dario Castiglione *Constitutionalism in Transformation: European and Theoretical Perspectives* (Blackwell Publishers Oxford 1996) 43.

need for certain procedures and forms. The problem in employing procedures and forms lies in the fact that the plurality of identities is no longer fluid and contextual; rather, identities are 'frozen'.[72]

One approach to addressing the dilemma is to view constitutionalism as discursive. The possibility of discursive constitutionalism has already been mentioned in earlier discussion; with reference to Jürgen Habermas, the idea will now be explained in more detail. Habermas first introduced the concept of normativity through discourse in his famous discourse theory.[73] He suggested that rules could be deliberated through communication. The purpose of discourse is to determine which norms meet with approval of all affected in their capacity as participants in a practical discourse.[74] He thus alters Kant's notion of the categorical imperative, turning it into a collective imperative, an imperative that reflects a general will. Habermas identifies such a norm as a truly universal norm with full legitimacy.[75] The discursive nature of law-making is directed towards participation, as was deemed necessary for a political process above. In application of the discourse theory, all those potentially affected by the norm would then stand in a participatory dialogue. A norm achieves validity when a general will as to its validity is recognisable. Such a form of discursive and political constitutionalism differs from liberal constitutionalism in that the constitutional provisions have no pre-political justification.[76] A discursive political designation allows for a flexibility and fluidity that a pre-political concept cannot provide.

Habermas' discourse theory must, however, be modified for the purposes of organic global constitutionalism. There are two factors that seem to be at odds with the idea of an organic global constitutionalism. Firstly, discourse theory attempts to identify a universal norm. While this is not directed to a pre-political norm, the identification of a universal norm could challenge the need for flexibility. Secondly, how is the normative outcome of the discourse theory to be understood in respect of the indeterminacy of norms? It was argued in Chapter 3 that norms are open to interpretation. Such indeterminacy could be counter to what discourse theory is in fact trying to achieve. Habermas himself is in favour of applying discourse theory in the international sphere in order to determine a common set of norms.[77]

This criticism brings us back to Tully's work. Tully claims that 'the presupposition of shared, implicit norms is manifestly false' in the predominant

---

[72] *Squires* (n 52) 216.

[73] Jürgen Habermas, William Rehg (tr), *Between Facts and Norms: Contributions to a Discourse Theory of Law and Democracy*, (The MIT Press, Cambridge MA 1998) 4.

[74] Christian Lenhardt and Shierry Weber Nicholsen (tr), Jürgen Habermas, *Moral Consciousness and Communicative Action* (The MIT Press, Cambridge MA 1990) 197.

[75] *Ibid* 67.

[76] *Squires* (n 52) 218.

[77] *Habermas 2006* (n 25).

forms of discourse theory. He explains that a constitutional dialogue should take place, not to determine sameness through agreements on universal principles and institutions, but to bring negotiators to recognise their differences and similarities.[78] Crucially, therefore, the global constitutional dialogue would not have the *aim* of ascertaining unity or sameness on the basis of a common moral order or common values. This criticism upholds the discursive methodology, but rejects the aim of ascertaining universal norms. While Tully criticised the predominant discourse theory for domestic constitutionalism, his argument seems even more fitting on a global scale. The world is, after all, by far more diverse than individual nation States. The discourse methodology itself is therefore not at odds with the need for flexibility and fluidity of organic global constitutionalism. On the contrary, it *encourages* flexibility. Tully suggests that by asking, explaining and rephrasing, participants will gradually be able to see things from the points of view of each other. This would enable an acceptable intercultural language capable of accommodating the truth in each of their limited and complementary views.[79] The use of the discourse methodology aimed at highlighting particularities rather than sameness alters the image of constitutionalism to be a 'humble and practical dialogue' rather than 'grand theory'.[80]

The second issue to be examined is whether discourse theory is compatible with what has been termed the indeterminacy of norms.[81] Despite its modification towards particularities, discourse theory is nevertheless to be regarded as a discourse theory of law. The norms that emerge through an employment of discourse theory could be contradictory to the observations in Chapter 3 on the indeterminacy of norms. However, it was already indicated that such indeterminacy is in fact correspondent to the flexibility of constitutional language. Recognition of the indeterminacy of norms is indeed useful for maintaining an 'organic' constitutionalism. Ulrich Fastenrath observes that the indeterminacy of norms, indeed of words, avoids the futile attempt to provide an exhaustive and finite meaning to the content of legal texts.[82] A certain indeterminacy of language is indeed necessary for flexibility in the constitutional language. What laws 'mean' and the aims they may appear to have will therefore depend on the judgment of application, which is a political act.[83] This is compatible with discourse theory. Indeterminacy is consistent with the

---

[78] *Tully* (n 44) 131.

[79] *Ibid* 134.

[80] *Ibid* 185.

[81] See Chapter 3.

[82] Ulrich Fastenrath 'Relative Normativity in International Law' (1993) 4 EJIL 310.

[83] Martti Koskenniemi 'Constitutionalism as Mindset: Reflections on Kantian Themes about International Law and Globalization' (2007) 8 Theoretical Inquiries into Law 11. Reference to Bonnie L. Paulson & Stanley L. Paulson (trs), Hans Kelsen, *Introduction to Problems of Legal Theory* 1934 (Clarendon Press, Oxford 1992) 81.

approach that constitutionalism should be determined by means of political and social processes, rather than pre-political legal norms.

While the possibility of participation of all is at the core of this point, it must nevertheless be considered whether there are some legitimate limits to such wide participation. For example, what of radical groupings such as nationalists that promote racism or xenophobia, groups that might be referred to as 'undesirable'? Considerations such as these lead to further questions. Does the identification of certain groups as 'undesirable' in a discourse of global constitutionalism lead back to a majoritarian form of discourse that – as has been argued in Chapter 3 – could raise concerns of hegemonic structures? Or, even broader, is the concept of participation 'free for all' simply too utopian? One might suspect that such an 'open' idea of discourse and participation places too much trust in humans. Does the example of radical groupings demonstrate the unfeasibility of organic global constitutionalism itself? Organic global constitutionalism can also be understood as being realistic, not utopian. Organic global constitutionalism recognises the need for law to be placed in its respective social context, and recognises that social contexts change depending on various factors of time and space. Thus, what is considered as acceptable here and now may be considered unacceptable elsewhere or in the future. The discursive nature of constitutionalism may be able to accommodate for these changes, whether they are self-corrective from a moral point of view or whether they are merely reflective of a change detached from morals. What the above example means to demonstrate is that constitutionalism should not adopt a presupposed ethical high ground since the adoption of such a position would automatically mean the exclusion of another possible ethical ground.

Politicisation of global constitutionalism is valuable in order to ensure the relevance of constitutional issues, and in order to place the emphasis on participation. An adjusted discourse theory that is not aimed towards a universal norm but that is directed towards an ongoing discursive process is a means of achieving this. Politicising the debate in this context means recognising the disunity of the world. Organic global constitutionalism is thus oriented, not to finding a common lowest denominator of values; rather, its purpose is to offer a diverse number of individuals and groups a space for representing their interests discursively.

C. *Global Constitutionalism as a 'Negative Universal'*

The third theme of organic global constitutionalism is that it is devoid of fixed content. This theme is closely linked to the idea of constitutionalism as process and specifically political process. It merits being considered a distinct theme since it highlights a balancing act that has been an underlying theme of the whole book: that of universalism on the one hand and particularism on the other hand. The work of Ernesto Laclau, specifically his book titled *Emancipation(s)*, is particularly illuminating.[84] Laclau argues that the universal should be regarded as an 'empty space' in the sense that it has a purely indicative character. Conceived in this 'negative' sense, the universal indicates the existence of something, but has no positive content of its own. It is suggested here that global constitutionalism should similarly be regarded as an empty space. It should indicate universality, but not on the basis of common values. The following will try to explain this.

Laclau begins his argument by questioning the independence of particularity from universality. In many theories, the particular is inherently dependent on the universal.[85] The particular identifies itself merely in relation to the universal, meaning there is a common ground in the sense of a common social reality. The emergence of the universal and the particular from a common ground would mean that the death of the universal would thus lead to the death of the particular.[86] Laclau explains that this outcome is unsatisfying for his purposes: there can be no true emancipation if there is a common ground between the element that the emancipation is sought from (the universal) and the element that is emancipating (the particular). The particular is and remains part of the universal in that case. For the purpose of organic global constitutionalism, such an outcome is also undesirable. If the particular is inherently linked to the universal, it cannot itself determine the nature of a constitutional discourse. The eternal chasm between the universal and the particular would signify an eternal hegemonic struggle; there can be no moment in which the particular finds an independent ground for discourse. In order to break this chain, Laclau suggests perceiving universality as a negative, that is to say, the lack of any particular content. Each new 'particular' or social antagonism would redefine this negative universal.[87]

To illustrate this, Laclau presents his reader with an example of a particular social antagonism: a national minority which is oppressed by an authoritarian State. He then invites the reader to imagine the intervention of other antagonistic forces such as a foreign invasion or the action of hostile economic forces. The national minority will view all the antagonistic forces as equivalent threats to its identity. This equivalence demonstrates that there is a commonality, albeit a *negative* commonality:

> This common element, however, cannot be something positive because, from the point of view of their concrete positive features, each of these forces differs from the other. So it has to be something purely negative: The threat that each of them poses to the national identity. The conclusion is that in a relation of equivalence,

[84] Ernesto Laclau, *Emancipation(s)* (Verso, London 2007).
[85] *Ibid* 4–6.
[86] *Ibid* 13.
[87] *Ibid* 14.

> each of the equivalent elements function as a symbol of negativity as such, of a certain universal impossibility which penetrates the identity in question.[88]

The negative commonality that is defined through the particular leads one to conclude that the universal can emerge from the particular. This negative universal is forever changing, organic, since the relation between the universal and the particular is defined through the respective social antagonism; and the respective social antagonisms are always *particular*. Laclau characterises this negative universality as a signifier, not of universality itself but the idea or possibility of universality.[89] The particular therefore incorporates universality as that which it is lacking.

Applying this to global constitutionalism, one could thus view global constitutionalism as such an empty space. Global constitutionalism has no content of its own; it has no predetermined values that it is based on and it has no common principles. Only the discourse of particularities, the above mentioned 'language of global constitutionalism' identifies the empty shell of global constitutionalism, and highlights that which is lacking in the respective particularities. Diverse interests may be represented on a global sphere that does not presuppose a common ground. The discourse itself is what makes the empty shell visible. Global constitutionalism as a negative universal can thus emerge from the particular. Such an idea of the foregrounding of the particular over the universal is in stark contrast to traditional liberal ideas of overlapping consensus, as suggested for example by Rawls.[90]

It is key that the discourse of the particular from which the universal can emerge is not something that happens by chance. In Laclau's example, the interventions did happen – from the perspective of the particular – by chance. The negative universal therefore also emerged by chance. Global constitutionalism, however, is necessarily to be viewed as an *available* space. It is a space that is designated to be used for discourse – a platform, so to speak. Not only the space is designated, the language is designated too. The availability of the space should not be viewed as another means of attaining a positive universal for the present, but should be viewed as a space for discourse in which the negative universal will involuntarily show itself. Global constitutionalism is therefore a distinct concept that has a character of its own. Going back to Bill Reid's sculpture of the *Haida Gwaii*, the various mythical creatures depicted there are, after all, *in the same boat*. Their variety points to the element of diversity, but the diversity is nevertheless situated in a common space. Furthermore, they are steering the boat together. Although the direction may not be predetermined, they have a shared course. The idea of global

---

88 *Ibid* 14.
89 *Ibid* 15.
90 John Rawls, *The Law of Peoples* (HUP, Cambridge MA 2002).

constitutionalism as an empty space reinforces the emphasis above on the discursive and political character of organic global constitutionalism.

D. *Organic Global Constitutionalism as a Promise for the Future*

The final theme that will be applied to global constitutionalism is the theme of organic global constitutionalism as a promise for the future. The work of Jacques Derrida is introduced in this context. The preceding sections have argued for a notion of constitutionalism as process, as discourse, and as an 'empty space'. So far, then, the flexibility and organic nature of global constitutionalism has been stressed. In all this change and movement, an aspect of stability must be present in order for this form of constitutionalism to be regarded as *normative*; Normativity is after all what makes the debate legal rather than merely political. It is suggested here that normativity as a positive aspect should be regarded as a feature belonging to the future. Normativity, stability, and possibly 'a constitution' are thus not features of the present, but are features of the promise of constitutionalism *to come*. This takes into account that the future of constitutionalism must remain open on the one hand – the necessity of openness to change – and must nevertheless include a prospect of being filled with content from time to time on the other hand.[91] The above-mentioned discourse is therefore directed to the future, more specifically to a *better* future. Due to the organic nature of the discourse, global constitutionalism will never accumulate to 'a global constitution'. The discourse will remain one of constitutional*ism* – an ongoing process. If the social reality of today is therefore seen as marked by limitations, global constitutionalism offers a tool with which current social reality can be amended and reconceived to do justice. While current social reality can be reconceived, it can only be reconceived as a future good, not for the present. This underlines the appeal of a shared project of global constitutionalism; it speaks to a desire for future justice and democracy. Derrida studied the idea of a better future as an abstract notion, a *promise*. He speaks of a promise that is empty of any meaning save for expectation: 'an *event* which cannot be mastered by an aprioristic discourse'.[92] Derrida believes this promise is so strong as to describe it as 'messianic':

---

[91] Nico Krisch also comes across the problem of normativity as regards his vision of global administrative law, explained above in Chapter 2, p. 84. In his view, global administrative law causes the 'disappearance of a clearly competent authority'. This implies, similarly to what is suggested for organic global constitutionalism, 'fluidity'. In his view, fluidity leads to the limitation of a 'lack of certainty'. (see Nico Krisch, 'The Pluralism of Global Administrative Law' (2006) 17 EJIL 275.) The characteristic of organic global constitutionalism as a promise for the future could possibly be a means to overcome the chasm between fluidity on the one hand and normativity on the other.

[92] *Laclau* (n 84) 73.

> A messianism without religion, even a messianic without messianism, an idea of justice – which we distinguish from law or right and even from human rights – and an idea of democracy – which we distinguish from its current concept and from its determined predicates today...[93]

Derrida is demonstrating a chasm between law and justice, which makes a better future necessary. Laclau rightly notes that we should not understand Derrida's idea of the 'messianic' as anything *directly* related to actual messianic movements of the past or the present. Indeed, it is distinct in that there is no eschatology, there is no 'Promised Land'. Derrida develops a concept of *democratie à venir* – the democracy to come.[94] Such ideas can be applied to organic global constitutionalism. Organic global constitutionalism in the *present* is devoid of fixed content; it is an open space. However, the concept promises justice for the *future*. This future cannot be concretised to a specific set of norms; rather the future remains to be realised. The tool that is employed to make the future promise realistic is the (adjusted) discourse theory. Organic global constitutionalism can therefore provide a means of expression to plurality and diversity – there is no positive universal that could assume a hegemonic power – and at the same time can provide a means of expression to the idea of a *shared* progressive project.

In order for organic global constitutionalism to acquire legitimacy, it must satisfy the features that make the concept appealing, as identified at the beginning of this chapter. A re-imagined global constitutionalism as an open space that requires wide-ranging discursive participation expresses the concern about the allocation of power in the international sphere. The open demand for 'politicisation' represents this element. Moreover, the belief in the potency of law to regulate global social reality is also captured by organic global constitutionalism. Although the normative aspect of organic global constitutionalism is by its nature not central, the ability of norms to regulate social behaviour is deeply rooted in the discursive element and in the element of a promise of a better future and finally, organic global constitutionalism, no matter how loose and flexible, would provide legitimacy to international law, at the very least in terms of a shared conception of constitutionalism on the global sphere.

E. *The Limitations of Organic Global Constitutionalism*

The above features are an attempt at re-imagining global constitutionalism in international legal perspective, but they are not without limitations of their own. There are two major limitations associated with the model of organic global constitutionalism. Firstly, the political mechanisms in which participation has to function risks exhibiting the inflexibility that was described as

[93] Jacques Derrida, *Specters of Marx* (Routledge Classics, New York 2006) 74.
[94] *Ibid* 81.

enabling marginalisations. Secondly, while organic constitutional language hopes to provide a forum of equal participation, not everyone comes to the discourse as equals. The vision of organic global constitutionalism cannot rid international law of these important limitations.

Constituting political procedures inevitably posits some stability of identity and requires exclusion of certain differences and therefore compromises the fluidity of heterogeneous differences.[95] Participation cannot take place outside of formal structures. In order to ensure representation of interests, some formal structures are essential. As discussed earlier, the feminist movement – the forerunner in many forms of participatory politics – adjusted its views with respect to participatory politics after having experienced the difficulties of an absence of formal mechanisms.[96] Learning from imperfections, many feminists began to promote a 'politics of difference', which seeks recognition of multiple and contingent differences, and does so through procedures and organisational structures.[97] Some form of institutionalisation of power will therefore be maintained for organic global constitutionalism.

A second possible limitation of organic global constitutionalism is that the participants to the discourse would be determined by current political and social structures, most notably, by current international law.[98] It follows that the consideration of *who* can participate in a discourse of global constitutionalism could be subject to the inequalities that are already present in current international law. There may therefore be an initial bias towards males, white, and Western participants. Despite this, the flexible nature of organic global constitutionalism could allow for its revisability in the future. The suggested themes of organic global constitutionalism may therefore also be subject to limitations, but – uniquely – incorporate the possibility of self-corrections. To offer some relief from this abstraction, the next chapter will apply the foregoing theoretical considerations in a more concrete form.

Conclusion

In sum, the idea of *a* global constitution should be abandoned; the idea of global constitutional*ism*, however, can be retained provided that the concept is reconfigured. The above has described the possible implications to the finding that prevailing visions of global constitutionalism are limited.

---

[95] *Squires* (n 52) 215.

[96] *Ibid* 212ff.

[97] *Ibid* 215.

[98] Nico Krisch has voiced a similar concern regarding the flexible and fluid global administrative law, mentioned in Chapter 2. He considers that the reliance on a free interplay through a pluralist approach could 'merely favour the powerful at the expense of the weak.' *Krisch* (n 91) 275.

Since abandonment of the entire discourse was found to be impractical, the reasons for the appeal of the concept were briefly examined. Against that background, the reconfiguration of global constitutionalism was proposed. Four defining features of organic global constitutionalism were suggested. Rather than trying to be an exhaustive account, this suggestion is one that attempts to initiate a new debate on global constitutionalism, one with a wider perspective than before. Organic global constitutionalism is different from the prevailing visions of global constitutionalism in that it:

(a) Rejects stability in favour of flexibility.
(b) Rejects any pre-political common values in favour of a discursive political determination of constitutionalism.
(c) Rejects viewing global constitutionalism as a 'positive universal', conceived along the lines of liberal democracy, in favour of viewing it as something that only emerges through contending particulars in the sense of a 'negative universal'.
(d) Suggests viewing the normative aspect of constitutionalism as a promise for the future, a *constitutionalism to come.*

It remains to be seen how the above features of organic global constitutionalism relate to the five key themes associated with prevailing approaches to global constitutionalism that were highlighted in Chapter 1. As will be recalled, these themes were criticised in Chapter 3, but in a way which pointed to their limitations rather than proposing their wholesale rejection.

The first key theme, the limitation of power, is also a theme of organic global constitutionalism. Constitutionalism as a process is a means of endeavouring to ensure that power cannot be concentrated or centralised. Moreover, the politicisation of constitutionalism tries to allow for a form of participation that does not lead to exclusions. The idea of constitutionalism as a negative universal and the idea of a constitutionalism to come are also means of providing for a limitation of power. They ensure that no specific set of values is designated normative status in the present and thus prevent a power structure from developing that could lead to the marginalisation of minorities. The second key theme, the institutionalisation of power, does not play a large role in the suggestion for organic global constitutionalism. This is chiefly due to the theoretical and rather abstract nature of the given suggestions. It prompts the examination of a very important issue: that of the universality of certain formalistic precepts not incompatible with the negative universal. It is a theme that is explored in more depth in the following chapter. Social idealism, the third key theme, was criticised in Chapter 3 for its normative aspect that entrenches present values as ideals for 'the good life' for the present. It was identified that specific values are designated as *ideal* and are thus set down in a normative form – largely in the shape of human rights. In modern visions of global constitutionalism, human rights are considered the only available way of enshrining societal values in a normative fashion. It was found that this is problematic since the alleged universal values are often in fact particular to a certain philosophical, historical, and ethical viewpoint and hence not universal at all. Such universalisation and objectification makes the concept open to criticisms of conceptual imperialism. The designations of specific norms as 'ideal' closes off discussion of ends, so that all that remains are technical issues relating to means. Organic global constitutionalism upholds the theme of social idealism, but does not predetermine the values considered as 'ideal'. Idealism is placed in the future rather than in the present. The remaining two key themes of global constitutionalism, standard-setting and individual rights, are distinctly problematic from the perspective of organic global constitutionalism. Standard-setting identifies a certain set of principles as 'constitutional' and these are put forward as guidelines for the functioning of the constitutional society. Such principles would provide a specific content to something that, from the perspective of organic global constitutionalism should remain an 'empty space'. Not only that, standard-setting in the sense of a systematisation of law means the direction of society according to a fixed plan or system. Such fixed plan or system is incompatible with the flexibility of organic global constitutionalism. The same applies to individual rights: pre-defining individual rights as fundamental or constitutional rights closes the door to a determination of different interests on the basis of discourse. These two themes of standard-setting and individual rights are too rigid to be compatible with an organic form of constitutionalism. Some, but not all, aspects of the key themes of global constitutionalism are therefore also part of the idea for organic global constitutionalism.

It must finally be noted that, while the discussion of organic global constitutionalism has proceeded in a mostly theoretical rather than practical register, global constitutionalism always also includes a *project* of constitutionalism. That is to say, concrete measures are needed to realise the abstract ideas. This aspect of organic global constitutionalism is the subject of the next and final chapter.

CHAPTER FIVE

A PRACTICAL APPROACH TO ORGANIC GLOBAL CONSTITUTIONALISM

I keep six honest serving-men; (They taught me all I knew); Their names are What and Why and When; and How and Where and Who.[1]

Introduction

How would the preceding theory of organic global constitutionalism be implemented into practice? In this final chapter, I return to the four dimensions of global constitutionalism that together make up the contemporary debate and address what a consideration of organic global constitutionalism may mean for them. The basic taxonomy used was that of Social Constitutionalism, Institutional Constitutionalism, Normative Constitutionalism and Analogical Constitutionalism. As clarified in the previous chapter, organic global constitutionalism does not hope to relinquish the entire discourse to date. It seems an impossible task to consider what organic global constitutionalism would look like under the circumstances of starting from scratch. While this may be theoretically possible, it is impossible in practice. And wiping the slate clean would not correspond with organic growth as organic growth requires something to already be present. Thus, it appears the best approach is to take the current debate as it is, as mapped out in the four dimensions of global constitutionalism, and to consider how global constitutionalism could proceed to change in a more organic fashion. Reconceptualising global constitutionalism would animate those aspects of the debate that have so far been overlooked, namely the emancipatory and anti-imperial aspects of a global constitutionalist debate. The limitations of the contemporary debate are manifested in the fact that it leaves the aspects of process, politics, and flexibility in the dark; in suggesting an organic approach, I would like to cast some light on these neglected aspects. While the previous chapters have primarily considered the theoretical underpinnings of organic global constitutionalism, this chapter seeks to consider its practical possibilities.

After dealing with some preliminary questions regarding a practical approach to organic global constitutionalism, namely Who? What? Where?

[1] Rudyard Kipling, *Just so Stories* (1902).

When? Why? And How?, the chapter examines what 'organic' may mean in a practical sense, beginning with what it does *not* mean. In considering what it means, this chapter cites various definitions from the Oxford English Dictionary and contextualises them within the global constitutional debate. With these definitions as guides, the chapter examines the four dimensions of global constitutionalism in terms of what their practical application would most likely look like. It almost goes without saying that the practical application of global constitutionalism, even Institutional Constitutionalism, does not mean commitment to a grand project to the ends of a federal world State in the vast majority of cases.[2] Bardo Fassbender describes the vision of a 'world State' as something 'which to many is still the epitome of horror'.[3] What is considered instead is to a great extent more humble. Nevertheless, these humble suggestions made through existing forms of global constitutionalism could manifest problems of international law and could stand in the way of the progressive possibilities of a more organic approach. This chapter provisionally considers how these default understandings could be ameliorated by use of an organic approach. For this organic approach, I draw upon the theory of the previous chapter and the definitions explored in this chapter. The problems with the implementation of the theory I freely admit: while theory could possibly be pure, practice is about compromise. Theory can be abstract, yet practice is contextual. In an interesting twist, practice is of course to be encouraged in global constitutionalism; contextuality that takes the place of abstraction is an important aspect of making the debate more organic. The practical approach below attempts to be as close to the theory as possible, at least to the extent that it does not betray it completely.

This chapter primarily focuses on two recent books: Jeffrey L. Dunoff and Joel P. Trachtman's edited book *Ruling the World?*[4] and the co-authored book by Jan Klabbers, Anne Peters and Geir Ulfstein *The Constitutionalization of International Law*.[5] In their opening chapter, Dunoff and Trachtman suggest a 'functional approach' to global constitutionalism in which they claim to avoid the 'definitional conundrums that mark so much of the literature on constitutionalism beyond the state' in favour of devoting attention to substantive analysis.[6]

---

[2] Mattias Kumm, 'The Cosmopolitan Turn in Constitutionalism' in Jeffrey L. Dunoff and Joel P. Trachtman (eds), *Ruling the World? Constitutionalism, International Law, and Global Governance* (CUP, Cambridge 2009) 259. I have in fact not considered a single author in the above that believes (or claims) world federalism stands at the end of the project of global constitutionalism.

[3] Bardo Fassbender, 'The Meaning of International Constitutional Law' in Nicholas Tsagourias (ed) *Transnational Constitutionalism: International and European Perspectives* (CUP, Cambridge 2007) 311.

[4] Jeffrey L. Dunoff and Joel P. Trachtman (eds), *Ruling the World? Constitutionalism, International Law, and Global Governance* (CUP, Cambridge 2009).

[5] Jan Klabbers, Anne Peters, Geir Ulfstein, *The Constitutionalization of International Law* (OUP, Oxford 2009).

[6] *Dunoff, Trachtman* (n 4) 9.

They therefore place the definitional questions aside in order to achieve a type of 'working definition' of global constitutionalism. In the opening chapter of his co-authored book, Jan Klabbers explains that the authors' purpose is neither a strictly descriptive account of global constitutionalism nor a strictly normative one; rather, they 'take the idea of constitutionalism and run with it, so to speak'. These scholars are also interested in the question of 'what happens next?'. This is the focus of my final chapter.

Section I: Preliminary Questions

Before discussing the possible emancipatory and anti-imperial properties of the debate of organic global constitutionalism, some preliminary questions should be addressed. I will approach these preliminary questions by inquiring into what in journalism and police investigations is referred to as the 'five Ws' (and one H): Who? What? Where? When? Why? and How? A review of the five Ws (and one H) will hopefully assist in focussing contemplations on what organic global constitutionalism could mean in a practical sense. Commonly, the five Ws are employed to assess what happened in the past – in order to reconstruct a past action; for example to determine whether the requirements for a specific crime were met. The five Ws will aid me in setting the scene for a *future* form of action. Who could take part in a discourse of organic global constitutionalism? What does it relate to? Where will the discourse take place? When will it take place? Why should there be a reconfiguration to an organic approach? and lastly, how can a reconfiguration transpire?

First then the question of 'Who?' I relate this question to the audience of a practical application of organic global constitutionalism: Who is it that could take an organic approach seriously? In the preceding chapters, I critiqued the contemporary contributors to the debate in some depth and so, of course, they are to be considered as an important part of the audience. But, the potential audience hopefully goes beyond this to include international lawyers that are not engaging directly in the debate, yet are somehow implicated in it. For example, international lawyers working for international institutions such as international courts and tribunals would hopefully also consider themselves as part of the debate and at the same time as the audience of this work. Organic global constitutionalism has a reformist agenda that can only be effective if practitioners partake in the debate.

The question of 'What?' is to be understood here as referring more specifically to what the ideas constituting organic global constitutionalism can be applied to. The question of what organic means in a practical sense will be explored below and is in any event not strictly a preliminary question. Most evidently, organic global constitutionalism relates to the contemporary debate on global constitutionalism. It was claimed at the beginning of this work that the contributions mostly fall into one of two categories: the descriptive (what global constitutionalism is) and the normative (what global constitutionalism should look like). The contributions were grouped together (irrespective of whether they had descriptive or normative accounts) according to the main emphasis of their work. The bulk of the debate was categorised into Social Constitutionalism, Institutional Constitutionalism, Normative Constitutionalism and Analogical Constitutionalism. What the application of organic global constitutionalism to the four dimensions would mean will be described in more detail below.

'Where?' is a significant issue for global constitutionalism. As previous chapters suggested, the various visions don't always justify the use of the term 'global'. Some scholars seem to be disproportionately more interested in theorising about global constitutionalism than others. Certainly, one might state that the centre of the debate is in Germany, with increasing attention from the Anglo-American academy. But, who, for example is writing about global constitutionalism in Asia – the region with the highest proportion of the global population? The aim is that by disassociating global constitutionalism from the Western liberal democratic tradition, it will become more global. Global constitutionalism should in a practical sense constitute an available space, a platform, for debates regarding social change through international law.

Will the matter only become pertinent when a policy-maker on the national or international scene becomes interested in global constitutionalism and employs the term in a particular way? Or should a reconfiguration of the contemporary debate occur immediately? These questions relate to the 'When?' of organic global constitutionalism. I am interested in organic global constitutionalism since I believe the debate is already closely related to the predominant political form of liberal democracy, possibly in a way that implies that a liberal democratic approach is the only available approach. Andreas L. Paulus claims that the term constitution 'implies comprehensiveness, hierarchy, and judicial control'.[7] It is a matter of urgency that the term be relieved of this one-dimensionality and parochialism for it to be a tool to be used on the international sphere that can generate social change. The longer the debate remains locked into a liberal democratic association, the less likely that it can be recognised *globally* as a useful tool and platform.

'Why?' is an immensely important question: Why reconceptualise global constitutionalism to be more organic? This question has hopefully already been answered to a certain extent in the previous chapters. One issue needs to be addressed here that has not been expressly addressed thus far: Is the idea of an organic global constitutionalism in fact a means to introduce an alternative to public international law in general? Organic global constitutionalism is to

---

[7] Andreas L. Paulus, 'The International Legal System as a Constitution' in Jeffrey L. Dunoff and Joel P. Trachtman (eds), *Ruling the World? Constitutionalism, International Law, and Global Governance* (CUP, Cambridge 2009) 76.

be understood as a platform for social change in the international sphere with the employment of the international legal language. But, is this not the purpose of public international law too? Angelika Emmerich-Fritsche and Jost Delbrück have followed this path by distinguishing World Law from public international law. In their view, public international law cannot adequately capture all the necessary issues of the international sphere, while world law can insofar as it is framed by a global constitution.[8] As was stated above and as will be emphasised again below, global constitutionalism, whether organic or not, is inescapably a framework. But what is it a framework for? A framework for public international law or a framework for a distinct area of law – possibly to be referred to as global law or global constitutional law? Without attempting to alienate the other thinkers in my field too much, I believe that these questions deserve some critical reflection. In light of fragmentation, international law is undoubtedly a field composed of various specialised areas. Furthermore, private law has become increasingly significant, with private military companies operating through contracts, with victims being granted reparations through the international criminal court and with arbitration taking on the terminology of public international law and vice versa. It is difficult, and maybe even undesirable to view public international law as a truly 'public' law. Certainly, constitutional law is in many ways the epitome of the 'public'. One could therefore conclude that global constitutional law has appropriated the 'publicness' that public international law no longer possesses. This would largely extinguish the emancipatory potential of organic global constitutionalism in that it too would be trapped within the exclusions that a public/private divide incur. I would encourage the following approach: Given that public international law has become and will continue to be fragmented, a void has been created for a framework – a framework that is about *inclusion* rather than exclusion, a framework that can take the private law issues into account and even embraces them, a framework that identifies the common course of the participants. Organic global constitutionalism can be viewed as filling this void. This necessarily means that it takes over some of the properties that public international law used to have – the all-encompassing potential, the determination of terminology and of participants. But, it can do this in a fashion that is suitable to the international sphere and its demands: with flexibility as well as with stability.

Lastly, the 'How?'. I neither intend to re-theorise organic global constitutionalism at this stage, nor do I want to anticipate the thoughts on an organic

[8] Angelika Emmerich-Fritsche, *Vom Völkerrecht zum Weltrecht* (Duncker & Humboldt, Berlin 2007); Jost Delbrück, 'Wirksames Völkerrecht oder neues "Weltinnenrecht"? Perspektiven der Völkerrechtsentwicklung in einem sich wandelnden internationalen System' in Klaus Dicke et al (eds), *Die Konstitution des Friedens als Rechtsordnung* (Duncker & Humboldt, Berlin 1996).

reconfiguration of the four dimensions of global constitutionalism set out below. Here, the question of 'How?' is to be understood as relating to the *initiation* of the debate: How should the initiation of a reconfiguration of global constitutionalism be approached? It should be recalled that in any event advocating an organic approach is a very minor and modest contribution, aimed at redirecting the debate from its current trajectory without suggesting a specific alternative model. The initiation of the debate itself poses a number of problems – problems that may be more easily dealt with in the abstract. In abstract, it would for example be necessary to deal with the important question of whether it is possible to suggest a reconfiguration while at the same time not being drawn into parochialism by universalising my ideas (is it possible to critique first and then reconceptualise without being a hypocrite?). I do, of course, not want to evade this important question. But, I have theorised to a great extent in the previous chapter so let it suffice to say that the placing of global constitutionalism in a liberal democratic tradition does not necessarily mean it is tainted irreconcilably. The biased history of global constitutionalism does not *necessarily* mean that the future debate will also be biased. While I felt it was necessary to place the predominant key themes into historical perspective in order to demonstrate that there are important overlaps between the four dimensions of global constitutionalism as they are today, this does not mean to say that aspects of the debate cannot be reconfigured. In order to animate the emancipatory dimension of organic global constitutionalism, some compromises have to be made. Some identities, which I have previously identified as fluid, will have to be frozen in time; some terms that I previously shied away from defining in order to embrace indeterminacy will have to be defined. Defining terms and freezing identities does not *necessarily* mean parochialism so long as the modus is regarded as an ongoing process. Indeed, defining terms and freezing identities for a short while at least seems to be essential for enabling the progressive possibilities of organic global constitutionalism. This leads us to the practical necessity of understanding – or rather defining – 'organic'.

Section II: What does 'Organic' mean?

In order to edge closer to what 'organic' means in a practical sense, I would like to begin by thinking about what organic global constitutionalism does *not* mean. It should have become clear that organic global constitutionalism does not entail a blueprint for a global constitution. Organic global constitutionalism is no precise framework that allows development according to a predetermined plan. However, some measure of normativity – and in that sense some measure of stasis – is necessary. Herein lies the greatest challenge: how to imagine a legal structure that manages to create a good balance between necessary flexibility (which enables change) and necessary stability (which enables certainty). For a practical approach, which includes the promise of realism, it makes sense to start with the contemporary visions of global constitutionalism. It appears that the approach of the contemporary debate is largely so fixed within its outlook on what ideological patterns a global constitution should follow that introducing some flexible aspects would already be a step towards such a difficult balance. A further defining term was mentioned in terms of what 'organic' does *not* mean: it is not *finite* stasis. The centrality of this was already demonstrated in the previous chapter. While some equilibrium may be necessary to avoid chaos, finite stasis, say in the form of a written global constitution, is not what 'organic' means. To summarise, organic global constitutionalism does *not* mean a blueprint for a global constitution and it does not mean finite stasis.

What is it that organic global constitutionalism proposes to be? The previous theoretical chapter explained that organic global constitutionalism is a rather eclectic collection of ideas. It is the idea of constitutionalism as process, the idea of making that which has become technical political, the idea of constitutionalism as a 'negative universal' in the sense of abandoning the search for commonalities, and finally the idea of constitutionalism as a promise for the future. The collection is of course not a random assortment; rather, the ideas share some important premises. As stated in the previous chapter, the links between these ideas are the procedural paradigms of communication, participation and inclusion. How does this translate into practice? For some signposts to guide this inquiry, it seems useful to gain an understanding of what 'organic' means in other contexts. According to the Oxford Dictionary, there are a whole host of meanings pertaining to biology, medicine, mathematics, music, economics, chemistry, and agriculture.[9] I would like to explore some of these in order to collect a number of inspirations for a sense of the word. I begin with the biological and medical definitions; organic is defined as: (2) (a) '*Of a part of the body: composed of distinct parts or tissues*' and (b) '*Having organs, or an organized physical structure; of, relating to, or derived from a living organism or organisms; having the characteristics of a living organism*'. This definition is apposite in that organic global constitutionalism is part of the body of international law, using its terminology and its assumptions about the universality of law. At the same time, the universality is 'empty' in the sense that there are no predetermined values (see the previous chapter on the negative universal). Global constitutionalism is a concept that is inescapably a framework – a 'body'. The challenge for organic global constitutionalism is to consider this framework as flexible and changeable rather than as a fixed blueprint. While the availability of the platform is determined, the content is

[9] Oxford English Dictionary online (OUP 2010).

both undetermined and indeterminate. This raises important questions of formalism, as agonised over by many scholars previously. However, this would lead to a re-theorising of the previous chapter, which as stated above is not the purpose of this chapter. Returning to the meaning of organic; the framework has an organised physical structure in the formal premises of communication, participation and inclusion. Communication is central to the idea of interests: law is a mechanism through which interests can be taken into account that would be over-powered if it were for a simple 'might is right' structure. Law offers a platform for communicating interests, and global constitutionalism in particular offers a platform for interests that need to be taken into consideration on a global rather than a local platform. Participation is central in that communication requires an objective: what is it that we are communicating about? What are we trying to achieve? Inclusion means that the space is available to anyone who has an interest and would like to give it a voice. This premise is highly complex in that it raises questions of equality, majority, representation, agency and similarly contested issues. For our purposes (to avoid re-theorising), inclusion should be understood in relation to its antonym: inclusion is not exclusion. Importantly, indeterminacy of the content of global constitutionalism requires a certain amount of constant movement and thus possibly to a certain extent chaos. Chaos of course has negative connotations, but I would invite the reader to understand a certain amount of chaos as something enabling, something that provokes change in contrast to stasis, which itself is disabling and prevents change. So far, the meaning of 'organic' relating to a *framework* has been confirmed as well as relating to an *organised structure*. The final part of the definition *having the characteristics of a living organism* is particularly apt for the idea of organic global constitutionalism suggested here. Organic global constitutionalism should be imagined as something shaped entirely by the participants in the debate, growing or shrinking with the interests and ideas put forward; becoming more or less comprehensive depending on the needs of the participants. In that sense, it has no life of its own – it is, as described in the previous chapter, an empty shell. The shell should however be understood as being both stretchable and retractable.

The following definition in the Dictionary has been described by Oxford University Press as obsolete, however, it seems key to what organic means in the context of constitutionalism: (3) (a) *Serving as an instrument or means to an end; instrumental.* (b) *Relating to an instrument or means.*[10] The purpose of organic global constitutionalism is to cater to the apparent demand for the discourse on global constitutionalism and view it precisely as an instrument for addressing the concerns of international lawyers today. As discussed in the previous chapter, international lawyers have concerns, even anxieties, about the status

[10] *Ibid.*

of their field. Global constitutionalism appears to be a forum in which they raise these concerns and it should continue to function as an instrument for debates on fragmentation, legitimacy, and the role of law in society. The instrumental property of organic global constitutionalism is its emancipatory potential. In the preceding chapters, I examined this *inter alia* with reference to Ernesto Laclau, who argues that emancipation is only possible if the particular is not conceived of as emanating from the universal; hence the necessity of the negative universal, which is established as an empty space – the absence of the universal – through a collection of various particulars.[11] This emancipatory potential of constitutional law is animated through the additional prefix of 'organic'. It is this potential of constitutionalism that has allowed the dominated to emancipate from their dominators for centuries that is often sidelined in the contemporary debate. Organic global constitutionalism could be *instrumental* to recalling this property of constitutionalism.

(5) (a) of the Oxford English Dictionary characterises 'organic' as meaning: *Belonging to or inherent in a living being; constitutional; natural.* This is of course interesting since reference is expressly made to 'constitutional' indicating how closely the terms organic and constitutional are related. Indeed the next relevant definition (6): *Of or relating to an organized structure compared to a living being* includes the subcategory referring to Law, which defines organic as *constitutive; that establishes or sets up; stating the formal constitution of a nation or other political entity.* Organic and constitutive are interlinked through the idea of the creation (constitution) of a social space (organic). The idea of constitutionalism therefore proceeds on the assumption of clearly differentiated containers of social space, particularly those that provide a space for politics.[12] It is the creation of something changing – compared to a living being. So although a product is achieved, it is not an end-product. Both organic and constitutionalism therefore incorporate the paradox of incorporating stability as well as flexibility. Summarising the above definitions, organic global constitutionalism does not mean a blueprint, but it does mean a framework; it does not mean finite stasis, but it does mean structure; it can be used as an instrument, but the instrument is to be considered as a living matter; and finally, it is constitutive without creating an end-product.

Section III: Organic Global Constitutionalism and the Four Dimensions

This section revisits the four dimensions of global constitutionalism. In the first chapter, the contemporary debate was mapped out into what I called the

[11] Ernesto Laclau, *Emancipation(s)* (Verso, London 2007).

[12] Neil Walker, 'Reframing EU Constitutionalism' in *Ruling the World? Constitutionalism, International Law, and Global Governance* (CUP, Cambridge 2009) 151, 152.

four dimensions of global constitutionalism. Here I consider how these dimensions can be reconfigured in practice to foster a more organic approach. It should be reiterated here, that this practical approach is not congruent with the theoretical considerations of the previous chapter. The application of the theory into practice carries with it some necessary compromises. The sections are divided into two parts. I examine first how the relevant dimensions are likely to play out in practice if *not* offset by organic global constitutionalism – the default, so to say. I then consider how these conditions could be reconfigured to become more organic.

A. *Social Constitutionalism*

Social Constitutionalism is a vision defined by the idea that the international sphere is an order of coexistence. Social Constitutionalism centres political concerns of participation, often relying on liberal democracy as a model framework through which participation can be achieved. Hermann Mosler's and Bardo Fassbender's work was used to describe the *international community school*. This school views the international community as a comprehensive international legal order, framed by a global constitution. Additionally, Gunter Teubner's and Andreas Fischer-Lescano's visions for a *global civil society* were described as belonging to a Social Constitutionalist vision. Due to his preoccupation with a future international society, Philip Allott's work was also portrayed as part of Social Constitutionalism. Social Constitutionalism emphasises the age-old key theme of the limitation of power – in this case through a community of individuals.

So what would the default implementation of Social Constitutionalism be? It appears that the danger lies in an attempt at democratisation in a hegemonic manner that gives preference to liberal democratic models – the policies of Reagan in the 1980s come to mind. Democracy promotion in conflict or post-conflict States is often predicated on the assumption that democracy brings about economic development and political stability. We bring democracy – it is for their own good. Latest democratisation projects include Iraq and Afghanistan. The tool for implementing democracy in such States is of course a new constitution. It is the constitution that sets out in which way democracy is to be implemented, whether there is an upper and a lower house, to what extent democratic principles are entrenched, the extent of separation of powers, who makes decisions and how they are made, etc. The democratisation process has been criticised for being primarily about securing oil and strategic interests rather than securing democracy in Iraq. The Iraqi constitution was adopted on 15 October 2005 and incorporates all the key themes of liberal democratic constitutionalism identified above – which are, as we know from Chapter 1, commonly extrapolated to the international sphere for global constitutionalism. Art. 1 of the unofficial but approved English version reads:

> The Republic of Iraq is a single federal, independent and fully sovereign state in which the system of government is republican, representative, parliamentary, and democratic, and this Constitution is a guarantor of the unity of Iraq.[13]

Elections and the implementation of constitutional provisions are overseen by a UN body – the United Nations Assistance Mission for Iraq (UNAMI), which receives its mandate from a Security Council Resolution, or rather multiple resolutions in which the mandate has been extended.[14] According to the *Los Angeles Times*, the US government had already allocated at least US$458 million to 'promote democracy' in Iraq by early 2004.[15] Promises were made of peace, stability, and self-rule. William I. Robinson observes that such monies overtly and covertly go towards the funding of political parties and other elite forums, organisations in Iraqi civil society such as trade unions, business councils, the media, student and women's groups, and professional associations.[16] The U.S. uses these funds in programmes, which have the 'overall objective … to force on the region a more complete integration into global capitalism'.[17] The Obama administration has recently announced that it is committed to promoting good governance in Afghanistan. President Obama stated that while the troops may be withdrawn from Afghanistan by July 2011, after that date 'we are still going to have an interest in making sure that Afghanistan is secure, that economic development is taking place, that good governance is being promoted'.[18] He has picked up on the modern parlance of democratisation: 'good governance'. The conception of a civil society, which is the focus of Social Constitutionalist visions of Gunter Teubner and Andreas Fischer-Lescano, is at the centre of ideas of democratisation and good governance and is worryingly key for the establishment of hegemony (although this is naturally not the intention of Teubner and Fischer-Lescano): Civil society programmes have been criticised for attempting to educate a group of elites, whose outlook is international and liberal democratic, and who can be employed as the instruments of a hegemon. As Susan Marks notes in *The Riddle of all Constitutions*:

> It is a familiar story. We start out singing of autonomy, justice, and solidarity, and of the great ideas through which those aspirations might be brought to social

---

[13] http://www.uniraq.org/documents/iraqi_constitution.pdf.

[14] UNSCR 1546, UNSCR 1710, UNSCR 1770, UNSCR 1830, UNSCR 1883.

[15] 'Iraq: One Year Later: Transition, But to What?' *Los Angeles Times*, March 20, 2004.

[16] William I. Robinson, 'What to Expect from US "Democracy Promotion" in Iraq (2004) 26 New Political Science 441 with reference to *idem*, *Promoting Polyarchy: Globalization, U.S. Intervention and Hegemony* (CUP, Cambridge 1996) and *A Faustian Bargain: U.S. Intervention in the Nicaraguan Elections and American Foreign Policy in the Post-Cold War Era* (Westview Press, Boulder 1992).

[17] *bid, Democracy Promotion*, 442.

[18] See the speech at http://www.cfr.org/publication/22114/remarks_by_presidents_obama_and_karzai_may_2010.html.

> reality (international law, democracy, even better a combination of the two), and end up legitimating domination.[19]

The possible pitfalls of associating global constitutionalism with this form of (liberal) democracy could bring global constitutionalism into disrepute. How could such a form be considered as a truly global principle? It could bring with it a manifestation of the private/public dichotomy leading to possible exclusions of those not associated with the public sphere; it could place too much weight on individual autonomy, bringing associations with it about formal equality, meaning the anticipated assimilation of minority cultures to majority cultures, overall there is the potential that it would assist in the marginalisation of some and the domination of others. Such limitations could lead to the concept of global constitutionalism itself being regarded as parochial at best and as a tool for hegemony at worst. So is democracy on a global scale necessarily subject to hegemonic advancements? Susan Marks argues in favour of recasting democracy according to the 'principle of democratic inclusion'. Much like constitutionalist ideas, democratic ideas too provide the potential of a 'framework for emancipatory claims'.[20] Drawing on David Held's idea of democratic cosmopolitanism, Marks suggests viewing the conception of democracy not only as entailing a particular set of institutions and procedures, but also, as an 'ongoing call to enlarge the opportunities for popular participation in political processes and end social practices that systematically marginalize some citizens while empowering others'.[21] Unfortunately rather inelegantly, David Held was categorised above as belonging to the tradition of Institutional Constitutionalism due to his preoccupation with a multilayered system underlined by his view that the articulation of international civil society in the international public sphere may lie 'within the grasp of the UN system'.[22] It is precisely this preoccupation that Marks hopes to redirect her readers from in favour of a democracy that centres processes and is open-ended. This brings us back to the descriptions of 'organic' that were set out above. Just as it was previously stated that it should be possible to reconceptualise global constitutionalism to be organic, so it is possible – indeed essential – to include an organic approach to democracy. How would this be possible in practice? An international civil society and its emancipatory activities are crucial, but they should not be couched exclusively within the terminology of government, or even governance. It should therefore not be a condition for participation in the international legal sphere and within the

[19] Susan Marks, *The Riddle of all Constitutions: International Law, Democracy, and the Critique of Ideology* (OUP, Oxford 2003) 101.
[20] *Ibid* 103.
[21] *Ibid* 109.
[22] David Held, *Democracy and the Global Order: From the Modern State to Cosmopolitan Governance* (Polity Press, Cambridge 1995) 269.

global constitutional forum that a State be regarded as a democratic State by others. For who decides whether a State is democratically legitimated or not? Those that have reached the status of fully democratic States? When is this status reached? Democracy in the international sphere should be viewed as an ongoing project, much as global constitutionalism should be. This requires caution when it comes to institutionalising governance or government in the international sphere. It certainly requires caution with projects of 'promoting democracy'. I have some sympathy with Teubner's vision of disassociating democracy from the State. The participants on the international sphere could be viewed as international civil society composed of individuals and groups. I am also sympathetic to Teubner's emphasis on digitalisation. It appears that internet accessibility is growing strongly across various States and demographics. Possibly, a virtual forum could be created. Such suggestions would of course require further in-depth analysis of possibilities of participation and exchange. Such analysis would have to include considerations of limitations and assumptions of literacy, current State censorship (for example in China or Turkey), and internet connectivity.

B. *Institutional Constitutionalism*

Institutional Constitutionalism places questions of accountability at the forefront of reflections on constitutionalism. In these contributions to the debate, the locus of power is identified in a first step, and this is then underscored by a constitutional order in a second step. The first vision of Institutional Constitutionalism that was described in Chapter 1 was the idea of global governance. Global governance advocates identify many power hubs that require legitimacy through accountability rather than only one locus of power. This type of global constitutionalism is put forward by a number of scholars including Anne Peters and Jürgen Habermas. The second variant of Institutional Constitutionalism focused on international institutions that are constituted through multilateral treaties. This is of course where the United Nations Charter becomes relevant. Bardo Fassbender is one of the most prominent proponents of the view that the UN Charter is the global constitution. Distinct from this idea, yet with many similarities, is the idea that specialised institutions and fields of international law are constitutionalising – referred to as microconstitutionalism becoming macroconstitutionalism. The prime example for this process is the WTO, which was first regarded as constitutionalising within the limits of trade law and is now considered as (at least part of the process of) constitutionalising the international legal order as a whole.

Much of the aforementioned thoughts on democracy also apply here: The advocates of Institutional Constitutionalism emphasise democratic features and thus regard discourses on government and governance as situated within global constitutional discourse. Specific to this view is quite plainly the institutional aspect. The default for Institutional Constitutionalism in practice revolves around either the establishment of new constitutional institutions or reform of existing institutions. Prominent are particularly the two views that (a) we are dealing with a multilayered and multifaceted phenomenon that requires streamlining, and (b) that one particular institution already provides a constitutional framework and it is a matter of either simply identifying this capacity or introducing some reforms to ensure this capacity. The UN Charter has some significance for the former view and is particularly relevant for the latter view. Within the global constitutional debate, considerable attention has been devoted to a descriptive or a normative engagement with the UN Charter as the global constitution. The default implementation of Institutional Constitutionalism would most likely be in the form of UN action or UN reform. Anne Peters, who has written extensively on global constitutionalism, views UN action as a necessary instrument for constitutionalism. In her view, global constitutionalism should be shaped to become a multi-unit democracy, or 'dual democracy', composed of democracy within nation States on the one hand and democratic governance 'above' States on the other hand.[23] Her views on UN action are a possible form of what Institutional Constitutionalism could look like if implemented.

The first step to achieving this 'fully democratized world order' is to promote democracy *within* States. It is worth noting here that democracy is, according to Peters, one of a number of constitutional principles including the rule of law, due process, and the protection of fundamental rights and minorities.[24] These principles are of course all central to the liberal democratic ethos and Peters' form of advocating democracy is to be understood as placed within this same tradition. Coming back to UN action *within* States, Peters praises the involvement of the UN as a vehicle of democracy. Examples she names include the 2005 World Summit Outcome, which asserted that democracy is a universal value,[25] the commitment to election monitoring through General Assembly resolutions,[26] and assistance through the UN Democracy Fund. So what happens when States fall short of this requirement of democracy? Peters considers this an infringement of global constitutional law. By speaking of 'requirements', Peters inevitably slips into interventionist rhetoric:

> On the premise that all states have a legal interest in compliance with international constitutional law, all, or at least those states which are 'specially affected', should be allowed to impose unilateral, non-military, and proportionate countermeasures against those states which breach the prohibition of retrogression.[27]

---

[23] *Peters* (n 5) 264.
[24] *Ibid* 261.
[25] UN Doc. A/60/1 of 24 October 2005.
[26] GA Res. 45/150 (1990); GA Res. 46/137 (1991).
[27] *Peters* (n 5) 284. Peters references Art. 54 ILC Articles here, which speak of 'lawful countermeasures'.

This, once more, raises questions of who decides when a breach has been committed? Who decides which States are 'specially affected'? and what is proportionate? Democratising global governance provides Peters with some significant challenges. She explains that democracy in this context cannot refer to 'formal' democracy involving voting, elections, and representation of citizens on a territorial basis but must be something fitting to the international sphere.[28] She refers to the UN 2004 Cardoso Report, which deliberates on three new shapes of democracy: Deliberative democracy, participatory democracy, and contestatory democracy.[29] To her mind, however, these alternatives to formal democracy are likely to be too weak, maybe even too weak to at all deserve the label 'democracy'. They form no real substitutes for formal democracy in that ideally the mechanisms would 'have to be linked to voting at some point'.[30] Peters is clearly inveterate in regard to the idea of a universal formal (liberal) democracy on the national and international sphere, even if this means democracy intervention. Peters always returns to the UN for inspiration – this is partly what qualifies her as adhering to a form of Institutional Constitutionalism. Suggestions include a UN Parliamentary Assembly, existing in addition to the General Assembly.[31] The UN Parliamentary Assembly would be constituted through deputies proportionate to the population of the UN member states (which must, according to her requirement above, be democratic States). Such an Assembly would consult with the General Assembly and other organs, deliberate on potential General Assembly resolutions before voted on by the General Assembly, convey opinions, have a procedure for questioning the principal organs, request for General Assembly policies to be extended or amended, and propose new policies.[32] Such determination to refer to the UN structure subjects her work to criticisms of hegemony, ignorance or management of fragmentation, and manifestations of marginalisation. Peters has an admirable style of confronting possible criticisms in her work. She summarises and addresses the criticism relevant to her vision very methodically. However, while being able to express the weaknesses of her suggestions, she remains locked to the current system in a way that restricts the potential for any meaningful alternatives.

This is not to say that Peters does not have some valuable ideas regarding global constitutionalism that capture its emancipatory potential and that

[28] *Ibid* 268.

[29] *We the Peoples: Civil Society, the United Nations and Global Governance, Report of the Panel of Eminent Persons on United Nations-Civil Society Relations*. UN Doc. A/58/817 (11 June 2004).

[30] Anne Peters, 'Dual Democracy' in Jan Klabbers, Anne Peters, Geir Ulfstein (eds), *The Constitutionalization of International Law* (OUP, Oxford 2009) 270, 271.

[31] See Campaign for the Establishment of a United National Parliamentary Assembly, http://en.unpacampaign.org/index.php.

[32] *Peters* (n 5) 326. Peters references here Erskinge Childers and Brian Urquhart, *Renewing the United Nations System* (Dag Hamarskjöld Foundation, Uppsala 1994) 179.

involve civil society beyond the State structure. For example, she raises interesting ideas of transnational referendums and consultations and explores modes of citizens' representation and interest groups.[33] It appears that such creativity is essential among the proponents of global constitutionalism. Indeed, at a more fundamental level, I would also agree with Anne Peters that democracy is a universal value. However, crucially, I disagree in terms of her idea of what a universal democracy should look like and in terms of her idea for (formal) democracy as a 'requirement' of international law.[34] Democracy and global constitutionalism as mentioned above should be considered as works in progress, not as a 'thing' that has the potential to reach a certain (predetermined) standard. Certainly, accordance with such a 'thing' should not be viewed as a *sine qua non* for participation in the international legal sphere.

The vast majority of contributors to global constitutionalism explore the role of the UN – this same vast majority is sceptical of viewing the UN Charter *as it is* as the global constitution but suggests some form of UN reform. Bardo Fassbender is a prominent supporter of the view that the UN Charter should be regarded as *the* global constitution as one visible document that is to be understood as

> an authoritative statement of the fundamental rights and responsibilities of the members of the international community and the values to which this community is committed – a document that is also the basis of the most important community institutions.[35]

Most authors do not share this view; in contrast, they tend to suggest that some form of reform is necessary. Peters is quite pessimistic about the potential for reform but other authors are more optimistic.[36] Suggestions for UN reform within a global constitutional project mostly include restructuring and strengthening the Security Council and establishing a more substantial role for the International Court of Justice.[37] If Institutional Constitutionalism were to be implemented without the corrective force of organic global constitutionalism, it would most likely be within the framework of UN reform. Jürgen Habermas enumerates the requirements for reform. First, he says, the UN Security Council composition and the modus of decision-making must be reformed in a way which reflects the altered geopolitical conditions in the world. This should be done with the aim of strengthening the body itself, to ensure adequate representation of the power distribution and the different

---

[33] *Ibid* 318–320.
[34] *Ibid* 273.
[35] Bardo Fassbender, 'Rediscovering a Forgotten Constitution' in Jeffrey L. Dunoff and Joel P. Trachtman (eds), *Ruling the World? Constitutionalism, International Law, and Global Governance* (CUP, Cambridge 2009) 137.
[36] *Peters* (n 5) 325.
[37] See http://www.un.org/reform/.

regions, and to meet the demands and interests of an integrated superpower. Second, the Security Council must be independent from national interests both when determining its agenda and in decision-making. It must be bound by justiciable rules that determine when the UN is authorised and when it is *compelled* to intervene. Third, the executive must be allocated more funds; it must be given the possibility of access to Member State resources so that it can guarantee the effective enforcement of Security Council resolutions. Fourth, a law of intervention should be developed that is analogous to domestic policing and has the purpose of protecting populations from the consequences of UN actions and interventions. Fifth, the legislative decisions of the Security Council and the General Assembly require a strengthened, albeit indirect, legitimacy by a well-informed civil society. This is *inter alia* to be achieved through a stronger role of NGOs in UN institutions. Sixth, the activity of the UN must be restricted to clearly defined rights such as the protection from a war of aggression, international acts of violence, and serious and widespread human rights violations.[38] Habermas' idea of UN reform is clearly within the boundaries of liberal democratic ideas and works within the (specifically Kantian) tradition of making complex procedures abstract in order to universalise them. This form of reform would lead to stasis, a feature of global constitutionalism that leads to exclusions and the manifestation of marginalisations. What could make Institutional Constitutionalism more organic? To be sure, some structures are necessary for a practical application of organic global constitutionalism. But the structures must be designed in a way that allows room for change – not just to the material content of global constitutionalism, but also to the structure itself. Civil society involvement from a bottom-up approach seems to be less susceptible to interventionist reproaches than the current formal institutions. UN reform is a step in the right direction but is clearly not far-reaching enough and carries the danger of just causing *different* marginalisations and a *different* kind of hegemony rather than attempting to address these limitations in a meaningful way. To my mind, the UN has no role to play in organic global constitutionalism unless it is so substantially restructured – and possibly also renamed – to include civil society proper.

C. *Normative Constitutionalism*

The term Normative Constitutionalism was employed to categorise those views of global constitutionalism that centre on the importance of a common normative (value) system. First, visions of a world law, as portrayed by Angelika Emmerich-Fritsche and Jost Delbrück were illustrated; second, visions pertaining to a hierarchy of norms put forward by Brun-Otto Bryde and Luigi Ferragoli were discussed; and third, visions of fundamental norms

[38] Jürgen Habermas, *Der Gespaltene Westen* (Suhrkamp Verlag, Frankfurt 2004) 172, 123.

were presented as ideas stemming from, *inter alia*, Michael Byers and Erika de Wet. The default global constitutionalist implementation of Normative Constitutionalism would most likely lie in the drafting of a human rights catalogue. Since this vision of global constitutionalism is strongly associated with a common global value system, efforts would most likely be directed towards codifying such values. In contemporary international legal scholarship, the predominant means of expressing common values is through the language of human rights.

The previous chapters argued that such pre-eminence of a common value system leads to significant limitations. The focus of civil and political rights preferred in the West, for example, is mostly at the cost of socio-economic rights. The former are largely associated with Western or liberal interests. The act of codifying fundamental norms is furthermore an enterprise that can lead to important exclusions. Which interests are not included in the relevant catalogue is highly relevant for the creation of a hierarchy of interests: the interests that are excluded are at the same time excluded from discussion. This can precipitate the ostracism of certain individuals and groups. How could a move to organic global constitutionalism act as a corrective to such exclusions? For one, it appears that the human rights language may not be suitable as a global constitutional language. In his article *International Law in Asia: The Limits of Western Constitutionalist and Liberal Doctrines*, Jean d'Aspremont considers the values-language and its reception in Asia. He explains that the liberal and values-oriented views of the international legal order, which are the preferred views of Western scholars have been received with hesitation and caution among Asian scholars.[39] His suggestion pertains to a minimising of the role of values in the international legal order. This indeed appears the only means to make the debate more 'global'. This is not to say that interests should not be given prominence in a global constitutionalist debate; indeed, it is impossible to engage in a debate about social change and law without awarding interests a central position. While d'Aspremont, like most Western scholars, is still focussed on the issue of finding common ground, the negative universal in the past chapter suggested an approach that looks at particularities rather than the universal. The idea of the negative universal gives prominence to interests, but it would not try to force the determination of a common ground. An example may make this more comprehensible: Take for example the much-debated question of counter-terrorism. For many Western scholars (and politicians), the debate concerns the establishment of the correct balance between the respect for human rights on the one hand and security measures on the other hand. Much scholarly attention has been dedicated to defining the term

[39] Jean d'Aspremont, 'International Law in Asia: The Limits to the Western Constitutionalist and Liberal Doctrines' (2008) 13 Asian Yearbook of International Law 89–111.

'terrorism' as a necessary component of addressing the issue from a legal perspective. It is thought that the establishment of a balance and the determination of a definition of 'terrorism' is key to social change. An organic approach however, would take seriously and revitalise the almost trite phrase 'one man's terrorist is another man's freedom fighter' and it would embrace the indeterminate nature of the term 'terrorism'. Various actors, which includes but is certainly not limited to States, would discuss what it is to their mind that captures the term 'terrorism' refers to in this moment in time. This discussion would clarify differences in perception. This is not to say that elucidating differences leads to chaos and inhibits change. Quite the contrary, illuminating differences is to be regarded as an engine for social change. To come back to the image of the *Haida Gwaii* in the previous chapter, all participants in a debate about differences would nevertheless be steering in the same direction: a global understanding of the differences of what terrorism means and the associations it has. Global Constitutionalism itself thereby becomes unavoidably a universal value. An organic approach to Normative Constitutionalism would abandon the idea of drafting a catalogue of rights and would rather centre on a discourse of varying interests. Where would such a discourse take place? Everywhere: It would take place in the work of scholars; it would take place among political actors; it would take place among drafters of legislation; it would take place among those that implement legislation; and it would take place in society at large.

D. *Analogical Constitutionalism*

Analogical Constitutionalism is advocated by scholars that find certain patterns in the international sphere which are familiar to them from their own legal systems; they then apply the familiar concept to the international sphere. This view is underpinned by the belief that there are certain universal concepts that apply in the international sphere as they do in the domestic system. Meta-Rules Constitutionalism was described as the first form of Analogical Constitutionalism. Since eminent scholars of this view, Alfred Verdross and Christian Tomuschat, have now departed from it in favour of a substantive focus on constitutionalism, the section was fairly brief. The idea that concepts and institutions in the international sphere are analogous to certain domestic constitutional orders was examined with specific reference to Robert Uerpmann's vision of global Constitutionalism as mirroring German constitutionalism. And finally, European constitutionalism was mentioned since it too is regarded as a model for global constitutionalism. Indeed, it appears that this latter type would be the favoured method for the implementation of Analogical Constitutionalism. It should be reiterated that of course all visions of global constitutionalism necessarily include analogies to domestic constitutionalism. Simply by the use of the term 'constitutionalism', which is a term that found its meaning in 17th and 18th century Western constitutional struggles, some form of analogy is employed. If some organisation, group of scholars, or politicians were to draft a global constitution, it is likely that the impetus will come from such an organisation, scholars or politicians who believe that their own legal system works well and who think that their constitution was key to facilitating the existing system. David Kennedy writes that in this case the interpretation of the world in constitutional terms can 'feel like a project of the utmost seriousness and urgency'.[40] The lesson from the EU has been that people are sceptical of a document named a 'constitution' that frames more than one legal order. Four years after it received the first draft for a constitutional treaty for the European Union, the European Council announced that it was abandoning this enterprise and was instead opting for the more modest 'Reform Treaty'.[41] EU constitutional debates have taught us that even for an entity that already has a common legal system in many areas, the word 'constitution' implies something stronger than a loose framework. We have also learnt that even for a fairly homogenous region such as Europe, a document labelled 'constitution', although appealing to lawyers and politicians, finds little appeal with populations outside of their own domestic legal setting. Mattias Kumm certainly has a point when he speaks of 'a general tendency to idealize national law and to cast a general shadow of suspicion on international [or generally supranational] law.[42] Finally, this experience has taught us that legal theorists are extremely pertinacious when it comes to constitutionalism at a supranational level. Although the constitutional treaty was rejected, thinkers are still adamant that this political defeat has no significance in terms of the actual reality of the existence of a constitution.[43] This clinging on is of course highly undemocratic. And more importantly, not all legal structures that work for State systems necessarily also work for the international legal sphere. If the term constitutionalism is employed it must itself be emancipated from the inevitably liberal democratic and formalistic associations it currently still bears.

Conclusion

This chapter has explored how the four dimensions of global constitutionalism could play out in practice and how they could be made more organic in

---

[40] David Kennedy, 'The Mystery of Global Governance' in Jeffrey L. Dunoff and Joel P. Trachtman (eds), *Ruling the World? Constitutionalism, International Law, and Global Governance* (CUP, Cambridge 2009) 40.

[41] Presidency Conclusions, Brussels European Council (21–22 June 2007), 11177/1/07 Rev. 1 Conc 2.

[42] *Kumm* (n 2) 323.

[43] Stefan Kadelbach and Thomas Kleinlein, 'International Law – a Constitution for Mankind? An Attempt at a Re-appraisal with an Analysis of Constitutional Principles' (2007) 50 GYIL 322.

order to prevent a manifestation of the already existing limitations in the international legal order. So is this all merely speculation? Is the concern about such manifestations indeed a straw man argument? I believe not. Judging by the prominence of global constitutionalism in international law, international relations, and political philosophy, the topic is very much at the forefront about concerns of the global legal arrangements. This study has already shown that the debate, although seemingly complex, is one-dimensional in that it appears to treat a vision of liberal democratic constitutionalism as the only available form of constitutionalism. Of course the debate is currently restricted to theory and therefore has limited scope in practice. How it will play out in practice, which it inevitably will, is a matter of terminology. It is possible that instead of 'global constitutionalism', the term 'global governance' will become prominent, or maybe it will be 'global civil society'. As shown in the mapping of the debate, these terms are all part of the discourse of how to capture and express the *de facto* changes in the international sphere. Global constitutionalism is an effort to rethink the global legal order and it is in this crucial time of rethinking that potential marginalisations must be ruled out and the emancipatory power of constitutionalism must be animated. David Kennedy reminds us that 'the traditional legal disciplines – public international law, private international law, international economic law, comparative law, UN law – are also projects of reinvention'.[44] Each of these disciplines began as a project for mapping the global regime more accurately. Such mapping includes both an element of description and an element of normativity: Some elements are described in order to be interpreted as meaning a particular principle. The object of this chapter has been to think about these projects from a practical perspective. In the manner of the previous chapters, an enumeration and summary follows:

1) *Social Constitutionalism* would most likely play out as democracy promotion if put into practice. Such democracy promotion could provoke interventions of a military or non-military kind and a forceful universalisation of Western ideology. But, democracy does not necessarily need to be viewed as pertaining to institutions and procedures; it too can be recast in a way that Susan Marks has coined the 'principle of democratic inclusion'. International civil society could be key to such reconfigured global political processes.
2) If implemented with no organic corrective, *Institutional Constitutionalism* would plausibly follow UN action or UN reform. The UN is structurally so flawed as it is that the designation of the UN Charter as the global constitutionalism would most likely bring with it concerns of hegemony.

[44] *Kennedy* (n 40) 43.

Organic global constitutionalism could work as a corrective to alert decision-makers to the necessity of viewing constitutionalism as an ongoing process. It could also accentuate the emancipatory potential of constitutionalism for those that may have been marginalised in the past.

3) *Normative Constitutionalism* would most likely be implemented in the form of a global constitutional rights catalogue. This would probably be a human rights catalogue, similar to the International Covenant on Civil and Political Rights and the International Covenant on Economic, Social and Cultural Rights. The problems with cataloguing certain rights range from difficulties in determinism, decisions on what and who to exclude, and the required protection, recognition and enforcement by a State. This kind of catalogue may be accompanied by the establishment of a World Constitutional Court, which would raise a number of similar concerns. In order to meet these concerns, organic global constitutionalism would encourage a reorientation towards interests and principles rather than a strict human rights language; it would be in favour of a more political process rather than a focus on pre-political rights; finally, it would give preference to alternatives that do not include a written document of substantive rights.
4) The default implementation of *Analogical Constitutionalism* would predictably be modelled on EU constitutionalism. Due to the unpopularity of EU constitutionalism with EU Member State citizens, this could mean that the idea of global constitutionalism could terminate before it has begun. To make this form of constitutionalism more organic, the flexibility of the vision must be stressed. Crucially, global constitutionalism must be reconfigured and must be seen as being reconfigured to a conception distinct from the international and transnational sphere.

The preceding speculations have shown that, although a minor and modest contribution, organic global constitutionalism could nevertheless have an important role to play if global constitutionalism were to be put into practice.

CONCLUSION

This book has highlighted some limitations of prevalent visions of global constitutionalism, and has made some suggestions for reducing such limitations. To begin with it was found that the relevant literature suggests a complex and multi-dimensional picture, but that in all its dimensions global constitutionalism takes its bearings from the same key themes, rooted in the same European legal-political traditions (Chapter 1). The historical roots of the key themes of constitutionalism were examined next (Chapter 2). The entrenchment within current trajectories of a particular political tradition was then shown to burden prevailing approaches to global constitutionalism with some important blindspots and biases (Chapter 3). However, rather than advocating the abandonment of the idea of global constitutionalism (were that possible), the above proposed its recuperation, in the shape of organic global constitutionalism (Chapter 4). Finally, it was examined how the contemporary theoretical debate is likely to play out in practice and how an organic approach may be implemented to correct some of the limitations (Chapter 5).

It seems sensible to close with going back to what I said I had set out to do. In the introduction to this book, I stated that this book critically examines public international law contributions to the debate on global constitutionalism. In examining the various contributions to the debate on global constitutionalism, I ventured outside of what is traditionally understood to be public international law. Here, I would like to return to public international law and consider the impact of the debate on it as a field. Again, these are thoughts that have been touched on throughout this work, but it seems worthwhile bringing them out specifically. Questions that arise in regard to public international law are: How does organic global constitutionalism affect longstanding debates over the existence of an international legal order? How does it affect more recent discussions of the fragmentation of international law? Might it help to reconcile two principles of international law that have been engaged in a constant tug-of-war: universality and particularity?

It was highlighted in the questions on legitimacy that it is an assumption underlying all ideas of constitutionalism that, just as there is no society without law, so too there is no law without society. With this in mind, the first point to be made is that global constitutionalism, 'even' organic global constitutionalism, puts an end to questions about *whether* an international legal order exists; the only – and vital – question is *what type of* international legal order exists, and should exist. As was discussed in Chapters 3 and 5, this would have the further effect of legitimising international law itself: inasmuch as the recognition of global constitutionalism requires the recognition of international law as a distinct and legitimate body of law that is itself independent of domestic law.[1] The second point regards the impact of organic global constitutionalism on the discussions of fragmentation of international law (see Chapter 3). It is widely argued that the field of international law has become fragmented into a collection of specialised and independent areas of law. Due to the differing principles of law, the differing definitions of norms, and the differing institutional procedures, it is maintained that there is no longer a comprehensive and overarching international law. This suggests that the field has become a compendium of particularities, rather than a universal order. Organic global constitutionalism could provide a way of recovering the sense that international law is to be understood as a universal order, albeit a 'negative universal', since it requires the recognition of both fragmentation *and* the universal. The final point follows on from this. One of the themes running through the entire book is the question of bringing universality (i.e. the global applicability of certain matters) together with particularity (i.e. the recognition of the great diversity of the world). Organic global constitutionalism seeks to reconcile the two in some distinctive ways. While laying emphasis on constant renegotiation of the terms of political association (the particular), it nevertheless has strong normative features (the universal). The latter provides the aspect of shared frameworks and all-encompassing regimes, while the former addresses issues of diversity and open-endedness. The need for such reconciliation could scarcely be more evident today. As the idea of a First, Second and Third World collapsed with the Soviet regime, the 1990s were dedicated to according a voice to the different ideologies that remained. The various cultures were not willing to give in to the hegemony of the Western world. Ernesto Laclau, writing in 1995, stated in the Preface to his book *Emancipation(s)*:

> If we wanted briefly to characterize the distinctive features of the first half of the 1990s, I would say that they are to be found in the rebellion of various particularisms – ethnic, racial, national and sexual – against the totalizing ideologies which dominated the horizon of the politics of the preceding decades.[2]

Indeed, there was a large amount of literature written by academics – including international lawyers – seeking to take these particularities into account. However, it could be asserted that 9/11 altered the political (and therefore legal) priorities of the international sphere. In the aftermath of the attacks on the World Trade Centre and the Pentagon, diversity and particularisms were

---

[1] Anne Peters observes: 'the constitutionalist reading should clarify that the legitimacy of norms and of political rule does not depend on the structures of government or governance being exactly state-like' in 'The Merits of Global Constitutionalism' (2009) 16 Indiana Journal of Global Legal Studies 410.

[2] Ernesto Laclau, *Emanicaption(s)* (Verso, London 2007) vii.

no longer at the forefront of concern. Rather, the fight against terrorism demanded a united front of those States that had similar values. 9/11 provided an excuse for implementing far-reaching measures in the name of counter-terrorism. Since the Western States were the primary victims of the attacks, their actions initially remained largely unquestioned. This, however, changed relatively quickly. There has been a great deal of questioning following the events taking place at the Guantanamo Bay detention camp and at the Abu Ghraib prison. Most recently, the military strategies in Iraq and Afghanistan have been called into question as well as US designs on a possible invasion of Iran. It has become clear that a delicate balance is required between common interests that can be considered universal on the one hand, and different interests that can be considered particular on the other hand. Since organic global constitutionalism requires the recognition of universality as well as particularity, it offers a new way of articulating these interests – and hence a new way of *balancing* one of the central *imbalances* of international law.

BIBLIOGRAPHY

Alkema, E. A. 'The European Convention as a Constitution and its Court as a Constitutional Court' in Paul Mahoney, Franz Matscher, Herbert Petzold and others (eds), *Protecting Human Rights: The European Perspective – Studies in Memory of Rolv Ryssdall* (Carl Heymans, Cologne 2000).

Allen, Michael J. and Thompson, Brian *Cases and Materials on Constitutional & Administrative Law* (7th edn OUP, Oxford 2002).

Allott, Philip *Eunomia – New Order for a New World* (OUP, Oxford 1990).

Allot, Philip 'Reconstituting Humanity – New International Law' (1992) 3 European Journal of International Law 219–252.

Allot, Philip *Eunomia – New Order for a New World* (2nd edn OUP, Oxford 2001).

Allott, Philip *The Health of Nations* (CUP, Cambridge 2002).

Allott, Philip 'The Emerging International Aristocracy' (2003) 35 New York University Journal of International Law and Politics 309–338.

Anaya, S. James *Indigenous Peoples in International Law* (OUP, 2nd ed Oxford 2004).

Anghie, Antony *Imperialism, Sovereignty and the Making of International Law* (CUP, Cambridge 2007).

Aquinas, Thomas; D'Entrèves, Alessandro Passerin (ed), Dawson, J. G. (tr), (*Summa Theologiae* I), *Aquinas Selected Political Writings* (Blackwell, Oxford 1948).

Arendt, Hannah *The Origins of Totalitarianism* (Allen and Unwin London 1951).

Aristotle; Barker, Ernest (tr), *The Politics of Aristotle* (Clarendon Press, Oxford 1948).

Aristotle, Rees, D A (ed) Joachim, H H (tr), *The Nicomachean Ethics* (Clarendon Press, Oxford 1951).

D'Aspremont, Jean 'International Law in Asia: The Limits to the Western Constitutionalist and Liberal Doctrines' (2008) 13 Asian Yearbook of International Law 89–111.

St. Augustine; Green, W. M. (ed) *De Libero Arbitrio* in *Corpus Christianorum: Series Latina*, vol. 29 (Brepols, Tunhout 1970).

Balot, Ryan Krieger *Greek Political Thought* (Blackwell Publishing, Malden MA 2006).

Beauvoir, Simone De; Parshley, H. M. (tr), *The Second Sex* (Vintage Books, New York 1989).

Beck, Ulrich *Cosmopolitan Vision* (Polity, Cambridge 2006).

Bederman, David J. 'Reception of the Classical Tradition in International Law: Grotius' *De Jure Belli ac Pacis* (2006) 10 Emory International Law Review 1–21.

Bederman, David J. 'The Classical Constitution: Roman Republican Origins of the Habeas Suspension Clause' (2007–2008) 17 Southern Californian Interdisciplinary Law Journal.

Bellamy, Richard 'The Political Form of the Constitution: the Separation of Powers, Rights and Representative Democracy' in R Bellamy and D Castiglione *Constitutionalism in Transformation: European and Theoretical Perspectives* (Blackwell Publishers, Oxford 1996).

Benhabib, Seyla *Situating the Self* (Polity, Cambridge 1992).

Benvenisti, Eyal 'The Conception of International Law as a Legal System' (2008) 50 German Yearbook of International Law 393–405.

Bodansky, Daniel; Brunée, Jutta; Hey, Ellen 'International Environmental Law: Mapping the Field' in Daniel Bodansky et al. (eds), *Oxford Handbook of International Environmental Law* (OUP, Oxford 2007) 1ff.

Bodansky, Daniel M. 'Is there an International Environmental Constitution?' (2009) 16 Indiana Journal of Global Legal Studies 565–584.

Bogdany, Armin von; Dann, Philipp; Goldmann, Matthias 'Developing the Publicness of Public International Law: Towards a Legal Framework for Global Governance Activities' (2009) 9 German Law Journal 1377–1400.

Bogdandy, Armin von and Bast, Jürgen (eds), *Principles of European Constitutional Law: Modern Studies in European Law* (Hart Publishing, Oxford 2005).

Bogdandy, Armin von 'Constitutionalism in International Law: Comment on a Proposal from Germany' (2006) 47 Harvard International Law Journal 223–242.

Breau, Susan C. 'The Constitutionalization of the International Legal Order' (2008) 21 Leiden Journal of International Law 545–561.

Braithwaite, William T. 'An Introduction for Judges and Lawyers to Plato's *Apology of Socrates*' (1994) 25 Loyola University Chicago Law Journal 508–533.

Bryde, Brun-Otto 'Konstitutionalisierung des Völkerrechts und Internationalisierung des Verfassungsrechts' (2003) 42 Der Staat 61–75.

Bryde, Brun-Otto 'International Democratic Constitutionalism' in Ronald St. John Macdonald and Douglas M. Johnston (eds) *Towards World Constitutionalism: Issues in the Legal Ordering of the World Community* (Martinus Nijhoff Publishers, Leiden 2005).

ButleRitchie, David T. 'Critiquing Modern Constitutionalism' (2004) 3 Appalachian Journal of Law 37–49.

ButleRitchie, David T. 'Organic Constitutionalism: Rousseau, Hegel and the Constitution of Society' (2006) 6 Journal of Law in Society 36–81.

Byers, Michael 'Conceptualising the Relationship between *Jus Cogens* and *Erga Omnes* Rules' (1997) 66 Nordic Journal of International Law 211–239.

Capps, Patrick 'The Kantian Project in Modern International Legal Theory' (2001) 12 European Journal of International Law 1003–1025.

Capps, Patrick 'The Rejection of the Universal State' in Nicholas Tsagourias (ed) *Transnational Constitutionalism: International and European Models* (CUP, Cambridge 2007).

Carlyle, Alexander James *A History of Medieval Political Theory in the West* (New York and London, 1903).

Cass, Deborah Z. 'Navigating the Newstream: Recent Critical Scholarship in International Law' (1996) 65 Nordic Journal of International Law 341–381.

Cass, Deborah Z. *The Constitutionalization of the World Trade Organization* (OUP, Oxford 2005).

Cassese, Antonio *International Law in a Divided World* (Clarendon Press, Oxford 1986).

Castiglione, Dario 'The Political Theory of the Constitution' in Richard Paul Bellamy, Richard Bellamy, Dario Castiglione (eds) *Constitutionalism in Transformation: European and Theoretical Perspectives* (Blackwell Publishers, Oxford 1996).

Caygill, Howard and Scott, Alan 'The Basic Law versus the Basic Norm? The Case of the Bavarian Crucifix Order' in Richard Bellamy and Dario Castiglione (eds) *Constitutionalism in Transformation: European and Theoretical Perspectives* (Blackwell Publishers, Oxford 1996).

Charlesworth, Hilary, Chinkin, Christine and Wright, Shelley 'Feminist Approaches to International Law' (1991) 85 American Journal of International Law 613–645.

Charlesworth, Hilary and Chinkin, Christine 'The Gender of *Jus Cogens*' (1993) 15 Human Rights Quarterly 63–76.

Charlesworth, Hilary 'Remarks' in *Contemporary International Law Issues: Opportunities at a Time of Momentous Change: Proceedings of the Second Joint Conference held in The Hague, The Netherlands July 22–23, 1993* (Martinus Nijhoff Publishers 1994).

Charlesworth, Hilary 'Feminist Methods in International Law' (1999) 93 American Journal of International Law 379–394.

Charlesworth, Hilary and Chinkin, Christine, *The Boundaries of International Law* (Melland Shill Studies in International Law, Manchester University Press 2000).

Chesterton, G. K. *The Thing: Why I am a Catholic* (Dodo Press, Gloucester 2009).

Childers, Erskinge; Urquhart, Brian *Renewing the United Nations System* (Dag Hamarskjöld Foundation, Uppsala 1994).

Chinkin, Christine, Wright, Shelley and Charlesworth, Hilary 'Feminist Approaches to International Law: Reflections from Another Century' in Doris Buss, Ambreena Manje (eds), *International Law: Modern Feminist Approaches* (Hart Publishing, Oxford 2005) 17–45.

Chroust, Anton-Hermann 'The Philosophy of Law of St. Augustine' (1944) 53 The Philosophical Review 195–202.

Cicero, Marcus Tullius; Yonge, C. D. (tr, ed), *De Natura Deorum, The Treatises of M. T. Cicero* (George Bell and Sons, London 1878) 15.

Cicero, Marcus Tullius, Keyes, Clinton W. (tr), *De Re Republica, De Legibus* (HUP, Cambridge MA 1948).

Cobbett, William *The Parliamentary History of England, from the Earliest Period to the Year 1803*, vol XVI (T. C. Hansard, London 1813).

Cogan, Neil H. (ed) *The Complete Bill of Rights – The Drafts, Debates, Sources and Origins* (OUP, New York 1997).
Coriden, James A. *An Introduction to Canon Law* (2nd edn Paulist Press, New York 2004).
Craven, Matthew; Marks, Susan; Simpson, Gerry; Wilde, Ralph 'We are Teachers of International Law' (2004) 17 Leiden Journal of International Law 363–374.
Davies, Howard 'Global Financial Regulation after the Credit Crisis' (2010) 1 Global Policy 185–195.
Delbrück, Jost 'Wirksameres Völkerrecht oder neues "Weltinnenrecht"? Perspektiven der Völkerrechtsentweicklung in einem sich wandelnden internationalen System' in Klaus Dicke et al (eds) *Die Konstitution des Friedens als Rechtsordnung* (Duncker & Humboldt, Berlin 1996).
Delbrück, Jost 'Laws in the Public Interest – Some Observations on the Foundations and Identification of *erga omnes* Norms in International Law' in Volkmar Götz (eds) *Liber amicorum Günther Jaenicke – zum 85. Geburtstag* (Springer, Berlin 1999).
Delbrück, Jost 'Perspektiven für ein "Weltinnenrecht"?' in Gedächtnisschrift für Jürgen Sonnenschein (De Gruyter Recht, Berlin 2003) 793.
Derrida, Jacques *Specters of Marx* (Routledge Classics, New York 2006).
Douglas, Eduardo De Jesus 'The Colonial Self: Homosexuality and Mestizaje in the Art of Nahum B. Zenil' (1998) 57 Art Journal 15–21.
Dunoff, Jeffrey L. 'Why Constitutionalism *Now*? Text, Context and Historical Contingency of Ideas' (2005) 1 Journal of International Law & International Relations 191–212.
Dunoff, Jeffrey L. and Trachtman, Joel P. (eds) *Ruling the World: Constitutionalism, International Law, and Global Governance* (CUP, Cambridge 2009).
Dupuy, Pierre-Marie 'The Constitutional Dimension of the Charter of the United Nations Revisited' (1997) 1 Max Planck Yearbook of United Nations Law 1–33.
Duverger, Maurice (ed) *Constitutions et Documents Politiques* (Presses Universitaires de France, Paris 1996).
Emmerich-Fritsche, Angelika *Vom Völkerrecht zum Weltrecht* (Duncker & Humboldt, Berlin 2007).
Fassbender, Bardo 'The United Nations Charter As Constitution of the International Community' (1998) 36 Columbia Journal of Transnational Law 529–619.
Fassbender, Bardo 'The Meaning of International Constitutional Law' in Ronald St. John Macdonald and Douglas M. Johnston (eds), *Towards World Constitutionalism – Issue in the Legal Ordering of the World Community* (Martinus Nijhoff, Leiden 2005).
Fassbender, Bardo 'The Meaning of International Constitutional Law' in Nicholas Tsagourias (ed) *Transnational Constitutionalism: International and European Perspectives* (CUP, Cambridge 2007).
Fassbender, Bardo 'Rediscovering a Forgotten Constitution' in Jeffrey L. Dunoff and Joel P. Trachtman (eds) *Ruling the World: Constitutionalism, International Law, and Global Governance* (CUP, Cambridge 2009).
Fastenrath, Ulrich 'Relative Normativity in International Law' (1993) 4 European Journal of International Law 305–340.
Ferrajoli, Luigi 'Beyond Sovereignty and Citizenship: a Global Constitutionalism' in Richard Bellamy (ed) *Constitutionalism, Democracy and Sovereignty: American and European Perspectives* (Avebury, Aldershot 1997).
Fischer-Lescano, Andreas 'Die Emergenz der Globalverfassung' (2003) 63 Zeitschrift für ausländisches und öffentliches Recht 717–760.
Fitzpatrick, Peter 'What are Gods to us now?: Secular Theology and the Modernity of Law' (2007) 8 Theoretical Inquiries in Law 161–190.
Friedrich, Carl J. *Transcendent Justice: The Religious Dimension of Constitutionalism* (Duke University Press, Durham N.C. 1964).
Friedmann, Wolfgang *The Changing Structure of International Law* (Stevens, London 1964).
Fukuyama, Francis *The End of History and the Last Man* (Free Press, New York 1992).
Gagarin, Michael and Woodruff, Paul (eds) *Early Greek Political Thought from Homer to the Sophists* (CUP, New York 1995).
Gallie, Walter Bryce (1956) 56 Proceedings of the Aristotelian Society 167–198.
Gilligan, Carol *In a Different Voice* (Harvard University Press, Cambridge MA 1982).
Goldsmith, Jack L. and Posner, Eric A. *The Limits of International Law* (OUP, Oxford 2005).

Grant, Edward *A History of Natural Philosophy: From the Ancient World to the Nineteenth Century* (CUP, Cambridge 2007).
Gray, Christopher B. *The Philosophy of Law: An Encyclopaedia* (Taylor & Francis, 1999).
Greer, Steven C. *The European Convention on Human Rights* (CUP, Cambridge 2006).
Grey, Thomas C 'Constitutionalism: An Analytic Framework' in J Roland Pennock and John W Chapman (eds), *Constitutionalism* (New York University Press, New York 1979).
Grotius, Hugo Schätzel, Walter (tr), *Hugo Grotius: De Jure Belli ac Pacis – Libri Tres* (Mohr Siebeck, Tübingen 1950).
Haakonssen, Knud *Natural Law and Moral Philosophy* (CUP, Cambridge 1996).
Habermas, Jürgen; Lenhardt, Christian; Nicholsen, Shierry Weber (tr), *Moral Consciousness and Communicative Action*, (The MIT Press, Cambridge MA 1990).
Habermas, Jürgen 'Struggles for recognition' in Amy Gutmann (ed) *Multiculturalism: Examining the Politics of Recognition* (Princeton University Press, Princeton 1994).
Habermas, Jürgen; Rehg, William (tr), *Between Facts and Norms: Contributions to a Discourse Theory of Law and Democracy*, (The MIT Press, Cambridge MA 1998).
Habermas, Jürgen *Der Gespaltene Westen* (Suhrkamp Verlag, Frankfurt 2004).
Habermas, Jürgen; Cronin, Ciaran (tr), 'Does the Constitutionalization of International Law Still Have a Chance?' in *The Divided West* (Polity, Cambridge 2006).
Haines, Charles Grove *The Revival of Natural Law Concepts* (Harvard University Press, Cambridge MA 1930).
Hallowell, John H *The Moral Foundation of Democracy* (University of Chicago Press, Chicago 1954).
Haltern, Ulrich 'Internationales Verfassungsrecht?' (2003) 128 Archiv des Öffentlichen Rechts 511–556.
Hanisch, Carol 'The Personal is Political' in Shulamith Firestone, Anne Koedt (eds) *Notes from the Second Year: Women's Liberation in 1970* (Radical Feminism, New York 1970).
Hannikainen, Lauri *Peremptory Norms (Jus Cogens) in International Law: Historical Development, Criteria, Present Status* (Lakimiesliiton Kustannus: Finnish lawyer's Publishing Co, Helsinki 1989).
Hansen, Mogens Herman *Polis: An Introduction to the Ancient Greek City-State* (OUP, Oxford 2006).
Hart, HLA *The Concept of Law* (OUP, Oxford 1981).
Hegel, G.W.F.; Knox, T.M. (tr), *Philosophy of Right* (OUP, Oxford 1952).
Held, David *Democracy and the Global Order: From the Modern State to Cosmopolitan Governance* (Stanford University Press, Stanford 1995).
Henkin, Louis *The Age of Rights* (Columbia University Press, New York 1990).
Hershey, Amos Shartle *The Essentials of International Public Law* (The Macmillan Company, New York 1912).
Hobbes, Thomas; Gaskin, J. C. (tr) *Leviathan* (OUP, Oxford 1998).
Hobe, Stephan 'Völkerrecht im Zeitalter der Globalisierung' (2003) 41 Archiv des Völkerrechts 453–282.
Hobsbawm, Eric *The Age of Empire, 1875–1914* (Pantheon Books, New York 1987).
Jaenicke, Günther 'Zur Frage des Internationalen Ordre Public' (1967) 7 Berichte der Deutschen Gesellschaft für Völkerrecht 31–93.
Jellinek, Georg *Allgemeine Staatslehre* (Athenaeum Verlag, Bodenheim 1982).
Johansen, Karsten Friis and Rosenmeier, Henrik (tr), *A History of Ancient Philosophy: From the Beginnings to Augustine* (Routledge, New York 1998).
Jones, W. T. *Masters of Political Thought: Machiavelli to Bentham*, vol II (Houghton Mifflin, Boston 1947).
Kadelbach, Stefan and Kleinlein, Thomas 'Überstaatliches Verfassungsrecht: Zur Konstitutionalisierung im Völkerrecht' (2006) 44 Archiv des Völkerrechts 235–266.
Kadelbach, Stefan and Kleinlein, Thomas 'International Law – a Constitution for Mankind? An Attempt at a Re-appraisal with an Analysis of Constitutional Principles' (2007) 50 German Yearbook of International Law 303–348.
Kadelbach, Stefan Völkerrecht als Verfassungsordnung? Zur Völkerrechtswissenschaft in Deutschland' (2007) 67 Zeitschrift für ausländisches öffentliches Recht und Völkerrecht 599–621.
Kant, Immanuel; Beck, Lewis White (tr), (*Zum Ewigen Frieden*) *Perpetual Peace* (Bobbs-Merrill, Indianapolis 1957).

Kant, Immanuel; Gregor, Mary J (tr, ed) (*Metaphysik der* Sitten) Metaphysics *of Morals*, (CUP, Cambridge 1998).
Kaplan, E. Ann *Looking for the Other: Feminism, Film, and the Imperial Gaze* (Routledge, New York 1997).
Kelsen, Hans; Paulson, Bonnie L. & Paulson, Stanley L. (tr) *Introduction to Problems of Legal Theory* (Clarendon Press, Oxford 1992).
Kelsen, Hans *Reine Rechtslehre* (Verlag Österreich, Wien 2000).
Kennedy, David 'The International Style in Postwar Law and Policy' (1994) 7 Utah Law Review 7–104.
Kennedy, David 'The Disciplines of International Law and Policy' (1999) 12 Leiden Journal of International Law 9–133.
Kennedy, David (2001) 'The Forgotten Politics of International Governance' 6 European Human Rights Law Review 117–125.
Kennedy, David 'The Mystery of Global Governance' in Jeffrey L. Dunoff and Joel P. Trachtman (eds) *Ruling the World? Constitutionalism, International Law, and Global Governance* (CUP, Cambridge 2009).
Kern, Udo *Was Ist und Was Sein Soll* (Walter de Gruyter, Berlin 2007).
Kipling, Rudyard *Just so Stories* (1902).
Klabbers, Jan 'Constitutionalism Lite' (2004) 1 International Organizations Law Review 31–58.
Klabbers, Jan *An Introduction to International Institutional Law* (2nd edn CUP, Cambridge 2009)
Klabbers, Jan; Peters, Anne; Ulfstein, Geir *The Constitutionalization of International Law* (OUP, Oxford 2009).
Koji, Teraya 'Emerging Hierarchy in International Human Rights and Beyond' (2001) 12 European Journal of International Law 917–941.
Kokott, Juliane 'Report on Germany' in Anne-Marie Slaughter, Alec Stone Sweet, J.H.H. Weiler (eds), *The European Court and National Courts – Doctrine and Jurisprudence: Legal Change in its Social Context* (Hart Publishing, Oxford 1998).
Koskenniemi, Martti & Leino, Päivi 'Fragmentation of International Law? Postmodern Anxieties' (2002) 15 Leiden Journal of International Law 553–579.
Koskenniemi, Martti *The Gentle Civilizer of Nations: The Rise and Fall of International Law 1870–1960* (CUP, Cambridge 2004).
Koskenniemi, Martti 'International Law and Hegemony: A Reconfiguration' (2004) 17 Cambridge Review of International Affairs 197–218.
Koskenniemi, Martti *From Apology to Utopia* (CUP, Cambridge 2005).
Koskenniemi, Martti 'Constitutionalism as Mindset: Reflections on Kantian Themes about International Law and Globalization' (2007) 8 Theoretical Inquiries into Law 9–36.
Krisch, Nico and Kingsbury, Benedict 'Introduction: Global Governance and Global Administrative Law in the International Legal Order' (2006) 17 European Journal of International Law 1ff.
Krisch, Nico 'The Pluralism of Global Administrative Law' (2006) 17 European Journal of International Law 247–278.
Kuhn, Thomas *The Structure of Scientific Revolution* (University of Chicago Press, Chicago 1962).
Kumm, Mattias 'The Legitimacy of International Law: A Constitutionalist Framework of Analysis' (2004) 15 European Journal of International Law 907–931.
Kumm, Mattias 'The Cosmopolitan Turn in Constitutionalism' in Jeffrey L. Dunoff and Joel P. Trachtman (eds) *Ruling the World? Constitutionalism, International Law, and Global Governance* (CUP, Cambridge 2009).
Laclau, Ernesto *Emancipation(s)* (Verso, London 2007).
Lammert, Norbert *Verfassung, Patriotismus, Leitkultur: Was Unsere Gesellschaft Zusammenhält* (Hoffmann und Campe, Hamburg 2006).
Lauterpacht, Hersch 'Japan and the Covenant' (1932) 3 Political Quarterly 174–194.
Lauterpacht, Hersch 'The Covenant as the Higher Law' (1936) XVII British Yearbook of International Law 54–65.
Lawrence, Thomas Joseph *The Principles of International Law* (D.C. Heath & Co, Boston 1910).
Leary, Virginia 'The Effect of Western Perspectives on International Human Rights' in Abdullahi Ahmed An-Na'im and Francis M. Deng (eds) *Human Rights in Africa: Cross-Cultural Perspectives* (The Brookings Institution, Washington DC 1990).

Lewis, Ewart 'Natural Law and Expediency in Medieval Political Theory' (1940) 50 Ethics 144–163.

Lippert, Stefan *Recht und Gerechtigkeit bei Thomas von Aquin – Eine Rationale Rekonstruktion im Kontext der Summa Theologiae* (N.G. Elwert Verlag Marburger Theologische Studien, Marburg 2000).

Locke, John *Two Treatise of Government* (C. and J. Rivington, London 1824).

Locke, John; Laslett, Peter (ed) *Two Treatise of Government* (CUP, Cambridge 1991).

Long, A. A. 'Law and Nature in Greek Thought' in Michael Gagarin, David Cohen (eds), *The Cambridge Companion to Ancient Greek Law* (CUP, Cambridge 2005).

Luhmann, Niklas *Das Recht der Gesellschaft* (Suhrkamp, Frankfurt 1993).

MacKinnon, Catherine *Towards a Feminist Theory of the State* (Harvard University Press, Cambridge MA 1989).

Malanczuk, Peter and Akehurst, Michael Barton *Akehurst's Modern Introduction to International Law* (7th edn Routledge, London 1997).

Macdonald, Ronald St. John 'The International Community as a Legal Community' in Ronald St. John Macdonald and Douglas M. Johnston (eds), *Towards World Constitutionalism – Issues in the Legal Ordering of the World Community* (Brill, Leiden 2005).

Machiavelli, Niccolo; Bull, George Anthony and Grafton, Anthony (tr), (*Il Principe*) *The Prince*, (Penguin Classics, London 2003).

Madison, James 'Notes for Speech in Congress' June 8 1789 in Charles F. Hobson et al (ed) *Papers of James Madison*, (University Press of Virginia, Charlottesville 1979).

Maduro, Miguel Poiares 'From Constitutions to Constitutionalism: A Constitutional Approach for Global Governance' in Douglas Lewis (ed) *Global Governance and the Quest for Justice* vol I (Hart Publishing, Oxford and Portland, Oregan 2006).

Manning, Patrick *Migration in World History* (Routledge, New York 2005).

Marks, Susan 'State-Centrism, International Law, and the Anxieties of Influence' (2006) 19 Leiden Journal of International Law 339–347.

Marks, Susan and Clapham, Andrew *Human Rights Lexicon* (OUP, Oxford 2005).

Marks, Susan *The Riddle of all Constitutions: International Law, Democracy, and the Critique of Ideology* (OUP, Oxford 2003).

Miller, David 'Citizenship and Pluralism' (1995) 43 Political Studies 432–450.

Miller, Jean Baker *Toward a New Psychology of Women* (Beacon Press, Boston 1976).

Montesquieu, Baron de, Charles de Secondat *The Spirit of Law* (Francis Douglass and William Murray, Aberdeen 1756) Volume I.

Morrison, Toni *Playing in the Dark: Whiteness and the Literary Imagination* (Harvard University Press, Cambridge MA 1992).

Mosler, Hermann 'The International Society as a Legal Community' (1974) 140 Recueil des Cours de l'Académie de Droit International 1–320.

Mosler, Hermann *The International Society as a Legal Community* (Sijthoff & Noordhoff, Alphen aan den Rijn 1980).

Mutua, Makau wa 'The Ideology of Human Rights' (1995–1996) 36 Virginia Journal of International Law 588–657.

Noortmann, Math *Enforcing International Law: From Self-Help to Self-Contained Regimes* (Aldershot, Ashate 2005).

O'Brian, Claire Methven 'Reframing Deliberative Cosmopolitanism: Perspectives of Transnationalisation and Post-national Democracy from Labour Law – Part I/II' (2008) 9 German Law Journal 1007–1042.

Oeter, Stefan 'Federalism and Democracy' in Armin von Bogdandy and Jürgen Bast (eds) *Principles of European Constitutional Law* (2005).

Okere, B. Obinna 'The Protection of Human Rights in Africa and the African Charter on Human and Peoples' Rights: A Comparative Analysis with the European and American Systems' (1984) 6 Human Rights Quarterly 141–159.

Orford, Anne 'Muscular Humanitarianism: Reading the Narratives of the New Interventionism' (1999) 10 European Journal of International Law 678–689.

Pagden, Anthony and Lawrence, Jeremy (eds), *Francisco de Vitoria: Political Writings* (CUP, Cambridge 1991).

Pagden, Anthony 'Stoicism, Cosmopolitanism, and the Legacy of European Imperialism' (2000) 7 Constellations 3–22.

Paulus, Andreas L. 'The International Legal System as a Constitution' in Jeffrey L. Dunoff and Joel P. Trachtman (eds) *Ruling the World: Constitutionalism, International Law, and Global Governance* (CUP, Cambridge 2009).
Perry, Michael J. 'Are Human Rights Universal? The Relativist Challenge and Related Matters' (1997) 19 Human Rights Quarterly 461–509.
Peters, Anne 'Compensatory Constitutionalism: The Function and Potential of Fundamental International Norms and Structures' (2006) 19 Leiden Journal of International Law 579–610.
Peters, Anne 'Global Constitutionalism in a Nutshell' in Liber amicorum Jost Delbrück, *Weltinnenrecht* (2005).
Peters, Anne 'Völkerrecht im Gender-Fokus' in Andreas Zimmermann and Thomas Giegerich, *Gender und Internationales Recht* (Duncker & Humboldt, Berlin 2005).
Peters, Anne 'The Merits of Global Constitutionalism' (2009) 16 Indiana Journal of Global Legal Studies 397–411.
Petersmann, Ernst-Ulrich 'The WTO Constitution and Human Rights' (2000) 3 Journal of International Economic Law 19–25.
Petersmann, Ernst-Ulrich 'Europäisches und weltweites Integrations-, Verfassungs- und Weltbürgerrecht' in Claus Dieter Classen et al (eds) *In einem Vereinten Europa dem Frieden der Welt zu Dienen…* Liber amicorum Thomas Oppermann (Duncker & Humboldt, Berlin 2001).
Pogany, Istvan 'Constitution Making or Constitutional Transformation in Post-Communist Societies?' in Richard Bellamy and Dario Castiglione (eds) *Constitutionalism in Transformation: European and Theoretical Perspectives* (Blackwell Publishers, Oxford 1996).
Polansky, Antony *The Little Dictators: The History of Eastern Europe since 1918* (Routledge and Kegan Paul, London 1975).
Prak, Maarten Roy and Webb, Diane (tr), *The Dutch Republic in the Seventeenth Century* (CUP, Cambridge 2005).
Pufendorf, Baron Kennet, Basil (tr) *The Law of Nature and Nations: Or, A General System of the Most Important Principles of Morality, Jurisprudence, and Politics in Eight Books* (5th edn J and J Bonwicke, London 1749).
Rawls, John *The Law of Peoples* (Harvard University Press, Cambridge MA 2002).
Rickaby, Joseph *Scholasticism* (Constable, London 1911).
Robinson, William I. *Promoting Polyarchy: Globalization, U.S. Intervention and Hegemony* (CUP, Cambridge 1996).
Robinson, William I. 'What to Expect from US "Democracy Promotion" in Iraq (2004) 26 New Political Science 441–447.
Ross, Kristin *Fast Cars, Clean Bodies: Decolonization and the Reordering of French Culture* (The MIT Press, Cambridge MA 1996).
Rosenau, James N. 'Governance, Order, and Change in World Politics' in James N. Rosenau, Ernst-Otto Czempiel (eds) *Governance Without Government* (CUP, Cambridge 1992).
Rousseau, Jean-Jacques; Cole, G.D.H. (tr) *Social Contract and Discourses* (Dent, London 1973).
Rubenfeld, Jed 'The Two World Orders' (2003) 27 The Wilson Quarterly 22–36.
Rubenfeld, Jed 'Commentary: Unilateralism and Constitutionalism' (2004) 79 New York University Law Review 1971–2028.
Ruddy, Francis Stephen *International Law in the Enlightenment: The Background of Emmerich de Vattel's Le Droit des Gens* (Oceana Publications, New York 1975).
Said, Edward W. *Culture and Imperialism* (Alfred A. Knopf, New York 1993).
Salcedo, Juan Antonio Carrillo 'Reflections on the Existence of a Hierarchy of Norms in International Law' (1997) 8 European Journal of International Law 583–595.
Schwarzenberger, Georg 'International *Jus Cogens*?' (1965) 43 Texas Law Review 455–478.
Schweber, Howard *The Language of Liberal Constitutionalism* (CUP, Cambridge 2007).
Shakespeare, William *The Tempest* (Courier Dover Publications, London 1999).
Schwöbel, Christine E. J. 'Organic Global Constitutionalism' 23 Leiden Journal of International Law 529–553.
Shih, Chih-yu 'Opening the Dichotomy of Universalism and Relativism' (2002) 2 Human Rights and Human Welfare 13–24.
Simma, Bruno 'The Contribution of Alfred Verdross to the Theory of International Law' (1995) 6 European Journal of International Law 33–54.

Slaughter, Anne-Marie *A New World Order* (Princeton University Press, Princeton 2004).
Sophocles; Fagles, Robert (tr), *The Three Theban Plays – Antigone, Oedipus the King, Oedipus at Colonus* (Penguin Books, Harmondsworth 1982).
Squires, Judith 'Liberal Constitutionalism, Identity and Difference' in Richard Bellamy and Dario Castiglione (eds) *Constitutionalism in Transformation: European and Theoretical Perspectives* (Blackwell Publishers, Oxford 1996).
Steyn, Johan 'Guantanamo Bay: The legal black hole' 27th F. A. Mann Lecture (25 November 2003).
Suárez, Francisco 'Tractatus de Legibus ac Deo Legislatore' in *Selection from Three Works*, Classics of International Law (Clarendon Press, Oxford 1944).
Tesón, Fernando R. *A Philosophy of International Law* (2nd ed Westview Press, Boulder CO 1998).
Teubner, Gunther 'Globale Zivilverfassungen: Alternativen zur staatszentrierten Verfassungstheorie' (2003) 63 Zeitschrift für ausländisches öffentliches Recht und Völkerrecht 1–28.
Tomuschat, Christian 'Obligations Arising for States Without or Against Their Will' (1993) 241 Recueil des Cours de l'Académie de Droit International 195–374.
Tomuschat, Christian 'International Law: Ensuring the Survival of Mankind on the Eve of a New Century' General Course on Public International Law (1999) 281 Recueil des Cours de l'Académie de Droit International 13–438.
Tsagourias, Nicholas 'Introduction – Constitutionalism: a theoretical roadmap' in Nicholas Tsagourias (ed), *Transnational Constitutionalism, International and European Perspectives* (CUP, Cambridge 2007).
Tully, James *Strange Multiplicity: Constitutionalism in an Age of Diversity* (CUP, Cambridge 1995).
Turner, Catherine 'Delivering Lasting Peace, Democracy and Human Rights in Times of Transition: The Role of International Law' (2008) 2 The International Journal of Transnational Justice 126–151.
Uerpmann, Robert 'Internationales Verfassungsrecht' (2001) 56 Juristen Zeitung 565–572.
Ulfstein, Geir 'Do We Need a World Court of Human Rights?' in Ola Engdahl and Pål Wrange (eds), *The Law as it Was and the Law as it Should Be* (Brill, Leiden 2008).
Ulpian; Watson, Alan (ed, tr), *The Digest of Justinian* (University of Pennsylvania Press, Pennsylvania 1998).
Veitch, Scott *Law and Irresponsibility* (Routledge Cavendish, 2007).
Verdross, Alfred *Die Verfassung der Völkerrechtsgemeinschaft* (J. Springer, Vienna 1926).
Verdross, Alfred *Völkerrecht* (5th edn Springer, Vienna 1964).
Verdross, Alfred '*Jus Dispositivum* and *Jus Cogens* in International Law' (1966) 60 American Journal of International Law 55–63.
Verdross, Alfred and Simma, Bruno *Universelles Völkerrecht: Theorie und Praxis* (3rd edn Duncker & Humboldt, Berlin 1984).
Vile, John R *The Constitutional Convention 1787: A Comprehensive Encyclopedia of America's Founding* (ABC-CLIO Press, Santa Barbara CA 2005).
Waldron, Jeremy 'Torture and Positive Law: Jurisprudence for the White House' (2005) 105 Columbia Law Review 1681–1750.
Walker, Neil 'Reframing EU Constitutionalism' in *Ruling the World? Constitutionalism, International Law and Global Governance* (CUP, Cambridge 2009).
Walter, Christian 'Constitutionalizing (inter)national Governance – Possibilities for and Limits to the Development of an International Constitutional Law' (2001) 44 German Yearbook of International Law 170–201.
Weil, Prosper 'Towards Relative Normativity in International Law? (1983) 77 American Journal of International Law 413–442.
Weiler, J. H. H. and Wind, Marlene (eds), *European Constitutionalism Beyond the State* (CUP, Cambridge 2003).
Werner, Wouter 'The never-ending closure: constitutionalism in international law' in Nicholas Tsagourias (ed), *Transnational Constitutionalism: International and European Perspectives* (CUP, Cambridge 2007).

Wet, Erika de 'The Emergence of International and Regional Value Systems as a Manifestation of the Emerging International Constitutional Order' (2006) 19 Leiden Journal of International Law 611–632.

Wet, Erika de 'The International Constitutional Order' (2006) 55 International and Comparative Law Quarterly 51–76.

Wilde, Oscar *The Picture of Dorian Gray* (Wordsworth Classics, London 1992).

Wilde, Ralph 'Casting Light on the "legal black hole": Some Political Issues at Stake' (2006) 5 European Human Rights Law Review 552–557.

Wildhaber, Luzius 'A Constitutional Future for the European Court of Human Rights?' (2002) 23 Human Rights Law Journal 161–165.

Wittgenstein, Ludwig; Docherty, Peter (ed), *The Blue and Brown Books: Preliminary Studies for the 'Philosophical Investigations'* (2nd edn Wiley-Blackwell, Oxford 1969).

Wright Jr, Benjamin F. 'American Interpretations of Natural Law' (1926) 20 American Political Science Review 524–547.

Wolf, Erik *Griechisches Rechtsdenken* Vol 2 (Vittorio Klostermann, Frankfurt am Main 1952).

Young, Iris Marion *Justice and the Politics of Difference* (Princeton University Press, Princeton 1990).

Zangl, Bernhard and Zürn, Michael 'Make Law Not War: Internationale und Transnationale Verrechtlichung als Baustein für Global Governance' in Bernhard Zangl, Michael Zürn (ed), *Verrechtlichung – Baustein für Global Governance?* (Dietz, Bonn 2004).

Documents

Charter of the United Nations. Done at San Francisco, 26 June 1945. Entered into force, 24 October 1945.

Draft Treaty Establishing a Constitution for Europe, European Convention Doc. 850/03; 18 July 2003.

ILC Articles on Responsibility of States for Internationally Wrongful Acts, UNGA Res. 56/83; 28 January 2002.

Report of the Study Group of the ILC, 58th session (2006) UN Doc. A/CN.4/L.682; 4 April 2006.

Rome Statute of the International Criminal Court, ICC-ASP/2/Res. 3; 12 September 2003.

UN 2004 Cardoso Report *We the Peoples: Civil Society, the United Nations and Global Governance, Report of the Panel of Eminent Persons on United Nations-Civil Society Relations*. UN Doc. A/58/817 (11 June 2004).

2005 World Summit Outcome UN Doc. A/60/1 of 24 October 2005

Websites

Daniszewski, John *et al.* 'The Tyrant is Gone but the Trauma Remains' <http://articles.latimes.com/2004/mar/20/world/fg-intro-chapter20>.

Bush, George H. W <http://bushlibrary.tamu.edu/research/public_papers.php?id=2217&year=1990&month=9>.

Obama, Barack <http://www.cfr.org/publication/22114/remarks_by_presidents_obama_and_karzai_may_2010.html>.

Plato; Jowett, Benjamin (tr) *Protagoras* (The Internet Classics Archive). <http://classics.mit.edu/Plato/protagoras.html>.

Campaign for the Establishment of a United Nations Parliamentary Assembly <http://en.unpacampaign.org/index.php>.

Beckett, Jason 'The Politics of International Law – Twenty Years Later: A Reply' EJIL:Debate <http://www.ejiltalk.org/author/jason-beckett/>.

2010 Freedom of the World Survey <http://www.freedomhouse.org/template.cfm?page=15>.

Oxford English Dictionary Online <http://dictionary.oed.com/cgi/entry/00333646?single=1&query_type=word&queryword=organic&first=1&max_to_show=10>.

'Kant's Social and Political Philosophy' Stanford Encyclopedia of Philosophy <http://plato.stanford.edu/entries/kant-social-political/>.
Former Soviet Constitution <http://www.servat.unibe.ch/icl/r100000_.html>.
Kaldor, Mary 'Beyond Militarism, Arms Races and Arms Control' <http://www.ssrc.org/sept11/essays/kaldor_text_only.htm>.
2005 Iraqi Constitution <http://www.uniraq.org/documents/iraqi_constitution.pdf>
UN Reform <http://un.org/reform/>.

Case and Opinion

ICJ *Case Concerning the Barcelona Traction, Light and Power Company, Limited (second phase) (Belgium v Spain)* [1970] ICJ Rep 3.
Legal Consequences of the Construction of a Wall in the Occupied Palestinian Territory, Advisory Opinion (9 July 2004).

INDEX

www.ingramcontent.com/pod-product-compliance
Lightning Source LLC
LaVergne TN
LVHW020652300926
849161LV00004B/917
* 9 7 8 9 0 0 4 1 9 1 1 5 0 *